PROGRESSIVE
Skills
in English

Level 4 Course Book

Terry Phillips and Anna Phillips

Garnet
EDUCATION

Published by
Garnet Publishing Ltd.
8 Southern Court
South Street
Reading RG1 4QS, UK

First edition 2012
Reprinted 2018

ISBN: 978-1-85964-685-4

British Library Cataloguing-in-Publication Data
A catalogue record for this book is available from
the British Library.

Production
Project managers: Richard Peacock, Nicky Platt
Editorial team: Emily Clarke, Richard Peacock,
                   Nicky Platt, Rod Webb
Research: Lucy Phillips
Design: Neil Collier, Ed Du Bois, Mike Hinks
Illustration: Neil Collier, Doug Nash
Photography: Clipart, Corbis, Neil Collier, Istockphoto
Audio and DVD: Silver Street Studios

Printed and bound
in Lebanon by International Press: interpress@int-press.com

PROGRESSIVE Skills in English

Contents

Book maps		4
Introduction		7
Theme 1	Geography and the modern world	9
Theme 2	Communication	39
Theme 3	Media and advertising	69
Theme 4	Living life to the full	99
Theme 5	The past, present and future of food	131
Resources		161
Transcripts		183
Word list		229

Topics

Listening	Speaking	Reading	Writing	Knowledge area
1 Geography and development	Geography and water problems	Geography and tourism	Geography and the economy	Geography and the modern world
2 Communicating far and wide	Communication aids	Communication inventors	Communication inventions	Communication
3 The case against television	The hidden persuaders	Conventions in narrative fiction	Reality TV – real or fiction?	Media and advertising
4 Life systems	A sporting life	Learning for leisure	Living longer, living better	Living life to the full
5 Agriculture through history	Interfering with nature?	Should man be a herbivore?	GM: The future or the end?	The past, present and future of food

Skills

Listening	Speaking	Reading	Writing
1 *lecture with headings and subheadings* • note-taking: scientific numbering	*discussion group* • clarifying • raising / dealing with an objection	*magazine article* • reading for a purpose: highlighting key words • making inferences	*Discussion essay* • linking sentences • restating (first steps to preventing plagiarism)
2 *lecture with sequence of events* • timelines • using handouts of slides	*presentation and discussion* • saying you are lost • helping a speaker	*article with biography* • reacting to a text: opinions and lessons for life	*Description essay* • adding extra information to existing sentences
3 *talk with argument* • understanding the argument • understanding the speaker's concessions	*tutorial* • linking to previous speaker / topic • expressing uncertainty	*textbook; academic website* • recording sources	*Outline essay* • supporting statements with evidence: statistics; quotations; reported speech
4 *talk with fractured text* • adding information (to notes) which comes out of order	*presentation and discussion* • summarizing • reacting to summaries	*student essay with sources and reference list* • highlighting key points • highlighting sources	*Outline essay; Evaluation essay* • writing about graphs: trends, reasons and results
5 *lecture with timeline / sections / problems and solutions* • recognizing digressions and end of digressions	*presentation and discussion* • referring to research • making V agree with S	*research extracts* • sentence relationships: reason, result, example, explanation	*Argument essay* • using lexical cohesions • using *despite / because of*

Grammar

Listening	Speaking	Reading	Writing
1 • comparing with *both / neither, and / but, whereas / while*	• correcting statements with *think* + past • showing surprise with *realize* + past • saying weak forms	• understanding linkage between information: *and / but / or, because / so, while / whereas, although*	• writing about the past: *for / since / ago* • linking past and present
2 • verb patterns (1): ditransitive verbs	• *was doing when did* • *did when did*	• complex sentences: understanding participle clauses with active sentences	• complex sentences: joining sentences with active participles
3 • verb patterns (2): verb + ~*ing*; verb + *that*	• noun phrases with relative clauses: subject noun phrases; object / complement noun phrases	• complex sentences: understanding participle clauses with passive sentences	• complex sentences: joining sentences with passive participles
4 • cleft sentences • pseudo-cleft sentences	• review of modals: *must* for rules / laws; *may / might / could* for possibility; *should* for advice	• statements with hedging	• tense choice • hedging with verbs / adjectives / nouns / modals
5 • complex sentences with *when / if, although, because*	• complex sentences with *when / if, although, because*	• interrogative clauses	• *because / although* + clause vs *because of / despite* + noun phrases

Phonology, Everyday English and Portfolio work

Listening	Speaking	Everyday English	Portfolio
1 • stress in two-word phrases	• saying weak forms	• expressing opinions politely; persuading	Island tourism
2 • hearing two consonants together	• linking and suppressing	• talking on the phone	Communication aids for the vision-impaired
3 • hearing two vowel sounds together	• intrusive sounds	• complaining	Media debate
4 • predicting pronunciation of new words	• sense groups • rising to pauses	• talking about health problems	The positive and negative aspects of ageing populations
5 • understanding phonemic symbols	• saying vowel letters *e, i, o* • stress in two-word phrases	• at the supermarket	Influences on the environment

Introduction

This is Level 4 of *Progressive Skills in English*. This course is in four levels, from Intermediate to Advanced. In addition, there is a remedial / false beginner course, *Starting Skills in English*, for students who are not ready to begin Level 1.

Progressive Skills in English is designed to help students who are at university or about to enter a university where some or all of their course is taught in English. The course helps students in all four skills:

Listening – to lectures
Speaking – in tutorials and seminars
Reading – for research
Writing – assignments

Progressive Skills in English is arranged in five themes. Each theme is divided into four sections, one for each skill. Each skill section has five core lessons as follows:

Lesson 1: *Vocabulary for the skill*
pre-teaches key vocabulary for the section

Lesson 2: *Real-time practice*
practises previously learnt skills and exposes students to new skills; in most cases, this lesson provides a model for the activity in Lesson 5

Lesson 3: *Learning skills*
presents and practises new skills

Lesson 4: *Grammar for the skill*
presents and practises key grammar points for the skill

Lesson 5: *Applying skills*
provides practice in the skills and grammar from the section; in most cases, students work on a parallel task to the one presented in Lesson 2

In addition, there are three extra elements in each theme:

Everyday English	presents and practises survival English for everyday life
Knowledge quiz	tests students on their learning of key vocabulary and knowledge
Portfolio	offers extended practice and integration of the skills in the theme

Theme 1

Geography and the modern world

- Geography and development

- Geography and water problems

- Geography and tourism

- Geography and the economy

Listening: Geography and development

1.1 Vocabulary for listening · The HDI

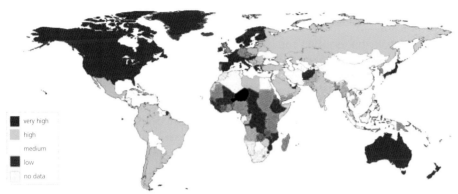

Data retrieved from the UNDP Human Development Report website: http://hdr.undp.org/en/statistics/ © UNDP

A Activating ideas

What does the map above show? Choose one item from below. Explain your answer.

☐ population, e.g., *total size*
☐ climate types, e.g., *desert*
☐ natural resources, e.g., *oil*
☐ minerals, e.g., *copper*
☐ cultivation, e.g., *crops for food*
☐ development, e.g., *economic*

B Understanding vocabulary in context
You are going to hear extracts from a lecture.

1. 🎧 **1.1** Listen to Extract 1. Check your ideas from Exercise A.
2. 🎧 **1.2** Listen to Extract 2. What questions does the UN ask about each country?
   a. How long ...?
   b. What percentage ...?
   c. How many ...?
   d. What is the average ...?
3. 🎧 **1.3** Listen to Extract 3. Why does the lecturer mention the following?
   a. Canada
   b. Norway
   c. Sierra Leone
   d. natural resources
   e. location
   f. fresh water

C Researching information
1. What colour is your country on the map? Find out the exact HDI for your country.
2. Find out the answers to the four UN questions for your country.

---

absence (*n*)
affect (*v*)
against (*prep*)
availability (*n*)
average (*v*)
copper (*n*)
cultivation (*n*)
density (*n*)
desalination (*n*)
fossil fuel
global (*adj*)
Human Development
  Index (*n*) [= list]
iron ore
lack (*n*)
literacy (*n*)
mineral (*n*)
natural gas
natural resource
population (*n*)
presence (*n*)
range (*n*) [= extent]
reflect (*v*) [= show]
rural (*adj*)
shortage (*adj*)
similarity (*n*)
split (*n*)
standard of living
sub-area (*n*)
temperate (*adj*)
underground (*adj*)
urban (*adj*)
with regard to

1.2 Real-time listening   Qatar and Lebanon

A   Activating ideas

1. What do you know already about the two countries, Qatar and Lebanon?
2. Study the maps and the photographs on the opposite page. What extra information do they give?

B   Understanding an introduction

1. Read the information from the faculty handout on the right. What does *the geography of a country* mean?
   its location, ...
2. ● 1.4 DVD 1.A Watch the first part of the introduction to the lecture. Make a list of the sections of the lecture.
3. ● 1.5 DVD 1.B Watch the second part of the introduction. Complete the subheadings column of the handout.

C   Understanding a lecture

1. ● 1.6 DVD 1.C Watch the main part of the lecture. Work in pairs.
   Student A: Make notes about Qatar.
   Student B: Make notes about Lebanon.
2. Ask your partner for information about the other country and complete the handout.
3. Which country do you think has the higher Human Development Index? Why? ● 1.7 DVD 1.D Watch the final part of the lecture and check your ideas.

Faculty of Human Geography

Does the geography of a country affect the human development of its population? In the next lecture, we compare countries and try to answer this question.

small countries:
Qatar and Lebanon

island nations:
Singapore and Tonga

large countries:
Turkey and Chile

headings and subheadings	Qatar	Lebanon
1. Location		
1.1. Region		
1.2. Borders		
2. Population		
2.1.		
2.2.		
2.3.		
3. Land		
3.1.		
3.2.		
3.3.		
4. Climate		
4.1.		
4.2.		
4.3.		
5. Natural resources		
5.1.		
5.2.		
6. Human Development Index		

D   Developing critical thinking

Compare the information about the countries for each area. Which parts of each country's geography affect its HDI figure?

A   Reviewing vocabulary

1. What could follow each word below?

a. natural	resources
b. temperature	
c. geographical	
d. population	
e. square	
f. agricultural	
g. fossil	

2. ⊕ **1.8** Listen to some sentences from the lecture and check your ideas.

3. Read the Pronunciation Check. What is the stressed word in each phrase above?

B   Identifying a new skill (1)

Read Skills Check 1. Correct the numbering of the notes below.

4. <u>Climate</u>
    1.4. Type
       Mediterranean
    1.5. Ave. rainfall
       900 mm

5. <u>Natural resources</u>
    1.6. Fossil fuels
       none
    1.7. Minerals
       limestone,
       iron ore

C   Practising the new skill (1)

⊕ **1.9** Listen to the introductions to three lectures.

1. Time management
2. Memory
3. Desertification

Organize your notes with scientific numbering.

D   Identifying a new skill (2)

1. Read Skills Check 2. Write one word in each space in the example sentences and questions.

2. ⊕ **1.10** Listen and check your answers.

E   Practising the new skill (2)

1. ⊕ **1.11** Listen to an introduction to a lecture about *communication*. Prepare a page for your notes with scientific numbering. Leave spaces in case you get lost.

2. ⊕ **1.12** Listen to the first part. Make notes.

3. Ask other students for missing information.

Pronunciation Check

Stress in two-word phrases

Two-word phrases can be:

'noun + noun   'temperature range

adjective + 'noun   natural re'sources

The first noun is stressed in noun + noun.

The noun is stressed in adjective + noun.

Skills Check 1

Note-taking: scientific numbering

This organization is very good for lectures with a **main subject**, e.g., *geographic features*, with several **areas**, e.g., *location, population*, etc., and several **sub-areas** under each area, e.g., *region, borders*.

<u>Qatar</u>
1. Location
    1.1. Region
    1.2. Borders
2. Population
    2.1. Total

Leave space under each sub-area for your notes.

Skills Check 2

Getting lost ... and recovering

During the lecture

1. Stop trying to take notes. Leave a space.

2. Wait until the lecturer moves on to the next topic or area. Then start taking notes again.

You will hear things like:

*OK. So _____ 's **climate**. Now, _____ 's look at **natural resources**.*

*Right. We've _____ about **fossil fuels**. _____ about **minerals**? _____, natural resources. Let's _____ on to **minerals**.*

After the lecture

Ask other students for information to complete your notes. You can say things like:

*I _____ the bit about **fossil fuels**.*

*What _____ she say about **climate type**?*

*Did you _____ the information for **average rainfall**?*

There are special words in English when two things are **the same or similar**. 🔊 **1.13** ①

Both	(countries)	are		located in the Middle East.	*positive thing is the same*
		have		hot, dry summers.	
			a	small land area.	
			some	natural resources.	
Neither	(country)	is		large in area.	*negative thing is the same*
		has	a	large population.	
			much	agricultural land.	
			any	mining industries.	

What differences in structure do you notice between *both* sentences and *neither* sentences?

There are special words in English when two things are **different**.

Qatar does not have much agricultural land	but	Lebanon has a great deal.
	whereas	
	while	
Qatar has a population density of 120 per square kilometre	against	413 in Lebanon.

| **One** country has less than 75 mm of rain per annum. | **The other** has 825 mm. |

Singapore

Tongan islands

A Identifying similarities

🔊 **1.14** Listen to an extract from a lecture about Singapore and Tonga. Tick (✓) if both countries have the feature. Cross (✗) if neither country has the feature. Some items are not mentioned.

Both countries are small in land area.

small land area	✓
surrounded by water	
small populations	
tropical climate	
desert areas	
high rainfall in summer	
high rainfall in winter	
high summer temperatures	
high winter temperatures	
mountains	
rivers and lakes	

B Identifying differences

🔊 **1.15** Listen to another extract about Singapore and Tonga. Tick (✓) the correct column for the country with the bigger, higher, larger number in each case.

Singapore has an area of 660 square kilometres and Tonga has 748.

	Singapore	Tonga
area		✓
population		
density		
highest point		
agricultural land		
highest rainfall		
urban %		
GDP per capita		
HDI		

A   Reviewing vocabulary

1. Put the words and phrases in the box into five groups. Give a heading for each group.

> agricultural   area   rainfall   borders   density
>
> fossil fuels   minerals   lakes and rivers
>
> temperature range   region   urban:rural split

2. 🌐 **1.16** Listen and check your answers. Mark the main stressed syllable in each word or phrase.

B   Activating ideas

You are going to watch a lecture from the Faculty of Human Geography. It is about Pakistan and Chile. What do you know about these two countries?

1. Where is each country?
2. Which population is larger? Which country is bigger in land area?
3. Which type of climate does each country have?
4. Which country is hotter? Which country has the higher rainfall?
5. What natural resources does each country have?
6. Which country has the higher HDI?

C   Understanding the lecture

1. 🌐 **1.17** DVD **1.E** Watch the lecture. Make notes about the two countries. Use headings and subheadings with scientific numbering. Leave space for information you miss.
2. Work in groups. Ask for missing information and complete your notes.

D   Developing critical thinking

1. Compare the two countries. Find similarities and differences.
2. Which parts of the geography of the countries explain the human development figure?

Speaking: Geography and water problems

1.6 Vocabulary for speaking   Water resources

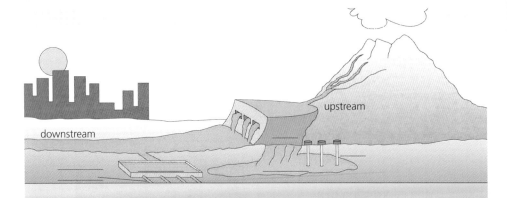

downstream

upstream

A Understanding a diagram

> aquifer   dam   irrigation channels   reservoir   wells

1. Label the diagram with words from the box above.
2. 🔊 1.18 Listen to an extract from a lecture about water resources and check your ideas.
3. Describe the water system.

B Using new vocabulary in context

1. 🔊 1.19 Listen and find an answer to each question about the water system in the diagram above.

☐ Yes, into the reservoir.

☐ No, because a lot of the rainfall is stored in the dam, the aquifer and the reservoir.

☐ No, because there is a lot of fresh water.

☑ a It comes from rainfall on the mountains.

☐ Several parts – the dam, the reservoir, the irrigation channels, the wells.

☐ The reservoir.

☐ There's a dam.

☐ They draw water from the wells and take it from the reservoir into irrigation channels.

☐ It could happen if there was a reduction in rainfall.

☐ It could result from the dam breaking.

2. Look again at each answer. What is the question?

C Building vocabulary

What is the *noun* from each of these *verbs*?
(In some cases, it is the same word!)

1. dam
2. divert
3. extract
4. flood
5. flow
6. irrigate
7. leak
8. shrink
9. supply

announce (v)
aquifer (n)
channel (n)
consensus (n)
crop (n)
dam (n and v)
deliver (v)
desalination (n)
destroy (v)
divert (v)
downstream (n)
draw (v) [= take out]
drought (n)
dry up (v)
extract (v)
extraction (n)
feed (v) [= supply]
flood (n and v)
flow (v)
grain (n)
irrigate (v)
irrigation (n)
leak (v)
limit (v)
pipe (n and v)
populous (adj)
privatize (v)
proposed (adj)
refill (v)
reservoir (n)
run out of (v)
shortage (n)
shrink (v)
shrinkage (n)
source (n)
store (v)
stream (n)
suffer (v) [~ from]
supply (v)
underground (adj)
upstream (n)
well (n)

A Reviewing vocabulary

1. Divide each word into syllables. Underline the stressed syllable.

> a̲/qui/fer   divert   extract
> irrigation   rainwater   reservoir
> shrinkage   underground

2. 🔊 **1.20** Listen, check your answers and repeat each word.

B Gathering information

1. Look at all the assignment details and one student's research on the right. Discuss the questions in the assignment for this research.

2. 🔊 **1.21** Listen to the student giving information to a discussion group.

 a. What points does the student get wrong?

 b. How do the other students show surprise?

 c. What do the other students think of the proposed solution?

C Studying the model

1. Study some extracts from the discussion below. Complete B's questions and statements.

2. 🔊 **1.22** Listen and check your answers.

A: Basically, the Ogallala Aquifer provides half of all the water for the United States.

B: Just a second. .... water?

A: Sorry. Did I say half? I meant a third.

B: .... and irrigation?

A: No, sorry. I mean just for irrigation.

A: The water was formed in the reservoir thousands of years ago.

B: .... ago? I thought these underground aquifers

....

B: So, what's the .... ?

A: Well, the farmers are going to stop growing crops which require irrigation.

B: I'... that's a very good solution.

A: Perhaps not, but it solves the problem in the short term.

D Practising the model

Practise the extracts of the discussion in pairs. Show you are surprised using stressed words and intonation in the key phrases.

E Developing critical thinking

What do you think of the proposed solution to the Ogallala Aquifer problem? Can you suggest any other solutions?

Department of Environmental Studies

Research ONE problem with water supply or usage in a developed country, e.g., the US. Be prepared to answer these questions at the next discussion group meeting:

1. What is the problem?
2. What is the proposed solution?

Ogallala Aquifer

Prob.

- Ogal. Aqu. = 1/3 of water for irr. in US.
- Water formed mya

BUT

- no longer fed by rainwater.
- level 1 m. p.a. = res. dry in 200 yrs.

Prop. sol.

- Farmers to stop growing crops that req. irr.

Pronunciation Check

Showing surprise

How does a speaker show surprise in English?

🔊 **1.23** Listen to these sentences.

Half of all the water?

Thousands of years ago?

Underline the stressed word(s). Mark the intonation with arrows.

🔊 **1.24** Listen and repeat some more sentences. Copy the stress and intonation.

Expressing opinions politely; persuading

poverty

poor sanitation

preventable disease

22,000 children die every day from hunger, thirst and preventable diseases

2.5 billion people do not have access to clean water and good sanitation

A Activating ideas

Look at the photographs and the newspaper headlines. What are some of the reasons for the problems in the headlines?

B Studying a model

1. 🔊 **1.25** Listen to the conversation below about the first headline. What do you notice about it?

2. 🔊 **1.26** Listen to a second version of the conversation. What differences do you notice?

3. Practise the conversation. Add words and phrases from the second version.

A: Did you know that over 20,000 children die every day unnecessarily?
B: You mean from poverty and hunger and so on?
A: Yes. Everyone should give money to charities.
B: The UN should do more.
A: Ordinary people can't just ignore the problems.
B: We can't leave it to charities. And we shouldn't just give aid. We should help the people in developing countries to help themselves.
A: In the long term. But people are dying, including thousands of children. It's terrible. We must do something about that.

C Practising the model

1. Complete these sentences about solutions to the problem in the second headline.

a. Governments should dig ....

b. The UN should provide money for ....

c. Factories should not ....

d. We should stop politicians stealing ....

e. People should not throw ....

f. Every child should be immunized ....

g. Celebrities should start ....

h. People in developing countries should find ....

2. Which solutions are the most effective? Discuss in groups. Be polite!

A Reviewing vocabulary

Discuss these questions.

1. How can you *extract* water from a river?
2. Why do lakes *shrink* and *dry up*?
3. How can you *refill* a reservoir?
4. Why are some areas *running out* of water?
5. Why do you have to *irrigate* crops?

B Saying vowels

1. What is the connection between the words below?

| a | are | do | have | the | was |
| and | but | for | of | to | were |

2. Read the Pronunciation Check and check your ideas.
3. Say all the phrases with the correct pronunciation of the underlined words.

C Identifying a new skill

1. Read the Skills Check. Answer the questions.

   a. When do you need to *clarify*?

   b. When do you *object* to something?

   c. How can you *deal with* objections?

2. Practise the conversation extracts.

D Practising the new skill: clarifying

Work in pairs.

Student A: Say the sentence.

Student B: Ask for clarification of the underlined words with *Did you say …*

Student A: Clarify with the word in brackets.

1. Visual learners like <u>sounds</u>. (colour)
2. Aural learners learn by <u>reading</u>. (listening)
3. American people <u>always</u> use the words *I apologize*. (nearly always)
4. American people <u>offer</u> to pay for damage. (never offer)
5. Consumption of oxygen by plants is called <u>breathing</u>. (respiration)
6. <u>Photosynthesis</u> is the production of oxygen by sunlight on water vapour. (photolysis)
7. Most of the carbon on Earth is stored in the <u>oceans</u>. (rocks)
8. More than <u>eight</u> per cent of energy usage comes from fossil fuels. (eighty)

E Practising the new skill: objecting

Work in small groups.

1. Each student reads one of the ideas from pages 164 to 181.
2. Students object to the ideas they hear.
3. Each student deals with any objections to his/her ideas.

Pronunciation Check

Saying weak forms

We normally use the schwa sound /ə/ for the vowel in articles, prepositions, conjunctions, the verb *be* and auxiliaries.

Mark the words with schwa in these sentences.

It provides <u>a</u> third of all <u>the</u> water <u>for</u> irrigation in <u>the</u> US.

The water was formed millions of years ago.

The farmers are going to stop growing crops.

They could grow crops which are local to the area.

🔊 **1.27** Listen and check your answers.

Skills Check

Sharing research

As you know, you should react to the contributions of other students in a discussion.

🔊 **1.28** Listen to some more contributions. Mark the main stressed word in each sentence.

Clarifying

- *Do you mean for drinking <u>and</u> irrigation?*
- *No, sorry. I mean just for irrigation.*
- *Did you say thousands of years ago?*
- *Sorry. I meant to say millions of years ago.*

Objecting and dealing with objections

- *They are going to stop growing crops.*
- *I'm not sure that's a very good solution.*
- *No, but it solves the problem in the short term.*
- *They could bring water from another area.*
- *But that would be very expensive.*
- *Yes, I think you're right.*

🔊 **1.29** Listen again. Copy the polite intonation.

We can show surprise at a statement with *think* or *realize*. ②
What change do we make to the main verb after *think* in this case?

statement		
subject	**verb**	**information**
The aquifers	are	thousands of years old.
The reservoir	provides	half of all the water for irrigation.

comment			
introduction		**subject**	**verb**	**information**
I thought	(that)	they	were	**millions** of years old.
		it	provided	**a third** of all the water.

🔊 **1.30** Listen to each statement and comment. In the comment, notice the strong stress on the information that the speaker is surprised about. Notice also the intonation.

A Showing surprise with *think*

These statements are wrong. Show surprise with *think* and the word(s) in brackets.

> *I thought it went round the Earth.*

1. The Moon goes round the Sun. (Earth)
2. Penguins live in the Arctic. (Antarctic)
3. Children start talking at six months. (one year)
4. They use the franc in France. (euro)
5. Most of the water on Earth is stored in the atmosphere. (oceans)
6. Plants don't release carbon dioxide into the atmosphere. (at night)

③

statement		
subject	**verb**	**information**
The aquifer	provides	a third of all US irrigation water.
The level	is falling	by one metre every year.

comment			
introduction		**subject**	**verb**	**information**
I didn't realize	(that)	it	provided	**a third**.
		it	was falling	by **one metre**.

🔊 **1.31** Listen to each statement and comment. In the comment, notice the strong stress on the surprising information, and the rise-fall in intonation at the end.

B Showing surprise with *realize*

These statements are correct but surprising. Show your surprize with *realize*.

1. They are greening the desert in the UAE.
2. There was a lot of water in the Sahara at one time.

> *I didn't realize they were greening the desert there.*

3. Sometimes ice can change straight to vapour.
4. Sugar is composed of carbon, hydrogen and oxygen.
5. Plants release carbon dioxide when they respire.
6. Whales are mammals.

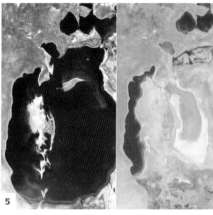

A Reviewing vocabulary

Use the verbs in the box to talk about the photographs above.

> dam   desalinate   dry up   extract
> flood   irrigate   run out of   shrink

B Researching information

Read the assignment on the right. Choose one topic from the **reading pack** and make notes.

C Taking part in a discussion

Divide into groups. Report your findings to your group. Other students in the group should check information and raise objections. Try to reach a consensus.

D Developing critical thinking

Discuss this question.

What problems, if any, are there with water supply or usage in your country or area?

Department of Environmental Studies

Water supply and/or usage can affect development of a whole country or a specific area of a country. In your reading pack, you have information on a number of problems with water around the world.

Discussion group assignment

Read about ONE of these problems and report back to our next discussion group meeting.

Water in the 21st century
Reading pack

Table of contents

Mexico City	p. 164
Southern Australia	p. 171
Southeastern Spain	p. 174
Turkey	p. 178
Chad	p. 182
Egypt	p. 175
Southern China	p. 169
India	p. 166

1

1.11 Vocabulary for reading   The impact of tourism

A   Activating ideas

Why do people go on holiday to the following types of places?

1. a modern city, e.g., *Dubai*
2. an old city, e.g., *Rome*
3. a coastal city, e.g., *Malaga*
4. a desert area, e.g., *Egypt*
5. a mountainous area, e.g., *the Alps*
6. a theme park, e.g., *Disneyland*
7. another part of their own country
8. a foreign country

B   Understanding new vocabulary in context

Cover the word list. Complete each sentence with a suitable word. Uncover the list and check.

> Join us on the c r u i s e of a lifetime!
>
> Go diving on beautiful coral r__fs.
>
> Take a s_____i into the rainforest to shoot wild animals – but only with your camera!
>
> Visit the r__ns of ancient civilizations.
>
> Enjoy the exciting n_____e on board every evening – we have clubs, a theatre and a cinema.
>
> Go shopping in our u_____t stores.
>
> Fly from London Heathrow (s_____l flights from other airports).
>
> Book early! D____d for our cruises is high.

C   Developing critical thinking

What is the impact of tourism around the world? How might it:

1. improve the HDI* of a country?
2. make life easier for local people?
3. make life harder for local people?
4. offend the local people?
5. damage the environment?

Use some of the words in the box.

> behaviour   carbon emissions
> customs   employment
> farming   fishing   noise
> pollution   tourist dollars
> water resources

*HDI = Human Development Index from the United Nations. It comprises life expectancy, educational level (including literacy) and income.

---

archaeological (*adj*)
archaeology (*n*)
available (*adj*)
carbon emissions
collapse (*v*)
comprise (*v*)
cruise (*n* and *v*)
damage (*v*)
demand (*n*)
direct (*adj*)
diving (*n*)
exceed (*v*)
follower (*n*) [of religion]
get by (*v*) [= manage to survive]
infer (*v*)
inference (*n*)
maintain (*v*) [= keep in good condition]
marina (*v*)
nightlife (*n*)
offend (*v*)
proximity (*n*)
reasonable (*adj*) [= quite good]
reef (*n*)
remains (*n*)
renovate (*v*)
republic (*n*)
restore (*v*)
ruins (*n*)
safari (*n*)
seasonal (*adj*)
serve (*v*) [= help]
shared (*adj*)
suffer (*v*) [~ from]
supplement (*v*)
treatment (*n*) [i.e., water]
upmarket (*adj*)
vast (*adj*)
widely (*adv*)

A   Preparing to read

Read the assignment on the right. A student has chosen to research Zarzis. Study the maps under the assignment. Discuss the questions in the assignment.

B   Understanding the text

Read and correct the notes below to complete the assignment. Refer to the web resources opposite.

Zarzis, Tunisia

1. Features
    1.1.   long, hot summers
    1.2.   nightlife
    1.3.   Greek ruins
    1.4.   marble statues at Zitha

2. Types of tourism
    2.1.   sun, sea and sand
    2.2.   cruise holidays
    2.3.   shopping
    2.4.   diving
    2.5.   archaeological
    2.6.   jungle safari

3. Development?
    3.1.   more flights, e.g., from Tunis
    3.2.   high-speed transport from airport
    3.3.   restore Greek ruins
    3.4.   extend 5-star hotels

4. Impact?
    4.1.   water shortages
    4.2.   damage fishing industry
    4.3.   offend local people
    4.4.   damage to agriculture = no water

C   Understanding new words in context

Think of a synonym for each of the words in _italics_ in the first text of the resources opposite.

direct = without any stops

D   Transferring information to the real world

1. Would you like to go on holiday to Zarzis? Why (not)?
2. Suggest some other locations for this assignment.

Faculty of Tourism and Hospitality

Seminar assignment

Research ONE area in Europe or Africa for an oral presentation.

1. What features of the area might attract tourists?
2. What type(s) of tourism might the area attract already?
3. How could the authorities develop tourism in the area?
4. What impact might an increase in tourism have on the area?

Tunisia

Tunisia is located in North Africa. It has borders with Algeria to the west and Libya to the southeast. The country has a long Mediterranean coastline. There are daily *direct* flights to the capital, Tunis, from Europe and the Middle East. However, there are none from the Americas or any part of Asia. Tunisia has been a *republic* since independence from France in 1956. Tunisia is an Arabic-speaking country, but you can *get by* in French. Italian is also widely understood, as a result of the *proximity* of the country to Sicily. The official religion is Islam but there are a very small number of *followers* of other religions.

Tunisia is small in terms of population (10.4m) but quite large in area 164,000 (km²). However, there are no people in large parts of Tunisia since most of the south of the country *comprises* the northern edge of the Sahara desert. The rest of the country is agricultural and Tunisia is famous for its *dates*.

There is only one permanent river, the Medjerda, in the west and north of the country, but Tunisia has *reasonable* access to water supply as the government has built dams and desalination plants which *supplement* the underground aquifers. However, the urban population is much better *served* (96 per cent) than the rural (52 per cent). The *vast* majority of water resources are required for agriculture but there is increasing demand for other uses as tourism and industry develop. From 1990 to 2010, *available* water resources increased as a result of water saving and the *treatment* of sewage water. However, some reports suggest that the country may *suffer* water shortages as demand increases.

Zarzis   Quick facts

population:	79,000 (2010)
climate:	long, hot, humid summers; mild, wet winters 23°C to 33°C
getting there:	
by air:	Djerba Airport (45 km)
by rail:	none
by road:	shared taxis, local buses
accommodation:	12 hotels (3- and 4-star)
restaurants:	plenty, cheap and upmarket
nightlife:	very little
markets:	Monday and Friday

Djerba Airport

Direct flights

Tunisia:	Tunis
France:	All major cities, seasonal to others
Germany:	All major cities, some seasonal
UK:	London, seasonal to Manchester
Holland:	Amsterdam
Belgium:	Brussels
Serbia:	Belgrade
Italy:	Verona
Switzerland:	Seasonal to major cities
Portugal:	Seasonal to Lisbon

HDI: 0.683 = 81st (up from 0.436 since 1980)

Zarzis, Tunisia

Zarzis is a coastal town in southeastern Tunisia, with white-washed buildings beneath shady palms and a few historic buildings with Arabic influences. The town has a busy commercial port, which has been the centre of the town's economy since Roman times. However, there is no marina for cruise ships or private vessels. Many kinds of Mediterranean fish are landed at the port, including red snapper, sea bass and octopus. Around the town are olive trees and palm groves. Some of these are watered by rain but most are fed by well water. Zarzis is on the edge of the Sahara and is also close to many sites of archaeological interest. It is possible to visit the Berber settlement of Chenini from Zarzis. The area has wide beaches of fine sand and sponge reefs off the coast.

Roman sites near Zarzis

Zitha

In Roman times, Zitha was an important city on the main road from Carthage (near Tunis) to Leptis Magna in Libya. The site was excavated at the beginning of the 20th century, revealing a forum surrounded by porticoes and paving slabs and many marble statues which have since been moved to the Louvre, Paris.

El-Hinche Kalakh

This is a site with two monuments – a medium-sized room with a dovecote, or columbarium, and a building with a few walls and a pool.

El Kantara

A Roman tower located on the beach near the road between Djerba and Zarzis. Today, the tower is in danger of collapsing since it has not been maintained, but there are plans to restore and renovate the tower as a museum.

A Reviewing vocabulary

Look at the beginning of some adjectives from 1.12.
What is the full word in each case?

1. reas_onable_
2. avai_____
3. incr_____
4. sea_____
5. his_____
6. comm_____
7. arch_____
8. upm_____

Ruins of Carthage, Tunisia

B Identifying and practising a new skill (1)

1. Read Skills Check 1. What should you:
   a. study? b. highlight? c. record?

2. Follow points 1 and 2 from Skills Check 1 with the assignment tasks below.

Research one country in Europe or Africa. Make a list of the key geographical features.
Read either the paper by Sengupta (2003) or the paper by Laukenmann (2003). Be prepared to talk about the main conclusions.
Research Eric Berne and Thomas Harris. What is the main similarity between their ideas of Transactional Analysis?
We can use the DIGEST approach for decision-making. 1. How can this approach reveal management style? 2. Describe a personal example of autocratic, participatory or democratic decision-making.
Read Robbins, pages 38–45. a. What are the main differences between an environment and an ecosystem? b. List three ways that animals adapt to changes in their environment.

C Identifying and practising a new skill (2)

1. Read Skills Check 2. How can you infer information?

2. Read the first text in 1.12 again. Is each inference below true or false? Explain your answer.

   a. Tunisia is a good destination for tourists from India.
   ☐ _____

   b. Tourists from Sicily might be interested in Tunisia.
   ☐ _____

   c. Egyptian tourists have no trouble in communicating with Tunisians. ☐ _____

   d. Tunisia has a low population density. ☐ _____

   e. It does not rain very much in southeastern Tunisia.
   ☐ _____

   f. Agriculture is more important than tourism at the moment. ☐ _____

3. Find three points which you can infer from the other texts in 1.12.

Skills Check 1

Reading for a purpose

Always do reading research for a purpose.

1. **Study** each assignment carefully **before** you start doing research.

2. **Highlight** key words in the task. Circle choices.

3. **Record only information** which meets the assignment task(s).

Do some research into one country in Asia (OR) Oceania.
1. What features of the country might attract tourists?

Skills Check 2

Making inferences

An inference is something you think is true because of facts in a text. You often have to use real-world knowledge to help with an inference.

Example:

fact in the text:	Tunisia has a long Mediterranean coastline.
real-world knowledge:	The Mediterranean is very hot in summer.
inference:	Tunisia would be a good destination for a summer beach holiday.

The words *as* and *since* can mean *because*, but each word also has other meanings.   ④

1	Tunisia has reasonable access to water supplies		as	the government has built dams ...
2	There is increasing demand for other uses			tourism and industry develop.
3	There are plans to restore and renovate the tower			a museum.
4	The tower is in danger of collapsing		since	it has not been maintained.
5	Tunisia has been a republic			1956.

When you read one of these words, think:

What is the meaning of the word in this sentence? What kind of information will come next?

		meaning	followed by ...
as	1	*because*	a sentence = the reason for an event
	2	*at the same time that*	a sentence = an action at the same time
since	3	*in the role of*	a noun phrase
	4	*because*	a sentence = the reason for an event
	5	*from a time in the past until now*	a date, period or moment in the past

A   Understanding *as* / *since* in context

Find more examples of *as* and *since* in the web resources in 1.12. What do the words mean in each case?

B   Predicting information after *as* / *since*

1. Read the start of each sentence. What kind of information do you expect to come next?

   a. There has been a great deal of research into memory since *date / time period – the 1960s.*

   b. It is better to spend a short time on memory retrieval every few weeks since _____

   c. Revise difficult ideas early in a revision period as _____

   d. Eric Berne believed that people behave as _____

   e. Thomas Harris worked in the Navy for several years as _____

   f. The cost of weddings in the US has risen by 30 per cent since _____

   g. Wedding dresses should be hired since _____

   h. You cannot use the creative side and the logical side of your brain at the same time, so you must not evaluate ideas as _____

   i. Tell other people about any decision since _____

   j. Many scientists say the Earth has been getting warmer since _____

   k. Fish in deep water see better in blue light since _____

2. Find an ending to each sentence from the phrases below.

☐ 1000 CE.	☐ they are only worn once.
☐ it might be difficult to stick to it later.	☐ you generate them.
☐ Parents, Adults or Children in interactions.	☐ a psychiatrist.
☐ ~~the 1960s.~~	☐ the start of the 21ˢᵗ century.
☐ retrieval and storage makes memory connections stronger.	☐ there is only blue light in the ocean.
	☐ you remember more from the start than from the end.

A Activating ideas

Study the map and photographs above. What do they tell you about the country?

B Preparing to read

Study the assignment. Mark the important points.

C Understanding a text

1. Do the assignment, using the texts opposite. Make notes under the assignment headings.

2. Discuss your findings in pairs or groups. Try to reach a consensus.

D Inferring information

Find the facts in the first text which support each inference below. Use real-world knowledge to help you.

1. Population density is very low in Cyprus.
2. Nicosia is not divided now.
3. Turkey took over the north because many people in the north are ethnic Turks.
4. There is tourism in the northern part of the island.
5. There is no fighting on the island.
6. Only certain parts of the Cyprus coast are suitable for bathing.
7. There were permanent rivers and lakes in the past.
8. You can't go skiing in Cyprus in summer.
9. Tourist hotels in Cyprus are a higher priority for water than local residents.
10. Tourists from Germany do not need to change money when they visit Cyprus.

E Reacting to information in a text

Would you like to visit Cyprus? Why (not)?

Faculty of Tourism and Hospitality

Case study 4: Island tourism

Tourism is already big business for Cyprus, but the government wishes to develop it further.

Research the island and make notes for an oral presentation on the following:

1. What geographical features may:
   1.1. assist
   1.2. restrict
   ... the development of tourism?

2. What non-geographical factors may:
   2.1. assist
   2.2. restrict
   ... tourism to the island?

Island in the sun

The island country of Cyprus is located in the eastern Mediterranean. It has an area of just over 9,000 square kilometres and a population of nearly one million. Its capital city, Nicosia, had the unhappy distinction of being the last divided capital in the world until quite recently. Cyprus is Greek-speaking in the south and Turkish-speaking in the north, but English is widely spoken in the tourist areas of both parts of the island, as the country was under British administration until 1960.

The country has a troubled recent past. It has been divided roughly in half since the occupation of the northern part by Turkish troops in 1974. The United Nations has kept the peace between the two halves for over 35 years. However, there are hopes now of a peaceful solution to the conflict.

Cyprus (which gave its name to the element copper) has a mainly rocky coastline, but there are sandy beaches in places, and lovely villages on the coast and in the low mountains. The island has been inhabited since at least 10 000 BCE. The Neolithic village of Choirokoitia is a UNESCO World Heritage Site and there are archaeological remains of many other peoples, including the Greeks and the Romans.

Cyprus has a Mediterranean climate so summers are hot and dry and winters are cool. Nowadays, there are no permanent lakes or rivers as there is almost no rainfall on the island, and the shortage of natural water is a constant problem, although supplies to hotels and restaurants are rarely cut. There is, however, thick snow in the Troodos mountains in the centre of the country in the winter months.

There are excellent transport links to the southern part of the island from all parts of the world, but many of the nicest beaches are some distance from the international airports at Larnaca and Paphos. Nicosia International Airport has been closed since 1974. Access to the northern part is only through airports in mainland Turkey.

Cyprus is part of the Eurozone, which means it has the same currency as 17 countries in Europe. The island nation is 35th on the UN HDI, with a score of 0.801. This puts it first in southern Europe.

Water resources in Cyprus

At one time, Cyprus was rich in water (with many rivers and lakes), but annual rainfall has gone down steadily since the 1970s, as the population and the number of tourists has gone steadily up. Now, there are 14 main rivers but none of them is permanent. There are also aquifers in several parts of the country but saltwater is moving into many of these. Demand for water in Cyprus now exceeds supply. According to one estimate, 40 million cubic metres per year are extracted above the natural recharge. As a result, reserves are at an all-time low and, from time to time, it is necessary to divert water from agriculture to domestic, industrial or tourist use. The government has responded by building dams, reservoirs and desalination plants, which now provide 50 per cent of domestic water. However, these plants use oil so this is not a long-term solution, since Cyprus has no oil reserves. Indeed, there is an energy shortage on the island and there are power cuts from time to time. One idea is to build a pipeline from Turkey in the north, which has a water surplus, but this would give control of water to the country which sent troops to the island in 1974.

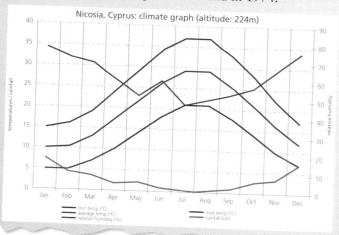

Nicosia, Cyprus: climate graph (altitude: 224m)

min temp (°C)
average temp (°C)
relative humidity (%)
max temp (°C)
rainfall (cm)

Government tourism strategy

There are more than two million tourist arrivals each year to Cyprus, 90 per cent from European countries. The government wishes to establish Cyprus as a quality tourist destination, which involves an increase in the average length of stay and in the average amount of money spent by each tourist. They also wish to spread tourism through the year.

Knowledge quiz **What? When? Where? How?**

1 Cover the final column. Try to answer each question.

1. What are *fossil fuels*?	a boat
2. What are *minerals*?	a large ship for passengers on holiday
3. What are *natural resources*?	an area for storing water
4. What can you *cultivate*?	being able to read and write
5. What can you *raise* on farms?	change planes somewhere
6. What do you have to do if there are no *direct* flights to a country?	crops or cattle
7. What does a *dam* do?	eat it – it is food like vegetables
8. What do you do with a *crop*?	from lack of maintenance or damage in war
9. What happens if a water pipe *leaks*?	into deserts or jungles
10. What happens in a *drought*?	land to grow crops
11. What is a *reservoir*?	1 oil, natural gas, coal
12. What is *desalination*?	some of the water gets out of the pipe
13. What is *literacy*?	stop water from flowing down a river
14. What is population *density*?	taking salt out of sea water to make drinking water
15. What is the *urban:rural* split?	the average number of people in, e.g., a square kilometre
16. What do you *cruise* in?	the ratio between people living in towns and people living in the country
17. What can you leave in a *marina*?	there is no rainfall, or very little
18. When do you *get by* in a language?	things like copper, iron, gold
19. When do you *irrigate* crops?	things like wood, oil, fish
20. When does water need *treatment*?	when it is dirty
21. Where do *safaris* go?	when there is not enough rainfall in a particular area
22. How can you make an *inference*?	when you don't speak it very well but can make and understand simple points
23. How does a building become a *ruin*?	with a well
24. How do people *extract* water from an underground aquifer?	you do work regularly to make sure there is no problem with the roof, the walls, etc.
25. How do you *maintain* a building?	you put pieces of information in a text together and use real-world knowledge

2 Uncover the final column. Match the questions and answers above.

3 Cover the first column. Make a good question for each answer.

1.16 Vocabulary for writing — Economic success – the factors?

Figure 1: Gross Domestic Product (GDP) per capita
Source: CIA Factbook

Figure 2: Deaths from infectious diseases
Sources: WHO, World Bank, Institut Pasteur, UNDP

A Activating ideas

1. Study the two maps. What does *GDP* mean? What is *per capita*?
2. What *infectious* diseases can you name?
3. What, *generally speaking*, links the two maps?
4. What are possible *contributory factors* for this linkage?

B Understanding new vocabulary in context

Read the basic sentences on the left. Rewrite the sentences with the extra information on the right. Add punctuation.

1. Geography contributes to success.	according to / a major survey / for the World Bank / economic
According to a major survey for the World Bank, geography contributes to economic success.	
2. Sachs and Gallup looked at data.	in 1998 / two / American / economists / for 150 countries
3. They reached a conclusion.	about / the economic performance / of countries
4. Factors affect the success.	they reported that / three / geographic / economic / of a country
5. They defined success.	in terms of / gross domestic product / (GDP) / per capita
6. Countries were successful.	firstly / they found that / in the northern hemisphere / more / in general / than countries in the southern hemisphere
7. Countries had a GDP ...	secondly / they discovered that / generally speaking / with temperate climates / higher / than hotter countries
8. ... these countries do not suffer from diseases.	perhaps / partly / because / tropical
9. Countries have access.	finally / they reported that / successful / usually / to a seaport / and / large navigable rivers / into the interior / so trade is easy
10. Countries met criteria.	24 / in the survey / all / three

Source: *The Oxford Handbook of Economic Geography* by Gordon L. Clark, et. al. OUP 2003
Chapter 9 Climate, Coastal Proximity, and Development, Mellinger, Sachs and Gallup

---

access (n)
account for (v)
because of
civil war
comprise (v)
consider (v) [= regard as]
contribute (v)
contributory (adj)
criterion (n) [pl. = criteria]
disease
economic indicator
exception (n)
exist (v)
extremely
GDP
generally speaking
gross domestic product
hemisphere (n)
in general
in terms of
infectious (adj)
invade (v)
invasion (n)
largely (adv)
mainly (adv)
market (n) [= general place to sell goods]
meet (v) [= equals]
member
membership (n)
navigable (adj)
partly (adv)
per capita
performance [= outcome]
place (v)
range (v)
reach a conclusion
seaport (n)
stable (adj) [= fixed]
suffer (v) [from]
the EU
the interior (n) [= of a country]
the WHO
the World Bank
tropical (adj)

A Previewing vocabulary

Write a verb to go with each noun or noun phrase. There are often several possibilities.

1.	reach	a conclusion
2.		data
3.		contributory factors
4.		criteria
5.	,	a disease
6.		a member of a group
7.		natural resources
8.		success

B Understanding the assignment

Study the assignment.

1. What kind of essay is required?
2. How successful is the UK in economic terms? Look at the student notes opposite to check your ideas.
3. Study the essay underneath the notes. What type of information is in each paragraph?

C Gathering information

Look at the notes at the top of the opposite page. Write one or two sentences for each point.

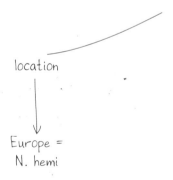

location

↓

Europe =
N. hemi

The UK is located in Europe, which is in the northern hemisphere.

D Writing the essay

1. Complete the essay with your sentences from Exercise C. Make any necessary changes.
2. Do the three geographical factors explain the economic success completely? Write the final paragraph with a summary of the findings and your opinion.

Faculty of Economics

The survey by Sachs and Gallup (1998) suggests that the economic performance of a country is largely the result of geographical factors.

To what extent is the economic performance of the United Kingdom explained by the Sachs and Gallup analysis?

The European Union

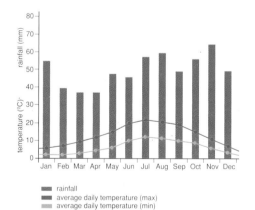

- rainfall
- average daily temperature (max)
- average daily temperature (min)

London climate graph

UK commercial port

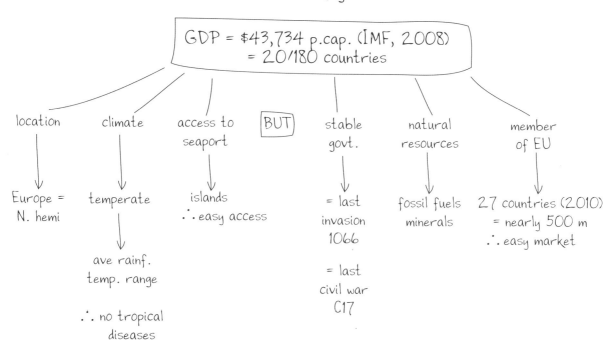

United Kingdom

GDP = $43,734 p.cap. (IMF, 2008)
= 20/180 countries

| location | climate | access to seaport | BUT | stable govt. | natural resources | member of EU |

Europe = N. hemi

temperate → ave rainf. temp. range ∴ no tropical diseases

islands ∴ easy access

= last invasion 1066

= last civil war C17

fossil fuels minerals

27 countries (2010) = nearly 500 m ∴ easy market

To what extent is the economic performance of the United Kingdom explained by the Sachs and Gallup analysis?

According to the Sachs and Gallup survey (1998), economic performance is largely the result of three factors. The three factors are _Locotion in the Northern hemisphere, a temperate climate and access to seaport_ In this essay, I will analyze _the data on the economic performance of the United Kingdom_ consider to what extent _the Sachs and Gallup explains it_ and then list _other possible contributory factors_. Finally, I _will reach a conclusion_

In this essay, I am defining economic success in terms of _gross domestic product GDP Per Capita_ The United Kingdom is _an extremely successful country_ in this terms The UK was placed _20th out of 180 countries in data produced in 2008 by the Internat_ The GDP _per capita was $43,734 in that year_ (monetory)

The United Kingdom meets all of the criteria for economic success in the Sachs and Gallup analysis. Firstly, it is located in Europe, which is in the northern hemisphere. Secondly, it has a temperate climate with an average temperature _between 5 on 15C_ and average rainfall _between 500 and 2,500 mm per annum_ As a result, the country does not _suffer from any tropical_ diseas Finally, the UK is _____. It is possible, therefore, that these three factors have contributed to the economic success of the United Kingdom.

However, there are other possible contributory factors. Firstly, the UK has a very long history of stable government. _____. Secondly, the UK has many valuable natural resources, including fossil fuels and minerals. _____.
This means it has an easy market of nearly 500 million people for its goods and services.

_____
_____
_____
_____

A Reviewing vocabulary and grammar

Complete each sentence with the correct prepositions.

1. According _to_ Sachs and Gallup, economic success is largely the result _____ three factors.
2. In this essay, I will analyze the data _____ the economic success _____ the UK.
3. The UK is a successful country _____ economic terms.
4. _____ 2008, the UK was placed 20th _____ of 180 countries, _____ a per capita GDP of $43,734.
5. The UK meets all three criteria _____ economic success _____ the Sachs and Gallup analysis.

B Identifying a key skill

1. What do you notice about each pair of sentences below?

   a. The UK climate is temperate.   The UK has a temperate climate.
   b. The UK has many seaports.   There are many seaports in the UK.
   c. The Normans invaded Britain in 1066. Britain was invaded by the Normans in 1066.
   d. The UK is a member of the EU.   The UK belongs to the EU.

2. Read the Skills Check. Which paraphrase method is used for each second sentence above?

3. Cover the first sentence in each pair above. Write a paraphrase from the second sentence.

C Practising the new skill (1)

Write synonyms for each of these words and phrases from the essay in 1.17.

1.	survey	report, analysis
2.	largely	
3.	partly	
4.	located in	
5.	therefore	
6.	goods and services	
7.	comprise	
8.	the result of	
9.	as a result	
10.	significant	

D Practising the new skill (2)

Paraphrase these sentences with the word(s) in brackets. Do not change the form of the new word(s).

1. Economic success is largely the result of three factors. (lead)
2. The UK is a successful country in economic terms. (economically / considered)
3. Average temperature ranges between 5 and 15 degrees Celsius. (There)
4. The UK meets all three criteria of the survey. (met)
5. The UK is a number of islands. (consists)

Skills Check

Reporting findings

You cannot use another writer's words unless you directly quote. You must **paraphrase** the words. Otherwise, you may be accused of plagiarism.

You can paraphrase the original words with:

synonyms	Geography **is responsible for** economic performance. *Geography accounts for* economic performance.
replacement subject *There* or *It*	**The UK has** many mineral resources. ***There are** many mineral resources in the UK.*
active to passive or passive to active	The IMF **placed** the UK 20th. *The UK was placed 20th by the IMF.*
a different order of information	**The GDP per capita in 2008** was $43,734. *In 2008, the per capita GDP was $43,734.*

What changes have been made to paraphrase the following original sentence?
original:
According to Sachs and Gallup (1998), geography is partly responsible for the economic performance of a country.
paraphrase:
The economic success of an area is partly accounted for by its location, landscape and climate, say Sachs and Gallup in a 1998 report.

Past Simple

We can write about past events in a number of ways: ⑤
1. with the past simple and a time preposition or *ago*

subject	verb	preposition	time expression	*ago*
The last civil war in the UK	was	in	the 17th century.	
		-	hundreds of years	ago.

2. with the present perfect and *since* or *for*   *Present perfect*

subject	verb	object	*since / for*	time expression
The UK	has not had	a civil war	since	the 17th century.
			for	hundreds of years.

3. with *It is* and *since*

subject	verb	time expression	*since*	sentence
It	is	hundreds of years	since	the UK had a civil war.

What kind of time expressions follow *since*? What kind of time expression follows *for*?

A Using *since* and *for*
Write *since* or *for* in front of each number or set of words.

1. _for_ ten years
2. _____ 1963
3. _____ 9.00 a.m.
4. _____ a long time

5. _____ ever
6. _____ half an hour
7. _____ he graduated
8. _____ I saw you

9. _____ midday
10. _____ the 15th century
11. _____ the whole of her life
12. _____ three months

B Paraphrasing
Study each sentence. Then rewrite it with each of the words or phrases.

1. The UK joined the EU in 1973.
   a. ago   The UK joined the EU over 30 years ago.
   b. since The UK has been a member of the EU since 1973
   c. for   The UK has been a member of the EU for nearly 50 years
   d. it   It is nearly 50 years since the EU joined the EU

2. The UK was last successfully invaded in 1066.
   a. ago   The UK was last successfully invaded nearly a 1000 years ago
   b. since The UK has not been successfully invaded since 1066
   c. for   _____
   d. it   _____

3. Oil was discovered off the coast of the UK in 1970.
   a. ago   _____
   b. have / since _____
   c. have / for   _____
   d. it   _____

C Using *in / ago / since / for / it is* + time period
Write one true sentence about your own country with the structures in Grammar box 5.

   1. in   2. ago   3. since   4. for   5. it

A Reviewing vocabulary and grammar

Rewrite each sentence with the same meaning. Use the word in brackets.

1. The UK is located in the northern hemisphere. (location)

   The location of the UK is the northern hemisphere.

2. The UK has a temperate climate. (is)

3. The UK does not suffer from tropical diseases. (exist)

4. Three factors contribute to the success of the UK. (contributory)

5. The UK has had a stable government for a very long time. (history)

6. The UK has an easy market for its goods and services. (sell)

The last successful invasion of the UK

B Thinking and organizing

You are going to write an essay about the Sachs and Gallup (1998) survey. You are going to write about your own country. Do some research into the following points.

1. How successful is your country economically?

2. To what extent does your country meet the three Sachs and Gallup criteria?

3. What other factors might contribute to your country's economic performance? These could be positive or negative factors.

Record your research in a diagram like the one in 1.17.

Offshore oil rig

C Writing

Write the essay. Follow the writing plan on the right.

Remember:

- use a range of sentence patterns
- paraphrase sentences from your research
- write about the past with the past simple + *in* or *ago*
- write about situations from the past to the present with the present perfect + *since* or *for*

	Writing plan
Para 1	Introduction
Para 2	Economic performance
Para 3	The Sachs and Gallup criteria
Para 4	Other contributory factors
Para 5	Conclusion

D Editing and research

Exchange drafts with a partner and mark his/her work with *?, S, G* or *P*.

Read your marked essay and correct the points. Write the essay again.

10 Downing Street

Malta   **Mauritius**   **Sri Lanka**

A   Activating ideas

Find the places in the photographs on a map. Describe their location and geography.

B   Gathering and recording information

Study the assignment. Do research and make notes on each point.

C   Preparing a presentation

Work with people who have chosen the same country. Prepare to give a talk about your country. Use slides or visuals to illustrate your points.

D   Giving and hearing a presentation

Work in different groups from Exercise C, with at least one student for each country. Make notes to answer these questions about each talk you listen to.

- Which factors are similar for the country which you researched?
- Which factors are different?
- Which country has the best chance of developing tourism?

E   Writing

Choose one of the following based on your notes from Exercise C.

- Make a poster presentation about one country. Illustrate key points with photos, etc.
- Write an essay for the following title: *To what extent does the Sachs and Gallup analysis (1998) explain the economic performance of Malta / Mauritius / Sri Lanka?*

Faculty of Human Geography
Assignment

Research Malta, Mauritius or Sri Lanka.
For your selected country, find out:

- geographical features: *location, climate, landscape*, etc.
- the HDI and the GDP per capita
- factors assisting economic performance, e.g., *seaports, natural resources, membership of trading groups*, etc.
- factors restricting economic performance, e.g., *civil war, corruption in government*, etc.

Then consider the following questions:

- Which kinds of tourism can the country develop?
- What impact might tourism have on the country?

Theme 2

Communication

- **Communicating far and wide**

- **Communication aids**

- **Communication inventors**

- **Communication inventions**

Listening: Communicating far and wide

2.1 Vocabulary for listening — Communication mediums: benefits and drawbacks

A Activating ideas

Study the mediums of communication.

1. What are the benefits and drawbacks of each medium? ⊚ 2.1 Listen to some students working with Table 1. Fill in the information for *posted letter*.

2. Work in groups. Fill in the table for the other mediums.

Table 1: *Benefits and drawbacks of certain mediums of long-distance communication*

medium	speed	cost	convenience for sender	convenience for receiver	security

B Word-building

1. Complete the table below with a word from the list on the right in each space.

2. Mark the stressed syllable in each word.

3. ⊚ 2.2 Listen and check your answers.

noun	adjective	opposite adjective
con'venience		`
security		
expense ↑		
	beneficial	
scarcity		common
complexity		simple

C Recognizing words in context

⊚ 2.3 Listen to some sentences. Number the words in the table above.

Example: 1. Mobile phone calls can be very *expensive*.

allocate (*v*)
analogue (*adj*)
beneficial (*adj*)
benefit (*n* and *v*)
browser (*n*)
cable (*n*)
code (*n*)
complex (*adj*)
courier (*n*)
customer base
deliver (*v*)
delivery (*n*)
device (*n*)
digital (*adj*)
drawback (*n*)
etailer (*n*)
high street (*n*)
inconvenient (*adj*)
infrastructure (*n*)
insecure (*adj*)
intercept (*v*)
market (*v*)
medium (*n*) [= way of sending message]
messenger (*n*)
navigate (*v*)
network (*n*)
personnel (*n*)
post (*v*) [= put in mail box]
postal system
principle (*n*)
relay station
retailer (*n*)
scarce (*adj*)
secure (*adj*)
security (*n*)
signal (*n*)
stand-alone (*adj*)
symbol (*n*)
technology (*n*)
telegraph (*n*)
useless (*adj*)

A   Activating ideas

1. What is the connection between all the illustrations on the opposite page?
2. Name each method of communication.
3. What is the correct chronological order?

B   Preparing for a lecture

Study the title slide from a Business Studies lecture. Number the headings of the slides underneath in a logical order.

C   Understanding a lecture

1. ● 2.4 DVD 2.A Watch the lecture. Check your ideas for Exercise B. Which slide(s) does the lecturer *not* deal with?

2. Study these bullet points from the slides. Put each one on the correct slide.

  5 • faster, more secure
  2 • first postal service
     • horse riders + relay stations
  4 • ~~benefits~~
  4 • infrastructure
     • invention of writing
  5 • Morse code
  4 • personnel
  3 • semaphore stations
  1 • smoke signals and drums

3. Which sort of information do you hear for each slide? Choose from the words in the box.

> biographical   chronological   classification
> exemplification   description   pros and cons

D   Developing critical thinking

What is the main point of the lecture? Write the phrases below in the correct order to make a two-sentence summary.

shows that	must provide
of long-distance communication	
successful businesses	the history
when it offers	greater benefits
people use	to customers
benefits	new technology

Business Studies Faculty
Module: 1463

Building a successful business

What does the history of long-distance communication teach us about business?

Three key business principles

4   **benefits**   ~ telegroph

Early systems: Sumeria, China, Egypt

Early systems: before writing

Only operator can deliver the mesoqfe

The telegraph: how did principles apply?

The telephone: how did principles apply?

Early systems: France   3

Early systems: A new approach

The telegraph: how did it work?   5

Tele - distant
Graph - second
machine print the
mesoqe in the poper

A   Reviewing vocabulary

1. Match words to make phrases from the lecture in 2.2.

   a. electrical   ☐ beings
   b. Morse   ☐ business
   c. postal   ☐ code
   d. skilled   ☐a device
   e. successful   ☐ message
   f. human   ☐ personnel
   g. urgent   ☐ system

2. 🔊 **2.5** Listen and check your answers.

3. How does the speaker say the end of the first word in each case? Read the Pronunciation Check and check your ideas.

4. Which word is stressed in each phrase? Why?

B   Identifying a new skill

Look at this slide from the lecture in 2.2.

> Three key business principles
>
> 1. benefits
>
> 2. trained personnel
>
> 3. infrastructure

1. How can you use this slide to *prepare* for the lecture?

2. How can you use the slide *during* the lecture?

3. Read the Skills Check and check your ideas.

C   Practising a new skill

1. Look at some slides from the next Business Studies lecture. Follow the advice in the Skills Check.

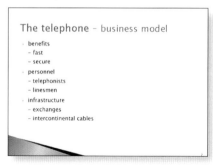

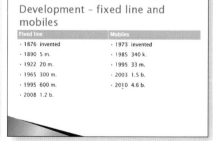

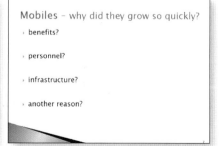

2. 🔊 **2.6** Listen and add notes to each slide.

Pronunciation Check

Hearing two consonants together

Look at the bold letters in the words below. They are both consonants. When two consonants occur together, we do not 'explode' the first consonant. Sometimes we do not say it at all.

Examples:
send messages   write letters
make progress   ask questions

🔊 **2.7** Listen to the pronunciation of some pairs of words. Can you hear the first consonant?

Skills Check

Using handouts of slides

Lecturers sometimes provide a copy of the slides *before* the lecture.

1. Look up any new words on the slides. Check the meaning and the pronunciation, especially the stress. Say the word several times.

2. Think: *What might the lecturer say about each slide?*

3. During the lecture, use the contents of the slides as headings for notes of the important points.

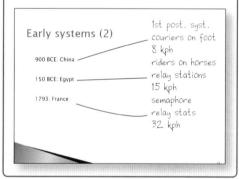

A number of verbs in English are followed by two objects. We can put the objects in two different orders. What do you notice about the two different word orders?

2.8 ⑥

Table 1

subject	verb	object: person	object: thing
New businesses	should offer	customers	better products.
Companies	give	them	details of products.
They	didn't teach	the couriers	the routes.

Table 2

subject	verb	object: thing		object: person
New businesses	should offer	better products		customers.
Companies	give	details of products	to	them.
They	didn't teach	the routes		the couriers.

Sometimes a verb takes two objects but there is a preposition before the second object. What do you notice about the objects in this case?

Table 3

subject	verb	object 1	preposition	object 2
Thieves	could steal	the messages	from	the courier.
Successful companies	supply	customers	with	benefits.
The machine	printed	the letters	on	strips of paper.

A Hearing the two objects

 2.9 Listen to each sentence. Number the two objects you hear in each case.

Example: 1. *I'm going to ask you a question.*

	object 1		object 2
[ ]	a message	[ ]	a lot of money
[ ]	customers	[ ]	a message
[ ]	her	[ ]	a present
[ ]	me	[1b]	a question
[ ]	the book	[ ]	for me
[ ]	the government	[ ]	for the government
[ ]	the Social Sciences lecturer	[ ]	his invention
[ ]	thousands of francs	[ ]	some money
[ ]	us	[ ]	the truth
[1a]	you	[ ]	to school

B Consolidation

Complete each sentence with a second object. Use a preposition if necessary.

1. He gave me *a message.*
2. The courier took the letter *to the government office.*
3. I offered her *a cup of tea*
4. The company sold its main business *to shareholder*
5. Mobile phone companies often give customers *the best offer*
6. Telegraph offices delivered telegrams *to the customers*
7. The employment agency found a good job *for me*

A   Activating ideas

Discuss these questions.

1. What *benefits* do people enjoy from using the Internet?
2. What *personnel* does a company need to have a presence on the Internet?
3. What *infrastructure* is involved in the Internet?

Business Studies Dept.

Module: 1464

Building a successful Internet business

In the last lecture, we looked at building a business by starting with a customer want – long-distance communication. In this lecture, we look at a different approach – starting with the infrastructure.

B   Preparing for a lecture

Study the handout from the Business Studies department and the slides from the lecture on the department intranet. Prepare to watch the lecture – see 2.3.

C   Following a lecture

🎧 **2.10** ☐DVD☐ **2.B** Watch the lecture. Add notes to the slides.

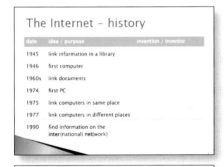

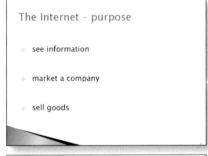

D   Developing critical thinking

Discuss these questions.

1. Amazon.com is one of the biggest etailing companies. Why? What does it do well?
2. Boo.com is one of the biggest etailing failures in Internet history. Why? What did it do badly? Think of some possibilities.

2.6 Vocabulary for speaking — Living with communication disability

sight

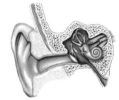
hearing

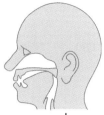
speech

A Activating ideas

Read the lecture information.

1. What are *communication disabilities*?
2. Why are the figures for unemployment so high?

B Understanding new vocabulary in context

🔊 **2.11** Listen to the case studies of Maria, Alfred and Elena from the lecture. Ask and answer these questions.

1. What disability does each person have?
2. How did they become disabled?
3. What aids do they use, if any?
4. What employment do they have, if any?

Department of Education and Social Work

Lecture 3:

Communication disabilities and employment

Statistics show that around 80 per cent of blind people in the world are unemployed. The figure for deaf people is around 90 per cent. There are no reliable figures for those without speech.

In this lecture, I will describe how we can help people with sight, hearing and speech disabilities get into the workplace.

C Recognizing vowel sounds

Find a word connected with communication in the list on the right that has the same vowel sound as each word below.

1. let	*deaf*	5. two		9. we're	
2. but		6. four		10. boy	
3. six		7. nine		11. how	
4. eat		8. way		12. go	

D Consolidating vocabulary

Find a word or words in the list on the right for each category below.

sense noun	sight,
parts of the body	eyes, brain,
disability nouns	blindness,
disability adjectives	blind,
verb phrases	can't see,
aids to disability	Braille,

accident *(n)*
adopt *(v)* [= take up]
alphabet *(n)*
binary *(adj)*
blind *(adj* and *v)*
blindness *(n)*
Braille
code *(n)*
consequence *(n)*
damage *(n* and *v)*
deal with *(v)* [= cope]
dot *(n)*
dumb *(adj)*
eyesight *(n)*
finger *(n)*
flat *(adj)*
give one's name to
go deaf / blind
go on to be [= result]
hand
hearing *(n)*
impaired *(adj)*
impairment *(n)*
infected *(adj)*
leather *(n)*
lip *(n)*
lose your sight / hearing / voice
lung *(n)*
mouth *(n)*
mute *(adj)*
nose *(n)*
raised *(adj)* [= above the surface]
result *(n)*
sight *(n)*
sign language
standard *(n)* [= norm]
symbol *(n)*
synthesis *(n)*
synthesizer *(n)*
teeth *(n pl)*
thumb *(n)*
tongue *(n)*
vocal chords
worldwide *(adj)*

A Activating ideas

You are going to hear about the life and work of Louis Braille. Think of questions you would like to ask with each question word.

> Did …?   Was …?   When …?   Where …?
> What …?   How …?   Why …?

B Gathering information

Look at the assignment details and the research notes underneath. Find the words in italics in the notes, and discuss these questions.

1. What's a *saddle*?
2. Where do we get *leather* from?
3. How do you *raise* something?
4. What are the main *symbols* in maths?
5. What does *adopt* mean, in this case?
6. What's a *standard*, in this case?

C Studying the model

1. ⊕ **2.12** Listen to a student giving information about Braille to a study group. How does she talk about dates, ages and time periods? Make a list of expressions.

   in 1809

   when he was three

2. Why does the speaker use a range of time expressions? Read the Skills Check.

D Practising the model

1. ⊕ **2.13** Listen and repeat some of the sentences from the presentation. Copy the pronunciation, including the pauses.

2. In pairs, make sentences from the first set of notes.

E Producing the model

1. In groups, present the remaining biographical information about Braille.

2. ⊕ **2.14** Listen to a student presenting the information. What extra comments do the students make?

3. Think about your questions in Exercise A. Did the presentation answer all of them?

Faculty of Education and Social Work

Tutorial assignment 3:
Research Braille, the system of reading and writing for blind people. Find out about the inventor and how the system works.

Braille

Inventor: Louis Braille (1809 –1852)
1809   b. small town near Paris – father = saddle-maker
1812   blinded in accident – playing with f's awl*
1815   leaves normal school
1819   goes to National Institute for Blind (NIB), Paris
1819–21   learns to read raised letters of the alphabet but does not like the system

Notes:
* awl = pointed tool for making holes in leather

1821–29   works on new system – raised dots* instead of letters
1828   becomes teacher at NIB, but not allowed to teach own system
1837   adds symbols for maths + music
1852   d. Paris
1853   NIB adopts Braille system
1868   Braille accepted as worldwide standard

Notes:
*dot = small circle

Skills Check

Giving biographical information

Biographies can be very boring if you just use *in* + date for every piece of information.

Use a range of time expressions, and vary the position – beginning or end of the sentence.

Pause after the time expression if you put it at the beginning of the sentence.

Everyday English — Talking on the phone

A Activating ideas

How long do you spend on your mobile each day?
Who do you call? What do you talk about?

B Studying models

1. Cover the conversations. Look at the sentences
   in the table. Match each sentence on the left
   with a situation on the right.
2. 🔊 **2.15** Listen and complete the conversations.

   a. Can you speak up?
   b. Sorry, I think you've got the wrong number.
   c. If you are calling about bus times, press 1.
   d. I'll text you later.
   e. Give me a call when you pick up this message.
   f. Certainly. It's d.marshall@hadford.ac.uk.

   ☐ leaving voice messages
   ☐ a bad line
   ☐ sending SMS messages
   ☐ a mistake in dialling
   ☐ an automated menu
   ☐ phoning the college for information

1 A: Hello. Could you give me David Marshall's
   e-mail address please?

   B: _____

   A: Thank you.

   B: You're welcome. Bye.

2 A: *[recording]* The person you have called is not
   available. Please leave a message after the tone.

   B: Hi Katia. It's Piera. _____ OK,
   talk to you later. Bye.

3 A: Hi Stef. It's Peter. How are you?

   B: Hi. Fine. I can't hear you very well.

   _____

   A: Do you know Alan's mobile number?

   B: You're breaking up. Can you hang up and
   redial?

4 A: Hi, is that Carlo?

   B: _____

   A: Oh, sorry.

   B: No problem. Bye.

5 A: *[recording]* _____ If you
   require information about family or student
   passes, or about Day Rover tickets, please
   press 2. For all other enquiries, please hold.
   … You are in a queue. One of our operators
   will be with you as soon as possible.

6 A: Send me a text this afternoon. My phone's
   always on.

   B: OK. What's your number?

   A: It's 0774 5559 173.

   B: Great. _____

C Practising the model

1. Practise the conversations.
2. Explain to your partner how to:

   a. say your phone number
   b. send a text
   c. use an Internet video phone system
   d. phone the tutors in your department
   e. use some of the applications on your phone

   f. find out times of trains by phone
   g. visit your social networking page on the web
   h. say your college e-mail address
   i. leave a message on your mobile's voicemail system
   j. use the college intranet

2.8 Learning new speaking skills   Repairing communication

A Reviewing vocabulary

1. What is the stressed syllable in each word?

   a. ac'cept   e. inventor
   b. accident   f. standard
   c. adopt   g. system
   d. institute   h. worldwide

2. 🔊 **2.16** Listen, check and practise.

B Saying consonants

1. Read the Pronunciation Check.

2. Mark the sentences below with linking (ᴜ) and suppressing (s̶).

   a. He was born in a small town near Paris.
   b. He wasn't blind from birth.
   c. He left normal school three years later.
   d. He invented a system of reading.
   e. He became a teacher at his old school.

3. 🔊 **2.17** Listen, check and practise.

C Identifying a new skill

1. Study the extract from the presentation in 2.7. Write a word or phrase in each space.

   A: He was playing with an awl when he hit his eye with the tool.
   B: _____. What's a nawl?
   A: It's not a nawl. It's an awl.
   C: _____. Was he blinded in both eyes at once?
   A: No. He damaged his right eye and then his left eye got infected.
   B: That's dreadful!
   A: Yes, it is. Anyway, _____
   B: _____
   C: _____
   B: Oh, yes. _____ the accident.
   A: That's right.

2. Read the Skills Check. Which words do you think should be stressed in each sentence?

3. 🔊 **2.18** Listen to the extract. Check your answers.

4. Work in threes. Practise the extract above.

D Practising the new skill

Work in threes. Use the research information about Braille on pages 169, 172 and 174. Use phrases in the Skills Check.

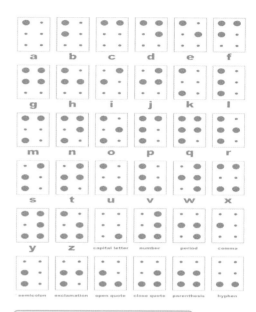

Pronunciation Check

Linking and assimilation

How do we say the consonant *d* in **bold** in each case below?

   He was blinded in an accident.
   It's a pointed tool.

The rules are:

- **consonant** end + **vowel** beginning = **link**
  e.g., blin – de**d** in an ac – cident
- **consonant** end + **consonant** beginning = **assimilate**
  e.g., poin – te**d** t ool

🔊 **2.19** Listen and copy the linking and suppressing.

Skills Check

Repairing communication

These phrases will help you in a discussion if you need to check information, or if one of you gets lost!

Checking information
Sorry, I don't understand.

Saying you are lost
Where was I?
What was I saying?
I've forgotten what I was going to say.

Helping a speaker
You were talking about …
You were going to tell us about …

Saying you can't help
Sorry, I can't remember.
I've forgotten, too.

We sometimes talk about an **action or situation** (1) which is **interrupted** by **another action** (2). ⑦
We often give the **result or consequence** of the interruption. We can make similar sentences with *While* …

action / situation 1				action 2						
S	V	O		S	V	O		**result or consequence 3**		
Braille	was playing with	an awl	when	he	hit	his eye.				
				S	V	O	S	V	O	
			When	he	hit	his eye,	he	damaged	it.	

	action / situation 1			action 2		
	S	V	A	S	V	O
While	the children	were studying	at the institute,	they	learnt	a system of reading.

What tense do we use for:
• action or situation 1?
• the interrupting action 2?
• the result or consequence 3?
How do we say *was / were* in the past continuous?

🔊 **2.20** Listen to the sentences in the tables. Notice the pronunciation of *was / were*, the stress and pausing.

I	was	
You	were	
He / She / It	was	
We	were	(doing)
You (*pl*)	were	
They	were	

How do we make questions with *was / were*?

A   What happened … and what happened next?

Complete each sentence, then give the result or consequence.

1. I was doing my homework when …
2. We were driving home when …
3. She was beginning to get worried when …
4. While I was studying yesterday evening, …
5. While they were waiting for the bus, …
6. While he was living in Paris, …

B   Describing action / situation, interruption and result or consequence

You are going to research one or more accidental discoveries or inventions on pages 164–180.

Fill in Table 1 with information from your research. Then find out about the other cases.

Example: There is a story that, in 1665, the British scientist Sir Isaac Newton was sitting under an apple tree when an apple fell on his head. He began to think about gravity. The falling apple probably didn't hit his head, but it did inspire his theory about gravity.

Table 1: *The top ten accidental discoveries or inventions*

date	person	situation / action 1	action 2	discovery / invention	T/F?
1665	Newton	sitting under apple tree	apple fell on head	gravity	?

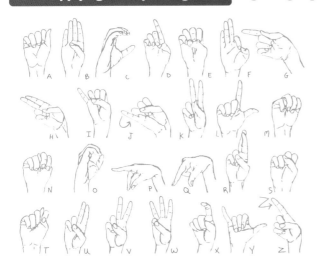

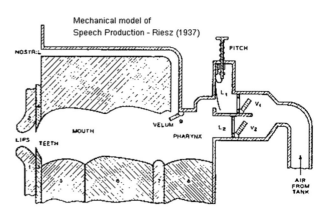

Mechanical model of
Speech Production - Riesz (1937)

A Previewing vocabulary

Look at the diagrams of two systems above.

1. Talk about each system with words from the box.
2. What is the purpose of each system?

| hands | fingers | teeth |
| mouth | lips | nose | thumbs |

B Researching information

Read the assignment on the right. Choose one topic then look at some student notes.

Sign language: page 180
Speech synthesis: page 167

Work with other people with the same topic. Practise making sentences from the biography.

* Use a range of time expressions.
* Try to make at least one sentence with *was / were doing*.

Divide your presentation into sections and decide who will present each section.

Faculty of Education and Social Work
Tutorial assignment: 4

Research the early days of
EITHER sign language for the deaf
OR speech synthesis.
Be prepared to give a talk on an inventor in your field.

C Presenting

Work in groups with two or three people from each topic.

Remember, when you are presenting:

* Introduce your turn.
* Use expressions about your research such as *Apparently, …; I understand that* … .
* Be prepared to explain any words or ideas in your research information if you are asked.
* Ask people to wait for explanations if you want to finish a sentence or section first.
* If you get lost, ask for help.

Remember, when you are listening:

* Check words and ideas but choose your time carefully.
* Help the speaker if he/she gets lost.

D Developing critical thinking

What help is given to people with communication disabilities in your country? Think about shops, offices, restaurants, public transport, etc. Think also about communicating with the government.

Reading: Communication inventors

2

2.11 Vocabulary for reading   Understanding phrases

A Understanding paragraph development

1. Read each topic sentence on the right.
    What sort of information do you expect
    to find in the rest of the paragraph?

2. Match each topic sentence with a
    paragraph below.

B Understanding phrases in context

Explain the meaning of each phrase in
italics in the texts on this page.

Example: ahead of its time – people
are not ready for this idea or
invention.

a An invention is sometimes *ahead
   of its time*.

b If you *feel strongly about* this
   issue, you should talk to the
   Principal of the college.

c In the 1950s and 1960s, many
   people thought the world was
   heading towards a nuclear war.

d Parents often *have a big
   influence on* their children.

e Einstein's teachers could not *get
   through to him* but he *went on to
   become* one of the most famous
   people in the world.

☐ Movies of the period *give an indication* of the way people felt. Several of
   them show 'end of the world' situations.

☐ He was an active campaigner for peace throughout his life, but science was
   his *first love*. His work in physics is *the basis of* many modern ideas in the field.

☐ A man called Charles Babbage invented a type of computer in the 1820s. He
   worked with Ada Lovelace, who *came up with* the idea of computer
   programming. However, it was 150 years before computers *came into their
   own*. An invention is often ignored if people can see *no commercial use* for it.

☐ Remember, however, that it is important *to put* the interests of the college
   ahead of your own personal interests.

☐ Clearly, children often *look like* their mother or father, but, in addition,
   they often have similar ideas and attitudes. However, sometimes parents
   get in the way of the development of their children.

C Predicting information from phrases

What do you expect to come next in each case?

1. The invention was ahead of its time so …

2. The Internet came into its own when …

3. The behaviour of pop stars clearly has an influence on …

4. You should not put work ahead of …

5. If you feel strongly about green issues, you should …

ahead of its time
bar-code *(n)*
be the basis of
bright *(adj)* [= clever]
bulb *(n)*
cellar *(n)*
come into its own
come up with
commercial use
constant *(adj)*
disability *(n)*
experiment *(v)*
expire *(v)*
feel strongly about
genius *(n)*
get in the way of
get through [= contact]
give an indication of
go on to do
have an influence on
head towards
hereditary *(adj)*
independence *(n)*
industrialist *(n)*
inspiration *(n)*
look like
make a fresh start
motion picture
observe *(v)*
original *(adj)* [= new]
patent *(n)*
perspiration *(n)*
put X ahead of Y
reasoning *(n)*
rebuild *(v)*
receiver *(n)* [= object]
recognize [= see the
  value of]
register *(v)*
save *(v)* [= stop death]
scanner *(n)*
speaker *(n)* [= object]
worth *(n)*
wrap *(v)*

_____

_____

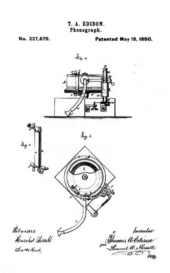

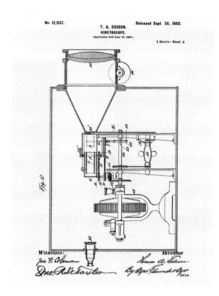

A   Activating ideas

Study the illustrations above.

1. What can you see, in general, in the illustrations above?
2. What do all these illustrations show?

B   Preparing to read

Study the assignment. Make a list of research questions.

C   Understanding the text

1. Scan the whole of the opposite page.

   a. Where can you see articles like this?

   b. What sort of information will the text contain?

   c. What order will the information be in?

2. Read the topic sentences (highlighted). What information will be in each paragraph?
3. Read the text. Find answers to your research questions in Exercise B.
4. How will you answer the question in the assignment?

D   Developing critical thinking

These statements are probably true. Find the evidence in the text.

1. Edison's mother taught him to read.
2. *Hereditary* means 'something you get from your parents'.
3. Edison knew sign language.
4. The telegraph was used on the railway system.
5. Edison knew people wanted the Stock Exchange device before he made it.
6. Edison stopped working as a telegrapher in about 1870.
7. A tape recorder is a kind of phonograph.
8. Before Edison, people made light bulbs with different materials.
9. A digital movie camera is a kind of kinetograph.

Institute of Technology

Module 3: The history of engineering

End-of-term paper

Q1: Thomas Edison is considered by many engineers as the greatest inventor of modern times. To what extent do you agree with this assessment?

Thomas Edison

Thomas Alva Edison was born in Ohio, USA on 11th February 1845. He moved with his family to Michigan when he was seven. Even then, there was an indication of his future life. 'He spent most of his time in the cellar,' his father told reporters later. 'He had a laboratory down there.'

Around 1855, Edison went to school for a short time. His teachers thought that he was not very bright. He stopped going and his mother spent some time teaching him at home. Once he could read, however, he did most of the teaching himself. Edison felt strongly about education. Most schools at that time, he believed, taught children to memorize facts. It was better, he thought, for children to observe nature and to make things with their hands. 'The present system,' he said, 'does not encourage original thought or reasoning.'

About the age of 12, Edison became almost completely deaf. He thought it was from an accident, but it was probably a hereditary disease since his father and later his son had the same hearing loss. He did not let his disability get in the way of his life, however, once telling a group of deaf people, 'I prefer the quiet of deafness to the noise of conversation.'

In 1862, the teenage Edison saved a little boy from being hit by a train. He was selling newspapers at his local railway station when a boy fell onto the tracks. Edison jumped down and pulled the boy back onto the platform. The boy's father was the station master, and thanked him by teaching him how to use the telegraph. Edison learnt well, getting a job as a telegraph operator. He travelled thousands of miles, doing the job in railway stations all over America. In 1867, Edison moved to Massachusetts to work as a telegrapher, but his first love was inventing things. He registered his first patent the following year; it was for an electrical vote recorder. However, nobody wanted to buy it. Edison said later, 'I learnt a good lesson then. Only invent things that people want to buy.'

Edison followed his own advice. He made a device for the New York Stock Exchange, selling it to them in 1870. He wanted $4,000 for the device but did not ask for this amount. When the manager of the exchange asked him, 'How much do you want?' Edison replied, 'Pay me what it's worth.' The manager paid him $40,000. Edison was now able to work full-time as an inventor. He was famous for working very long hours and making constant improvements to his inventions. He once said, 'Most people miss opportunity because it wears overalls and looks like work.'

Edison's favourite invention appeared in 1877. Wrapping tin foil around a cylinder, he connected a receiver and a speaker and said, 'Mary had a little lamb' into the receiver. The speaker played his words back. He called the device a *phonograph* (from two Greek words), which literally means 'sounds writing'. Today we call it a sound recorder. It is the basis of the whole recorded music industry.

Edison went on to work on a large number of inventions. Perhaps his most famous is the electric light system. He didn't actually invent the light *bulb* but, in 1879, he discovered the best materials to make it from. Experimenting with hundreds of materials, he finally found the one that really worked. He once said, 'I haven't failed. I have just discovered 10,000 ways that don't work.' In 1888, Edison told reporters, 'I am experimenting with a device which does for the eye what the phonograph does for the ear, which is the recording and reproduction of things in motion.' Edison's kinetograph (or 'movement writing') appeared in 1891, starting the motion picture industry, 'the movies'.

On 9th December 1914 fire destroyed Edison's laboratories. He said, 'I am 67, but I'm not too old to make a fresh start.' Edison rebuilt the laboratories and went back to work.

Edison died on 18th October 1931, holding 1,093 patents for inventions covering mass communication devices and energy distribution. *Time* magazine called him a genius, but during Edison's lifetime he said, 'Genius is 1 per cent inspiration and 99 per cent perspiration.'

A   Reviewing vocabulary

Complete the final word in each sentence.

1. As a child, Edison had a laboratory in his c_____.
2. His teachers didn't think he was very b_____.
3. He thought children should observe n_____.
4. His deafness was probably h_____.
5. In 1868, he registered his first p_____.
6. He constantly improved his i_____.
7. He didn't actually invent the light b_____.
8. His phonograph is the basis of the recorded music i_____.
9. His kinetograph was the start of the m_____.
10. In 1914, his laboratories were destroyed by f_____.

B   Identifying a new skill

Discuss these questions in pairs then read the Skills Check.

1. What does the quote show about Edison's opinions? (see right)
2. How true is the popular saying for Edison's life? (see right)

C   Practising a new skill

1. Find more quotes in the text in 2.12. What does each quote show about Edison's opinions and attitudes? Do you agree with them?
2. Read the 'lessons for life' below. Which of these apply to Edison? Find evidence in the text in 2.12.

   a. If at first you don't succeed, try, try again.
   b. A poor workman blames his tools.
   c. Behind every great man there's a great woman.
   d. Concentrate on what you can do, not on what you can't do.
   e. Count your blessings.
   f. Forgive and forget.
   g. God helps those who help themselves.
   h. If a job is worth doing, it's worth doing well.
   i. Life is what you make it.
   j. One good turn deserves another.

I haven't failed. I have just discovered 10,000 ways that don't work.
Edison

If at first you don't succeed, try, try again.
popular saying

Skills Check

Reacting to a text

While you are reading a text, you must distinguish between facts and theories, you must recognize bias and make inferences.

After reading a text, you must react to it. Ask yourself some questions:

- *What are the opinions / attitudes in the text? Do I agree with them? Why (not)?*
- *What can I take from the text, e.g., lessons for life?*

Examples:

opinion in the text	Schools teach children to memorize facts.
my opinion	*I agree, but that is not true at university in my country.*
fact in the text	Fire destroyed Edison's laboratory when he was 67 but he rebuilt the laboratory and went back to work.
lesson for life	*It's never too late to start again.*

Study the information in Table 1 and Table 2. What is similar about them? What is different?   ⑧

Table 1

sentence 1				sentence 2			
S	V			S	V		
Edison	learnt	well	.	He	got	a job	as a telegraph operator.

Table 2

clause 1				clause 2			
S	V			S	V		
Edison	learnt	well	,		getting	a job	as a telegraph operator.

Study Table 3. What is the subject and tense of the verb in clause 1? How do you know?

Table 3

clause 1				clause 2		
V	O			S	V	O
Wrapping	tin foil	around a cylinder	,	he	connected	a receiver and a speaker.

In the tables above, *getting* and *wrapping* are **present participles**. When you see present participles on their own, think:
*What is the **subject / tense** of this verb?* It is **the same** as the main verb in the other clause.
But be careful! **Gerunds** have the same form as participles and can be the subject of a clause themselves.
Working hard all his life, Edison registered 1,093 patents.   = **participle** with subject *Edison*
Working hard came naturally to Edison.   = **gerund** = subject of *came*

A   Recognizing participle clauses

Look again at the text in 2.12. Find five more participle clauses.
What is the subject of each one? What is the original verb, before clause joining?

B   Participle or gerund?

Find the ~*ing* form(s) in each sentence. Is the word a participle or a gerund? If it is a participle, what is the missing subject, and what tense is the original verb in?

1 As we all know, forgetting is a natural process. 2 If you use information many times, it becomes fixed, staying in your memory for years. 3 As the graph shows, the first review actually boosts memory, taking it to 100 per cent. 4 Reviewing information regularly helps you remember it for a long time.

5 Being part of a complex web of relationships, animals are affected by climate change.
6 Removing one part of a food web has an enormous effect on the rest of the web.
7 Adapting to a changing environment takes animals and plants many thousands of years.

8 It is clear that making good decisions is not easy. 9 Participatory managers involve their workers, asking them to take part in decision-making and listening to their ideas.

10 Moving to New York in the 1930s, Berne trained as a psychiatrist. 11 Berne believed that people often play games with their friends, family and workmates, making other people feel worse so they can feel better. 12 Some people are happy to work with others, respecting their contribution but also feeling confident about their own.

A   Activating ideas

Study the illustrations above.

1. What are these items? What are they for?
2. What is the connection between the three items?

B   Preparing to read

Study the assignment. What do you have to look for in your research? Make a list of questions.

C   Understanding the text

1. Read the text and answer your research question.
2. Discuss your answers in pairs or groups.

D   Showing comprehension

1. How did these people feature in Hedwig's life?
   a. Fritz Mandl   c. Louis B. Meyer
   b. Hedy Lamarr   d. George Antheil
2. Which of Hedwig's opinions do you agree with?
3. These statements about Hedwig are true or probably true. Find evidence in the article.
   a. She was very intelligent.
   b. She had many abilities.
   c. She didn't admire Hitler.
   d. She lived to see her invention in use.
   e. She realized the importance of her invention.

E   Understanding vocabulary and grammar in context

1. Find five words in the text beginning *in~*. What does each word mean?
2. Find five participle verbs. What is the subject and tense of each one?

F   Developing critical thinking

1. What lessons for life can you learn from the story of Hedwig's life?
2. Find some connections between Edison and Kiesler.

Institute of Technology

The history of telecommunications

End-of-term test

Question 1:

'Hedwig Kiesler did not get the recognition she deserved in the field of telecommunications.'

To what extent do you agree with this assessment?

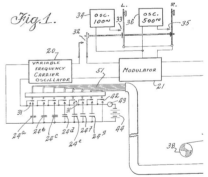

Aug. 11, 1942.   H. K. MARKEY ET AL

SECRET COMMUNICATION SYSTEM

Filed June 10, 1941

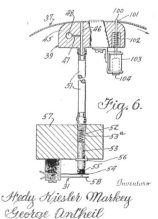

Hedwig Kiesler

Hedwig Kiesler was born in Austria in November 1913, one year before the start of the First World War. Perhaps her experience of growing up during a war had a strong influence on her later life.

Hedwig became an actress, making her first full-length movie in 1931. It was called *Storm in a Glass*. Over the next few years, she made several more movies. It seems that they did not require much acting. She just had to look beautiful. She said later: 'Being glamorous is easy. All you have to do is stand still and look stupid.'

Meanwhile, the world was heading towards the Second World War. In 1933, Hitler came to power in Germany. In the same year, Hedwig married Fritz Mandl. He was an industrialist, producing guns for Hitler. Going to all his business meetings, Hedwig learnt a lot about weapons. In 1937, she divorced Mandl, escaping from Austria to America. One year later, Hitler took over Austria.

While she was travelling across the Atlantic, Hedwig met an important Hollywood producer, called Louis B. Meyer. He offered her a movie contract in Hollywood, also giving her a new name, Hedy Lamarr (from La Mar, 'the sea'). In America, she continued her movie career. She made her first film for Meyer, *Algiers*, in 1938. The world moved closer to war, and Hedy Lamarr still knew a lot about weapons, especially the weapons on submarines.

Submarines have special weapons called torpedoes. After a torpedo is fired, the sailors on the submarine control it with radio signals. However, enemy sailors can also send radio signals and stop the correct messages getting through. In 1941, in the middle of the Second World War, Hedy Lamarr had an idea. 'Is it possible,' she thought, 'to change the control signal constantly, so that the enemy cannot intercept the signal?' Working with an American composer, George Antheil, she came up with a device which they patented in 1942, using the title Secret Communication System.

The US Navy never used the invention. The problem was, it was years ahead of its time. Only today has the invention come into its own, forming the basis of all wireless communication. It is used in mobile phones, in wireless Internet systems, even in the bar code scanner and reader in your local supermarket.

Hedy Lamarr went on to make many more films. Her last starring role was in 1957. In her later life, she also wrote songs and, in 1966, she published her autobiography, *My Life as a Woman*. The patent did not earn Hedy or George a penny, expiring before any commercial use was found for the device. However, she was never poor, believing that money was a by-product of activity. 'I know why most people never get rich. They put the money ahead of the job. If you just think of the job, the money will automatically follow. This never fails.'

Although she was an inventor, Hedy was not sure about inventions in general. 'The world isn't getting any easier,' she once said. 'With all these new inventions, I believe that people are hurried more and pushed more. The hurried way is not the right way. You need time for everything, to work, to play, to rest.' Hedy was also uncertain about marriage, although she had six husbands during her life. 'Perhaps my problem in marriage – and it is the problem of many women – was to want both intimacy and independence. It is a difficult line to walk.'

Finally, scientists began to recognize Hedy Lamarr's role in radio technology, awarding her the Electronic Frontier Foundation prize in 1997. Some people call it the Oscar of inventing. Austria, Germany and Switzerland celebrate invention on Inventor's Day, holding it on 9th November, her birthday.

Hedwig Kiesler died in Florida on 18th January 2000.

Aim

Some of the sentences below are grammatically correct but some are wrong. Identify the correct sentences and then go to the auction. Try to buy the correct sentences. The winner is the person or group with the most correct sentences.

How to play

Each person or group has £10,000 to spend. Bids begin at £200 and increase by £100 each bid. Each sentence is sold to the highest bidder.

1. Humans have being able to communicate since they first learnt to speak.
2. As you probably know, the Sumerians invented writing thousands of years.
3. In Ancient Egypt, messages with couriers were not very fast or not very secure.
4. New businesses should offer better products customers.
5. Successful companies supply customers of benefits.
6. Telegraph offices delivered telegrams to people's homes.
7. The employment agency found for me a good job.
8. Berners-Lee realized that every document needed an address, so you find it on another computer.
9. In the second phase of the Internet, it became a marketing tool.
10. Although etailers use the virtual infrastructure of the Internet, they have to use the real infrastructure of postal delivery to get goods to customers.
11. Statistics show that around 80 per cent of blind people in the world is unemployed.
12. Braille played with an awl when he hit his eye.
13. While Braille was studying at the institute, a soldier came to teach night writing.
14. Give me a call when you pick up this message.
15. In 1928, Alexander Fleming was studying a bacteria that it causes food poisoning.
16. He left some slides overnight and, next morning, found that there was not bacteria on them.
17. He realized that a mould grew on the slides.
18. Friedrich Kekule was studying the structure of carbon compounds when he was having a day-dream.
19. In his dream, he was seeing a snake with its own tail in its mouth.
20. His dream led to the discovery that the structure of benzene was a ring of carbon atoms.
21. I've forgotten what was I going to say.
22. You were going to telling us about the accident.
23. Edison saved a little boy from hit by a train.
24. He was selling newspapers when the boy fell onto the tracks.
25. Jumping down, Edison pulled the boy back onto the platform.
26. Inventing things it was Edison's first love.
27. Edison's deafness was probably hereditary since his father also suffered from the disability.
28. Hedwig Kiesler married Fritz Mandl who was an industrialist produced guns for Hitler.
29. Hedy Lamarr's invention was years ahead for its time.
30. After firing a torpedo, sailors control them with radio signals.

2.16 Vocabulary for writing   Types of competition

A Developing critical thinking

1. Are the animals above in competition? In what way(s)?
2. What happens if …

   a. the number of sheep increases sharply?

   b. the number of rabbits rises rapidly?

   c. the number of foxes declines sharply?

B Understanding structure in context

Read the text from a marketing journal on page 170. Choose a word, phrase or sentence below to complete each *which* clause. Write the number.

1. 'We do the same thing, but better.'
2. a rapid decline in sales of the old products.
3. because of the competition.
4. cassettes in the recorded music market.
5. every day.
6. clearly much better than MP3s.
7. new-born lambs.
8. Products B, C, D, etc.
9. their disappearance from the market.
10. with CDs and MP3 players.

C Transferring information to a table

Copy and complete Table 1 below, which appeared with the article.

Table 1: *Some competition types*

type	markets	effect on sales	strategy	example
1	both products in same market	each product takes sales from other	'we do the same thing but better'	different mobile phone companies

D Understanding vocabulary in context

Look again at the words in italics in the text. Choose five and write a sentence for each to show the meaning.

---

analogue *(adj)*
analysis *(n)*
analyze *(v)*
brand *(v)*
cancel *(v)*
cancellation *(n)*
cartridge *(n)*
CD *(n)*
compete *(v)*
competition *(n)*
compress *(v)*
compression *(n)*
contract *(n)*
conversion *(n)*
convert *(v)*
correct *(v)*
correction *(n)*
demonstrate *(v)*
demonstration *(n)*
design *(n* and *v)*
digital *(adj)*
dry *(v)*
existing *(adj)*
experiment with
flow *(v)*
handmade *(adj)*
ink *(n)*
laser *(n)*
luxury *(n)*
manufacture *(v)*
manufacturer *(n)*
manuscript *(n)*
marketing strategy
MP3 *(n)*
patent *(n)*
practical *(adj)* [= able to work]
proofreader *(n)*
react *(v)*
rebrand *(v)*
recover *(v)* [e.g., sales]
refill *(v)*
scan *(v)*
smudge *(v)*
suffer *(v)*
tube *(n)*

A Preparing to write

Study the assignment on the right.

1. Make a list of paragraph topics for this essay.
2. Look at the introductory paragraph of the essay on the opposite page and check your ideas.

B Previewing vocabulary

1. Label Figure 1 and Figure 2 with words from the box.

cartridge	ink	nib	tube

2. What is the connection between pens and each verb below?

refill	leak	flow	smudge

C Previewing grammar

How do fountain pens and ballpoint pens work?

1. Read the explanation for the fountain pen. There are mistakes. Rewrite the explanation correctly.

> As the nib was moving across the paper, ink flowed down a pen from cartridge. In the same time, air is flowing up the pen.

2. Write an explanation for the ballpoint pen, using the information in Figure 2.

D Gathering data

1. Study the notes below and the graph opposite.
2. Rewrite paragraphs 2, 3 and 4, adding the extra information from the notes and the graph.
3. Add the two sections from Exercise C.
4. Read the start of the final paragraph. Complete the paragraph with information from the table on the opposite page.

Institute of Marketing
End-of-term test
Answer ONE of the following:

What effect did the invention of the ballpoint pen have on sales of the fountain pen? Describe with reference to the analysis of competition by Smitalova and Sujan.
OR
What effect did the invention of

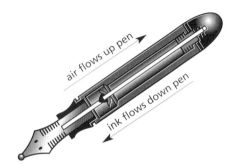

Figure 1: fountain pen

air flows up pen

ink flows down pen

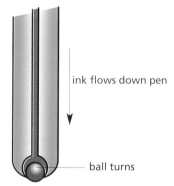

ink flows down pen

ball turns

Figure 2: ballpoint pen

Fountain pen —1st practical pen – improved existing product

Inventor = Lewis Waterman (US)

1883   W. wanted client to sign imp. contract   bought new pen for the purpose
insurance
salesman bought fount. pen, leaked, destroyed contract

   W.: 'I will make better pen!' → diff. designs —in brother's workshop

1884   patent
Ballpoint pen   1885 started making handmade pens

Inventor = Ladislo Biro (Hung.)

1930s   Biro = proofreader – checked manuscripts, made corrections

   used fount. pen but ink = long time to dry, so often smudged corrections ②did not hold
            ①   ╱chemist   much ink so had
   B.: 'I will make better pen' → asked George (brother) 'Make a thicker ink'   to refill often

   but ink not flow thru normal nib so put small ball in tip of pen = ballpoint pen

1938   patent 1943 began manufacturing

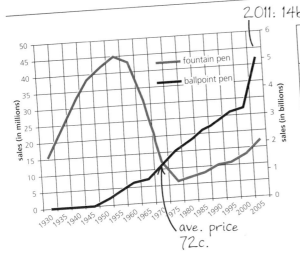

2011: 14b.

period	comp. type*	fountain pen	ballpoint pen
'51–'56	1	sales suffer	sales suffer
'56–'74	5	affected by b. pen	not affected by f. pen
'74–now	6	not competing; rebranded as luxury	not competing; everyday use

ave. price 72c.

* Smitalova and Sujan (1991)

What effect did the invention of the ballpoint pen have on sales of the fountain pen? Describe with reference to the analysis of competition by Smitalova and Sujan.

In this essay, I will describe the invention of the fountain pen and the ballpoint pen. I will then give details of the global sales of each product. Finally, I will analyze the competitive relationships between the two products, as explained by Smitalova and Sujan (1991).

The fountain pen was invented by an insurance salesman called Lewis Waterman. In 1883, Waterman wanted a client to sign an important contract. However, as the client was signing, the pen leaked and destroyed the contract. Waterman set out to make a better pen, experimenting with many different ideas. Finally, he produced a design which worked. Waterman obtained a patent in 1884.

The ballpoint pen was invented by Ladislo Biro. In the 1930s, he was working as a proofreader, checking manuscripts from writers and making corrections on them. He used a fountain pen but the ink took a long time to dry so he often smudged his corrections. Biro decided to make a better pen, asking his brother, Georg, to make a thicker ink. However, the thicker ink did not flow through a normal nib so Biro decided to put a small ball in the tip of the pen, producing a pen which wrote reliably and did not leak. Biro obtained a patent in 1938.

Ballpoint pens became widely available in 1951. From then until 1956, sales of fountain pens continued to rise, reaching a peak of 45 million per annum in that year. Then, from 1956 to 1974, sales of fountain pens declined as sales of ballpoint pens rose. The manufacturers of fountain pens reacted by dropping the price of their product. However, their market share continued to go down, and the product was facing extinction. Then, in 1973, sales of fountain pens began to recover. By 2007, they were back to 17 million per annum. In the same year, the sales of ballpoint pens reached more than 5 billion.

According to Smitalova and Sujan (1991), there are six possible types of competition between two products. We can identify three types in the competition between fountain pens and ballpoint pens. During the first stage, from 1951 to 1956, the newly-invented ballpoint pen took sales away from fountain pens and vice versa. This was competition type 1. Each product suffered from the existence of the other product. In the second stage,

A Reviewing vocabulary and grammar

Correct the mistakes in the title and introductory paragraph.

> ### What effect the invention of the ballpoint pen have on sales the fountain pen?
>
> In this essay, I describe the invention the fountain pen and the ballpoint pen. I then will give details of the global sales of every product. Finally, I will analysis the competition relationships between two products, as is explained by Smitalova and Sujan (1991).

B Identifying a key skill

1. What is the basic S V O of this sentence from the essay in 2.17? What extra information has the writer added?

> The biro was invented in 1938 by a Hungarian called Ladislo Biro, with the help of his brother, Georg, who was a chemist.

2. Read the Skills Check and check your ideas.

C Practising the key skill

Study the first draft sentences and the extra information. Rewrite each sentence, including the extra information correctly.

1. The first component of knowing a word is meaning.

   dict. definition of word
   The first component of knowing a word is meaning, which is the dictionary definition of the word.

2. Two researchers conducted an experiment into memory recall.

   Lloyd and Margaret Peterson (1959)

3. Acme Engineering is located in Causton.

   pop. 10,000

4. The company occupies premises of 5,000 square metres.

   employs 14

5. There is a major motorway close to Bellport.

   links city to London

6. When heat energy reaches the Earth, some of it is absorbed by the land.

   = taken in

7. Some is reflected by the clouds.

   = sent back

8. Most scientists believe that gases in the air cause the greenhouse effect.

   e.g., CO_2

9. According to Sachs and Gallup, economic performance is largely the result of geography.

   survey of 150 countries, 1991

10. The UK is a member of the EU.

    27 countries, market of 500 m.

Skills Check

Adding extra information

While you are writing the second draft of an essay, you often want to add information. Choose the best place and use correct sentence structure. Make any necessary changes to the first draft sentence.

type of extra information	S V O + extra information
about a noun	The **first practical fountain pen was invented by an American called** Lewis Waterman. Waterman, **who was an insurance salesman**, met an important client.
about a linked action	He wanted the client to sign a valuable contract, **and he bought a new pen for the purpose.**
about a location or time	**For several months,** Waterman experimented with different designs **in his brother's workshop.**

Look again at the tables in Grammar box 8 (2.14).   ⑨
Look at the sentence on the right below and answer the questions.

1. How many clauses are there?
2. What is the subject of each clause?
3. What is the verb of each clause?
4. What form is each verb in?
5. What do you notice about the punctuation?

> Waterman set out to make a better pen, experimenting with many different ideas.

We can use a present participle, e.g., *experimenting* to describe **the next action** if the subject of the second clause is the same as the first, e.g., *Waterman*.
Remember to put a comma before the present participle, e.g., *a better pen, experimenting with …*

A   Forming the present participle

1. What is the present participle form of each verb?

a. write	writing	e. speak		i. begin	
b. put		f. lie		j. offer	
c. make		g. dry		k. prefer	
d. try		h. set		l. know	

2. What must you do before you add ~*ing* to the infinitive? Tick the correct rules.
   Find examples in A1 above.
   a. ✔ take off final *e*   writing, making
   b. ☐ change final *ie* to *y*
   c. ☐ change *y* to *ie*
   d. ☐ with one-syllable verbs, double the final consonant letter after a single vowel letter
   e. ☐ with multi-syllable verbs, double the final consonant letter after a single vowel letter

B   Joining with a present participle

Study each pair of sentences. Can you join them, using a present participle? If so, rewrite the information in a single sentence.

1. The pen leaked. It destroyed the contract.
   The pen leaked, destroying the contract.

2. The contract was destroyed. Waterman had to get a new one.
   (no, different subjects)

3. Biro checked manuscripts. He made corrections on them.

4. Acme Engineering makes car components. It sells 75 per cent of its finished goods to customers in Britain.

5. A major motorway runs near Bellport. It links the city to London.

6. The company employs 14 people. Most of them are unskilled.

7. People can send a text message to Freedom Fone. They get a call back from the organization.

A Thinking and organizing

Study the assignment and complete the writing plan underneath. Check with the essay in 2.17.

B Writing and editing

1. Write the essay. Use the notes and resources at the bottom of the page. Remember:
   - Use a range of expressions.
   - Paraphrase your research notes.

2. Exchange drafts with a partner and mark his/her work with *?, S, G, P*.

3. Read your essay and correct the points.

C Rewriting

1. Look at your additional research – page 182. Add the information to your essay in logical places. Change the sentence structure if necessary.

2. Write the second draft of your essay.

Institute of Marketing

End-of-term test

Answer ONE of the following:

What effect did the invention of the MP3 player have on sales of CDs? Describe with reference to the analysis of competition by Smitalova and Sujan.
OR
What effect did the invention of the ballpoint

	Writing plan
Para 1	Introduction
Para 2	
Para 3	
Para 4	
Para 5	

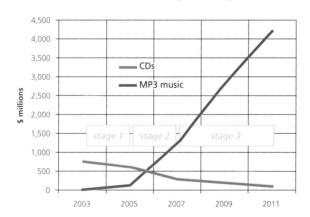

st.	type	CDs	MP3s
1	1	affected but already in decline	affected – many people still choose to buy music on CDs
2	4	sales fall sharply	sales rise quickly
3	5	not competing, rebranded as gifts, high-quality items	not competing, only real choice for everyday use

CD
inventor: James Russell
1970   R. patented the technology
1976   Sony demonstrated first workable CD
1982   Commercial manufacturing began
        1st CD player produced
1983   Very good reviews from audio magazines
        for quality
1985   'Brothers in Arms' sold one million copies

MP3 player
inventor: Karlheinz Brandenberg
1977   Br. began researching music compression
1987   Br. developed MP3 technology for
        Fraunhofer company
1991   Project nearly cancelled
1998   patent to Fraunhofer
        1st MP3 players manufactured

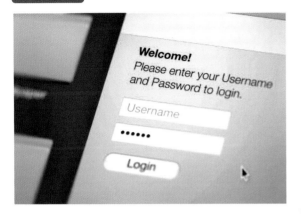
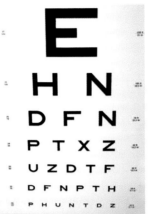
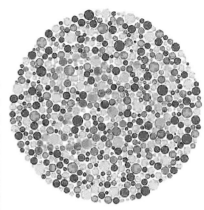

A   Activating ideas

1. What do the photographs above show?
2. What difficulties might a vision-impaired person have using a computer?

B   Gathering and recording information

1. Study the assignment. Make your choice and do some research.
2. Work in pairs. Exchange notes and make comments.

C   Preparing a presentation

Prepare to give a talk about your research. Use slides and/or visuals to illustrate your points.

D   Listening to a presentation

Work in groups. Make notes to answer the three questions in the assignment about each aid that is presented.

E   Writing

Choose one of the following:

- Write an article about the aid that you researched for Exercise C.
- Make a poster presentation of all the aids that help one particular group of people, e.g., people who are colour-blind. Use the notes you made in Exercise D.

Faculty of Education and Social Work

Computers and the vision-impaired

Around 250 million people in the world have low vision. About eight per cent of men and one per cent of women are colour-blind. People with vision impairment may have great difficulty in reading or producing written communication. However, the infrastructure provided by modern computers can assist people who are vision-impaired in many ways.

Research ONE of the following areas:
- Putting information into the computer, e.g., using a keyboard or mouse.

OR

- Receiving information from the computer, e.g., from the screen, from the speaker.

Choose ONE communication aid and find answers to these questions:
1. Who does it help?
2. What benefit(s) does it offer?
3. How do you access it?
4. How does it work?

Be prepared to give a presentation at the next tutorial.

Theme 3

Media and advertising

- The case against television

- The hidden persuaders

- Conventions in narrative fiction

- Reality TV – real or fiction?

3.1 Vocabulary for listening Violence in stories for children

A Activating knowledge

Study the illustrations above.

1. Which fairy tale is illustrated? What is the basic story?
2. Do you have a similar story in your culture?

B Understanding vocabulary in context

1. ⦿ **3.1** Listen to part of a talk about fairy tales. Answer the questions.
   a. How has the story of Little Red Riding Hood changed through history?
   b. Why has it changed in those ways?
   c. What was the message of the story originally?
   d. What is the message now?
   e. What other stories are mentioned in the talk?

2. ⦿ **3.2** Listen to part of the talk again. Number each word from the list on the right as you hear it.

3. Write a numbered word from the list in each sentence. Make any necessary changes.
   a. Young children need to _experience_____ fear.
   b. Fairy tales were very _violences__ d__, originally.
   c. The _violence_____ is often against children or young people.
   d. The Father Bear in the Goldilocks story deals with Goldilocks with _oggression_____.
   e. _Initialy_____, in the Little Red Riding Hood story, the weak people died.
   f. Nowadays, extreme violence is _obviously___ in fairy tales.
   g. The violence and aggression _tone down___ in recent years.
   h. Some people say that the _Message_____ has changed, as a result.
   i. Now the message of the story for children is: 'Don't speak to _Strangers___.'
   j. Perhaps there is a message for adults too, _Incidently__.
   k. 'Always _Supervise____ your children when they are young.'
   l. Some people say this is _dumb down_____ – in other words, taking a complex idea and making it so simple that it is not useful.

4. ⦿ **3.3** Listen and check your answers.

C Developing critical thinking

What do you think about changing fairy stories? Do you think we should remove the violence?

---

accept *(v)*
aggression *(n)*
aggressive *(adj)*
argument *(n)* [= thesis]
authorities
ban *(v)*
brand *(n)* [= named product]
calculate *(v)*
childminder *(n)*
clearly *(adv)*
commit *(v)*
conform *(v)*
counter-argument *(n)*
deny *(v)*
dependency *(n)*
dependent *(adj)*
dumb down
eliminate *(v)*
experience *(v)*
fairy tale
fictional *(adj)*
golden age
incidentally *(adv)*
initially *(adv)*
media *(n pl)*
mediate *(v)*
medium *(n)*
message *(n)* [= meaning]
model *(v)* [= copy]
obviously *(adv)*
proposition *(n)*
sedative *(n)*
socialize *(v)*
stranger *(n)*
supervise *(v)*
supervised *(adj)*
tone down
unsupervised *(adj)*
unvarying *(adj)*
violence *(n)*
violent *(adj)*
vulnerable *(adj)*

A   Activating ideas

1. 🔊 **3.4** Listen to statements about television from adults and children. Who is making each comment?

2. Study the transcript on page 199. What is your reaction to each comment?

3. Study the department information. Discuss the question in pairs. Make a note of your ideas. (We will return to this later.)

> ## Media Studies Department
> **Guest lecture**
> 'Does violent television produce violent children?'
> A talk by Gillian Marsh, educational psychologist.
>
> There will be an opportunity to ask questions at the end of the talk.

B   Preparing for a lecture

You will hear all the words and phrases below in the talk. What sort of information will follow in each case?

- Let's start with some facts.   *facts*
- Nobody can deny that ...   *opinion of speaker*
- According to research ...
- Just think about that for a minute.
- Now, I accept that ...
- Clearly, ...

- So that's the first point.
- It's true that ...
- What should we do about this issue?
- We must consider the counter-arguments.
- Some people say ...
- Incidentally, ...

C   Understanding a lecture

🔊 **3.5** DVD **3.A** Watch the talk. For each slide:

1. Add notes to the bullet points.

2. Make notes of arguments against each point.

Violent TV and young children	Violent TV and young children
○ children watch a lot of television	○ children are visual learners
○ children see a lot of TV violence	○ children 'model' behaviour
○ children become violent	
1	**2**

Violent TV and young children	Violent TV and young children
○ TV is like a stranger in your house	○ Studies
○ children shouldn't watch unsupervised	• Berkowitz
	• Parke
	• Williams
3	**4**

D   Developing critical thinking

1. Have the points in the talk changed your mind, or reinforced your opinion?

2. Think of some questions about TV violence and young children to ask the speaker.

A Reviewing vocabulary

What is the noun from each verb? Where is the main stress in each case?

> advertise appeal compete endorse
> exaggerate present produce release register

B Gathering information

1. Study the assignment. Answer the question.
2. Study Table 1. What does the Youth4U advertisement probably contain?
3. ● **3.23** Listen to some students and complete the information about the second method.

Marketing Institute
Module 325/7

Tutorial assignment

How do advertisers try to sell their products?

Research the methods, then choose one and find an example of a current TV advertisement which uses the method.

Be prepared to talk about the method and the ad at the tutorial.

Table 1: *Common TV advertising methods*

method	Contents of the ad	science behind the ad	current TV example
the big lie (= not true)	exaggerated claims, e.g., this product will make you richer, more attractive, etc.	people believe big promises more than little ones; people believe what they want to believe	Youth4U – anti-ageing cream
BOGOF (= _____)			

C Studying a model

1. Study extracts from the discussion below. Find expressions which:
   - introduce the presentation
   - ask for clarification
   - clarify
   - introduce research
   - ask people to wait
   - explain that you are lost
   - help the speaker

2. ● **3.24** Listen to some expressions from the extracts. Repeat, copying the stress and intonation.
3. Practise the extracts.

S1: I worked with Sarah on this research. We chose BOGOF, which means Buy One, Get One Free.

S2: Sorry. I don't understand. Is it a word?

S1: No, it's the initial letters.

S2: I still don't get what you mean.

S1: What I'm saying is, it's the first letter of each word. Buy One, Get One Free.

S2: Oh, I see.

S2: So what's the science behind this method?

S1: I'm just coming to that. Apparently, people don't want cheap products. They want expensive products cheaply.

S2: Did you find any good examples of BOGOF on TV at the moment? We couldn't find any.

S1: Sorry. Can I deal with that in a second? So they pay full price for one product and get the second one free. And, um, ah. I've forgotten what I was going to say.

S2: You were going to give us examples on TV at the moment.

D Producing a model

1. Research an advertising method – see pages 164–176. Think of current TV examples.
2. Work in groups. Make sure people have researched different methods. Discuss your research and examples.

A Activating ideas

Look at the photographs. Have you ever complained in any of these places? What was the result of your complaint?

B Studying the models

1. ● **3.25** Listen to the conversations below. What is the complaint in each case?
2. Write one word in each space.
3. Practise the conversations.

1
A: Hello, reception.
B: Ah, yes. This is Mr Adams in Room 306.
A: Yes, Mr Adams. How _____ I help you?
B: I'm afraid the air conditioning _____ working.
A: Have you _____ changing the thermostat?
B: Yes, it _____ do anything.
A: OK. _____ send someone up.
B: Thank you.

2
A: Excuse me.
B: Yes, madam?
A: Well, we have _____ waiting a long time.
B: I'm sorry. _____ you ordered yet?
A: No. We haven't even _____ the menu.
B: OK. Sorry. Here you _____.
A: Thanks.
B: Now, what _____ you like?
A: _____ you give us a moment?
B: Oh, yes. Sorry.

3
A: Can I help you?
B: I hope so. I _____ this iPod here a few days ago but when I unpacked it, I found the screen _____ cracked. See?
A: Oh, dear. OK, so have you _____ the receipt?
B: No, I _____ I've lost it.
A: Well, we _____ replace the item but I'm afraid we _____ give you a refund.
B: No, that's OK. I _____ a replacement.
A: Right. Just, _____ me a moment. I'll get the form.
B: Thanks.

C Building vocabulary

What could each word apply to, in a hotel or a restaurant, or with a product?

a. broken	d. damaged	g. missing	j. scratched
b. blocked	e. dirty	h. overcooked	k. wrong
c. cold	f. faulty	i. past its sell-by date	l. not working

D Practising the model

Role-play a conversation about a problem in each of the locations in the photographs.

A Saying vowels

1. Read the Pronunciation Check.

2. Mark the sentences below with intrusive sounds.

   a. BOGOF products are often loss-leaders.

   b. I worked with Sarah on this research.

   c. It's on TV at the moment.

   d. So I did a bit more research.

   e. The word *free* is very powerful.

   f. You get two of them.

3. 🔊 **3.26** Listen, check and practise.

B Identifying a key skill

1. Read the Skills Check.

2. Study the extracts from the tutorial in 3.7. Mark the pauses and the stressed words in the sentences in *italics*.

3. Practise the extracts.

Joe:	Customers who buy a packet of biscuits get another packet free.
Sarah:	Superbuys is using BOGOF at the moment.
Mark:	*But going back to Joe's point, BOGOF is the same as half price, isn't it?*

Mark:	So BOGOF sells more than half price?
Joe:	Yes. Apparently, it does.
Mark:	That's weird.
Joe:	Not really. *As Sarah has said, people want something for nothing.*

Debbie:	*I don't know if this is relevant, but I read that BOGOF products are often loss-leaders.*
Tutor:	Yes, that's a good point.

Pierre:	Sorry, I'm late.
Tutor:	That's OK. We're talking about BOGOF.
Pierre:	Right. *Has anyone mentioned that BOGOF products are often loss-leaders?*
Tutor:	Yes, we've just talked about that.

C Practising the new skill

🔊 **3.27** Listen to some sentences about information in this course so far. Repeat the information, beginning with a phrase from the Skills Check.

Example: Visual learners don't like noise.

As Joe has said,
Going back to
   Sarah's point,   visual learners don't
Has anyone   like noise(?).
   mentioned that

Pronunciation Check

Intrusive sounds

What do we do when two vowels occur next to each other?
Examples:
They are all in the promotion.
Have you all looked at the examples?

🔊 **3.28** Listen and copy the intrusive sounds /r/, /j/ and /w/.

Skills Check

Linking to a previous speaker

In a tutorial or discussion, we often need to link to a previous speaker.

Agreeing with a previous speaker
As [Joe] has said, …
Taking up [Sarah's] point …

Referring to a previous point
Going back to [Joe's] point, …
Returning to [Sarah's] point, …

Expressing uncertainty about relevance
I don't know if this is relevant but …
I'm not sure if this is related but …

Expressing uncertainty about previous contributions
Has anyone mentioned that …?

When you make long sentences, you must divide them into **sense groups**, pause between each sense group and stress the key words.
Example:
As <u>Sarah</u> has <u>said</u>, / people / want <u>expensive</u> products / <u>cheaply</u>.

🔊 **3.29** Listen to some sentences with linking expressions.
Which words are **stressed**?
Where are the **pauses**?

3.9 Grammar for speaking Noun phrases with relative clauses

We can add extra information about the **object / complement** with a **relative clause**. ⑫

S	V	object			
		N	relative	V	O/C
We	are talking about	adverts	which	use	BOGOF.
Adverts	are targeted at	people	who	might buy	the product.

When do we use *who*? When do we use *which*?
What is the basic SVO sentence in each case in the table above?
🔊 **3.30** Listen to the sentences. Where do the speakers pause?

A Adding extra information about objects and complements

1. Underline the object / complement in each basic sentence (left column). Then find the extra information about it (right column).
2. Write the complete sentences and mark where the pause should be in each.
3. 🔊 **3.31** Listen and check.

Example: There are many ads / which use BOGOF.

a. There are many ads. ☐ He or she endorses the product.
b. A jingle is a tune. ☐ He or she is famous for movies, sport or television.
c. A tag line is a slogan. ☐ It contains the name of the product.
d. A big name is a person. ☐ It encourages someone to do something.
e. A big name ad contains a personality. ☐ It is funny and it makes people laugh.
f. A bribe is money. ☐ It is memorable.
g. A punchline is an ending. ☐ It is usually in many episodes.
h. Ads with punchlines have a set-up. ☐ It prepares people for a particular ending.
i. A narrative is a story. ☐ They appear in narrative ads.
j. People may like the characters. ☐ They use BOGOF.

We can add extra information about the **subject** with a **relative clause**. ⑬

subject			O/C	V	extra information
N	relative	V			
Customers	who	buy	a packet of biscuits	get	another packet free.
Twenty products	which	are	basics	are	in the promotion.

🔊 **3.32** Listen to the sentences. Where does the speaker pause?

B Adding extra information about subjects

Each sentence below contains a subject with extra information in a relative clause.

1. Divide each sentence into sense groups with /. Underline the stressed word(s) in each sense group.
2. 🔊 **3.33** Listen and check your ideas.
3. Practise saying each sentence.

a. Advertisers who use BOGOF / start the advert / with the normal price.
b. People who are aural learners need to hear new information.
c. Farmers in the States who use irrigation are worried about the future.
d. A third of the water which is used for irrigation comes from the Ogallala Aquifer.
e. People who apologize a lot often give a reason for their actions.

A Previewing vocabulary

You are going to need the words in the box in this lesson.

> cartoon delicious disgusting dull eye-catching
> famous intriguing live action obvious one-off
> series unknown

1. Find pairs of words.
2. What part of speech is each pair?
3. Where is the stress in each word?

B Researching information

1. Study the assignment and the dictionary definition.
2. Research one of the sets of methods, 1, 2 or 3. Decide which of the three methods is most effective.
3. Prepare sentences to explain your research to other students.
   Example: *Advertisers use reviews which praise the movie.*

C Taking part in a discussion

Work in groups. There should be students in each group who have researched all three sets of methods.

1. Report your findings to the group. Other students should clarify information. Make notes of the methods you hear about.
2. Discuss the effectiveness of each method. Remember, you are a focus group, so you can give your personal opinion. Try to reach a consensus.
   Example:
   We think reviews that praise a movie are the most effective method. Number 2 is ...
3. How useful are focus groups in helping companies to decide if a product will be effective?

D Taking part in a discussion

1. Prepare a presentation on EITHER the most effective OR the least effective method of selling a film.
2. Give your presentation.

E Developing critical thinking

Choose a billboard from a film's website or magazine. Which methods have the advertisers used to sell the film?

Marketing Institute
Module 325/7

Focus group assignment
How do film studios try to sell their films? Which are the most successful methods?

1. Research ONE group of methods below.
2. Have a focus group meeting with fellow students. Rank the methods in order of effectiveness with the focus group.

Methods:

1
• the CGI	page 173
• the trailer	page 182
• the tag line	page 174

2
• the billboard	page 169
• the franchise	page 178
• the review	page 167

3
• the megastar	page 176
• the genre	page 180
• viral	page 164

> **focus group** (*n*) /ˈfəʊkəs gruːp/ a term from marketing; a small number of people, typically between six and nine, brought together to focus on a specific product or topic. Focus groups discuss rather than answer formal questions. They produce data on preferences and beliefs.

3.11 Vocabulary for reading   Schema theory

A Activating ideas

Study the film posters above. Find words in the list on the right connected with:

1. each film genre (type)
2. characters

B Understanding words in context

1. Complete each **bold** word in the encyclopedia text with an item from the list on the right. Make any necessary changes.

2. The items in green are in a referencing code. Which item means:

> copyright   pages   journal
> author   date of work
> from the same author and same work

3. Find four adjectives ending in ~al.

C Understanding the text

True or false? Explain your answer.

1. The participants in the experiment were Native Americans.
2. *Conflict* is another word for *war*.
3. The participants retold the story, using schema from their own culture.
4. Conventions are rules.
5. *Labelled*, in this context, means 'put into a genre'.
6. According to Bartlett, we label fiction when, for example, we see a poster for a film.

Bartlett Sir Frederic Charles (1886–1969): British psychologist who studied memory. Bartlett's most famous experiment was conducted in 1928. He asked a group of participants who were not Native Americans to read a **f**_____ narrative from that culture called 'The War of the Ghosts'. The story of a **c**_____ between two tribes was entirely logical in the original culture but, for the participants, there were strange **c**_____ and illogical parts. He asked the participants to repeat the story several times, after a few days and eventually after a few months. He found that they reconstructed the **n**_____, leaving out the strange parts, and turning it into a story with the pattern of stories from their own culture.

Bartlett concluded that stories are controlled by patterns, or **c**_____, so understanding a story involves decoding. 'A story,' he said, 'is at once labelled as being of this or that type ... The form, plan, type, or scheme of a story is ... the most persistent factor of all' (Bartlett, 1928). In other words, stories have to follow certain **c**_____. If they do not **c**_____ to this code, they will be changed in the memory so that they do fit. 'In fact all incoming material, if it is to be dealt with in any manner, must be somehow labelled' (ibid.). Bartlett called these labels '**s**_____', and pointed out that they are cultural.

R_____
Bartlett, F. C. (1928). 'An experiment upon repeated reproduction', **J**_____ *of General Psychology* Vol 1: pp. 54–63.
* This **s**_____ by courtesy of *Journal of General Psychology*, © 1928.

adventure *(n)*
alien *(n)*
animation *(n)*
antagonist *(n)*
character *(n)*
code *(n)*
conflict *(n)*
conform *(v)*
constraining
convention *(n)*
copyright *(n)*
creative *(adj)*
critic *(n)*
decode *(v)*
distinguish *(v)* [= mark the difference]
donor *(n)*
drama *(n)*
encounter *(v)*
equilibrium *(n)*
establish *(v)* [= make clear]
fantasy *(n)*
feature *(v)*
fiction *(n)*
fictional
genre *(n)*
hero *(n)*
ibid.
ignorance *(n)*
journal *(n)*
monster *(n)*
narrative *(n)*
obstacle *(n)*
plot *(n)*
protagonist *(n)*
reconciliation *(n)*
reference *(n)*
romance *(n)*
schema *(n)*
stable *(adj)* [= fixed]
stage *(n)*
stock *(adj)* [= unchanging]
strict *(adj)* [= very clear]
struggle *(n)*
synopsis *(n)*
thriller *(n)*
victim *(n)*
villain *(n)*
volume *(n)* [= journal]

A Preparing to read

Study the assignment. Make a list of research questions.

B Understanding the text

1. Read the heading and the introduction. Why are conventions important in narrative fiction?

2. Read the rest of the article. What did each of these people say about narrative conventions?

Aristotle   Lévi-Strauss   Todorov   Propp   Bartlett

3. Answer these questions about the detail in the article.

   a. What types of conflict are there, according to Aristotle? *(Conflict, stages and charact-*

   b. What are possible binary oppositions, according to Lévi-Strauss?

   c. What are the three stages of narratives, according to Todorov?

   d. What are the main roles in a narrative, according to Propp?

   e. How do we use schema in everyday life, according to Bartlett?

4. How many of your research questions have now been answered?

5. Use the words in the box to summarize an answer to the assignment question.

basic ideas, story and characters   conventions in narrative fiction   help in terms of   the audience   to understand   what to expect

School of Language and Literature

Narrative studies
Narrative in media texts, such as fiction films and novels, contains a large number of conventions. In what ways do these conventions assist the audience to understand the narrative?

C Understanding new words in context

1. Find a synonym in the text for each of these words.

   a. conflict   *struggle*   d. disequilibrium   *disorder*

   b. binary   *opposed*   e. protagonist   *hero*

   c. equilibrium   *Stable*   f. antagonist   *bitin*

2. Find each word below in the text. Tick the correct meaning in this context.

	1	2
a. encountered	seen and dealt with ✓	met a person
b. originated	created	happened for the first time ✓
c. emerging	coming out of a difficult time ✓	appearing
d. established	made clear	fixed ✓
e. strict	having lots of rules	very clear, cannot be changed ✓
f. stable	not liable to be changed easily ✓	place for horses
g. idyllic	very happy	very beautiful ✓
h. critic	a reviewer of art or literature	person who says bad things about behaviour
i. distinguish	show bravery or judgement ✓	mark the difference
j. stock	unchanging ✓	supply of goods

D Transferring information to the real world

Think of a film or novel that you know well.

1. What is the basic conflict, in Lévi-Strauss terms?

2. What are the three stages, in Todorov terms?

3. How many of Propp's characters can you identify?

Decoding narrative: conflict, stages and characters

Whenever people read a novel or watch a film, they have to decode the fictional narrative, understanding the role of each character in the unfolding drama, and seeing how the characters interrelate. This complex process poses no difficulties most of the time. It is very rare that people come out of a cinema or put down a novel and say 'What was that all about? What were all those people doing?' Human beings are experts at understanding fictional narrative, written in code, because we have encountered the code thousands of times since we first heard fairy tales. In this article, we look at three conventions of fictional narrative – conflict, stages and characters.

Theories of narrative structure originated with the Ancient Greeks. According to Aristotle, all dramatic narrative is conflict, 'either in the sense of struggle within a person or ... the clashing of opposed principles' (as cited in Belfiore, 2000; p. 64). In rites-of-passage stories, for example, teenagers or young adults are taken through formative episodes, emerging as adults at the end. Conflict in other stories is usually more a clash of principles. The conflicts are governed by strict conventions, in the view of the French theorist Lévi-Strauss, who suggested that all narratives have binary opposition (Lévi-Strauss, 1990). In other words, there are two opposite parts. The most obvious ones are good and evil, right and wrong, strength and weakness, youth and age, but there are many others.

The Russian theorist Tzvetan Todorov (1969) stated that narratives conventionally follow a structure of three stages. The narrative begins with a state of equilibrium, or order, established in the early scenes. The main characters are in a stable situation, married happily, successful at work or enjoying an idyllic childhood. Then something happens to disrupt the equilibrium, producing disequilibrium or disorder. An event occurs, unnoticed at first perhaps, which eventually turns the characters' lives upside down. In thrillers, it is usually a murder. In other genres, it can be something quite innocuous. At the end, the equilibrium is restored, although this might be at great cost to one or more of the main characters.

According to the literary critic Vladimir Propp, control of narrative does not end with binary opposition and overall structure. In most fiction, the main characters perform roles, defined by convention, which Propp calls 'spheres of action' (Propp quoted in Lacey, 2000, pp. 51–52). Firstly, there is the *hero*, who is usually male, and a *victim.* It is the hero's role to restore the equilibrium. The *hero* may be the *victim* himself, or he may help the victim. Others have called the hero character the *protagonist*, to distinguish him from the other main character, the *villain* or *antagonist*, who causes the disruption to the equilibrium. Supporting these two central characters, other stock characters appear, although they do not all feature in all plots. There might be a *donor*, who gives the hero something real, like a letter, or something abstract, like information or advice, which helps him to return life to normal. The protagonist may have a *helper*, whose role is self-evident. Another central character is the *victim,* who is threatened by the antagonist, the villain. Many narratives have a female character, called the *princess* by Propp (ibid.). Other characters appear frequently, including the *dispatcher*, who sends the hero on the journey, real or emotional. Also, the *false hero,* who turns out to be a villain, or at least does not help in restoring equilibrium. One character can perform more than one role – for example, the *donor* can also be the *false hero*.

It may seem strange that the majority of human narratives have recurrent types of opposition, structure and characters. However, the British philosopher Frederick Bartlett demonstrated the importance of a schema, or picture, of a real-world situation in order to make sense of it (Bartlett, 1932). We need to know what can happen when we step into a restaurant, an office or a church. We can extend this need for a schema to fictional situations. Stepping into an unknown world, we need convention to guide us. Unless the narrative follows conventions, it will be hard for the audience to make sense of it.   © Kristin Powell

References
Bartlett, F. (1932). *Remembering: A Study in Experimental and Social Psychology*, Cambridge: Cambridge University Press.
Belfiore, E. (2000). 'Narratological plots and Aristotle's mythos', *Arethusa. Vol. 33, No. 1*, 37–70.
Lacey, N. (2000). *Narrative and Genre*, London: Palgrave Macmillan.
Lévi-Strauss, C. (1990). *The Naked Man*, Chicago: University of Chicago Press.
Todorov, T. (1969). *Grammaire du Décameron*, The Hague: Mouton.

A Reviewing vocabulary

1. Complete each word connected with fictional narrative.

   a. conf*lict*   e. prota
   b. stru   f. anta
   c. conv   g. equi
   d. char   h. vic

2. Complete the binary opposites.

   a. good and   *evil*
   b. strength and
   c. youth and
   d. wealth and
   e. knowledge and
   f. beauty and
   g. real and
   h. progressive and

B Identifying a new skill

1. Read the Skills Check and study the cards below it.

2. Discuss these questions.

   a. What information must you record for a book?

   b. What about a journal article?

   c. What information do you think you need for an Internet article?

C Practising the new skill

The teacher will give you blank index cards, or you can use the cards on page 181.

1. Fill in cards for the other references in 3.12.

2. Study the information for the following publications and articles. Fill in an index card for each one.

a

Ambrose Nelson

Studying narrative

Published by Taylor Press
30 West 29ᵗʰ Street
New York, NY 11001
© 2010 Ambrose Nelson

Book

c

'Schema in fictional narrative'
Bill Andrews …   26–30

Media today
Vol. 23
July 2009

journal

Skills Check

Recording sources

You must record sources of information from reading research. It is good to use index cards – see below.

Prepare the cards in advance so you record full information. Record the author's gender, so you can refer later to *he* or *she*. Write (author, date) beside relevant information on your notes,
e.g., *schema theory (Bartlett, 1932)*

---

book / ~~journal~~ / ~~Internet~~

author(s)	Bartlett, F. (m)
date	1932
title	Remembering: A Study in Experimental and Social Psychology
pub. place	Cambridge
publisher	Cambridge University Press
journal	
volume	
page nos	
retrieved	
full URL	

~~book~~ / journal / ~~Internet~~

author(s)	Belfiore, E. (f)
date	2000
title	'Narratological plots and Aristotle's mythos'
pub. place	
publisher	
journal	Arethusa
volume	33
page nos	37–70
retrieved	
full URL	

---

b

Conflict in film

by Alison Hughes and Brian Dean

Jones and Miller,
Publishers
London
© 2006 Alison Hughes
and Brian Dean

article

---

d

File Edit View Favorites Tools Help

http://mediastudiesonline/todandpropp.html

Todorov and Propp – convention in narrative   *website* *title*   20/12/12

notes –

Study the sentences in the tables. What is similar about them? What is different? ⑭

Table 1

clause 1				clause 2		
S	V	O/C		S	V	extra
The characters	are	in a stable situation	,		married	and happy.

Table 2

clause 1				clause 2		
S	V	O/C		S	V	extra
Humans	understand	fiction	,		written	in code.

In the tables above, *married* and *written* are **past participles**.
The full sentences are: *The characters* **are married** *and happy. Fiction* **is written** *in code.*
Note that these sentences are passive.
When you see past participles on their own, think: *What is the* **subject** *of this verb?*
It may be **the same** as the **subject** or the **object / complement** of the **first clause**.

A Recognizing participle clauses

Look again at the text in 3.12. Find five more participle clauses.
What is the subject of each one? What is the original verb, before clause joining?

B Predicting the next information after a past participle

Study the start of each sentence. Find an ending on the right.

1. James Bond was in a locked room, tied ...   [3] and frightened.
2. Cynthia arrived at the church, dressed ...   [4] and ready to fire.
3. The two children wandered through the wood, lost ...   [5] in the shadows.
4. The gun was on the desk, loaded ...   [2] in white.
5. The spy was waiting in a shop doorway, hidden ...   [1] to a radiator.

C Understanding sentences with participles

Find a verb in the box to complete each sentence. Put it into the correct form.

> break   bring   capture   take   tie

1. The sheriff found his horse, *tied* to a fence post.
2. Malcolm looked at the photograph of his brother, *taken* many years before in France.
3. The soldiers arrived at the town, *captured* from the enemy the previous day.
4. The aliens inspected the humans, *brought* from all over the planet Earth by their spaceships.
5. The thief was delighted when he saw the window, *broken* some time before by a child's ball.

D Finding the subject of participle clauses

Find the start of the second clause. What is the subject and the original verb in each case?

1. Collins returned to the camp in the centre of the forest, injured and broken in spirit.
2. Marlon left Stewart, locked in the basement.
3. The Captain got out of the small boat and approached the natives, assembled on the beach.
4. Sophie looked up at the young man nervously, scared of making a fool of herself.
5. Kit Carson pushed Billy to the ground and grabbed for his gun, loaded with one final bullet.

A Activating ideas

1. What conventions of narrative fiction do you know already?
2. Why are these conventions required by audiences?

B Preparing to read

Read the assignment. What do you have to research before you can complete the assignment?

School of Language and Literature

Narrative studies

Evaluate Booker's thesis concerning plots in narratives (Booker, 2004) with regard to films OR novels in a genre you are familiar with.

C Understanding the text

1. Read the topic sentences of the text and check your answers to Exercise B.
2. Read the whole text. Use the references to find out the source of each statement below.

   a. Adventure, comedy and sci-fi / fantasy are the most popular film genres. wordpress.com

   b. Romance is the most popular novel genre.

   c. Humans require schema to make sense of something new.

   d. There are seven basic plots in fictional narrative.

   e. All authors have used the same images.

   f. Fairy tales do not all conform to particular basic plots.

   g. All comedies contain movement from ignorance to knowledge.

   h. All narratives end with a return to equilibrium.

   i. Hubris is the most common theme in tragedies.

   j. The princess is a common character in fictional narrative.

D Applying information from the text

Read the synopsis of each story. Discuss the questions.

1. Which genre is it probably in?
2. Which type of plot does it probably conform to?
3. Which Proppian character types does it probably contain?
4. How is equilibrium probably restored at the end?

a   Identical twins are separated at birth when their parents get divorced. They meet at summer camp and decide to reunite their parents.

b   An unemployed single mother becomes a legal assistant and destroys a California power company which is accused of polluting a city's water supply.

c   A man has a meal in a café but he doesn't have enough money for a tip for the waitress. So he says, 'If I win the lottery this week, I'll give you half.'

d   A wizard gives Frodo a magic ring, telling him that it must be destroyed in a magic mountain which is controlled by Sauron.

e   Bud Fox is an ambitious man, prepared to do anything to become rich and powerful. Finally, he discovers that his boss wants to destroy his father's company in order to make a lot of money.

f   The daughter of a rich man is kidnapped and the pirate Jack Sparrow sets out to rescue her, sailing off to the Caribbean in his ship, *The Black Pearl*.

E Completing the assignment

Choose a genre of films or novels that you are familiar with. To what extent is Booker's thesis accurate?

File   Edit   View   Favorites   Tools   Help

      http://www.mediawise.org.uk/genreandplots.htm

Genre

In the world of narrative fiction, a genre is a type of artistic work. Adventure is the most popular film genre, in terms of box-office takings, followed by comedy and sci-fi / fantasy, then romance, drama and animation. Biopics, which tell the fictionalized story of a real person, are a popular sub-genre of drama.[1] For novels, the situation is rather different. Romance takes more than 50 per cent of the market, followed by crime thrillers (26 per cent), reflecting the different audiences for the two types of fictional narrative.[2] Young adults constitute far more of the audience for movies than for book-buying.

Genre is another way of tapping in to schema, required by humans to make sense of something new.[3] It is also useful for producers and marketers of narrative fiction. Writers can become specialists and film stars can associate themselves with a particular genre, so the writer's name or the star's face becomes part of the code. If you see a billboard with *that* name or *that* face, you know the genre. Ads for a particular market go where that demographic is, so ads for romantic comedies don't usually appear in men's magazines.

Plot

Once attracted to a particular film or book, an audience will find, according to Christopher Booker, one of seven plots.[4] Booker did not invent the idea of a limited number of basic plots, although different commentators have suggested different numbers. The famous English lexicographer Dr Johnson said, '... the same images, with very little variation, have served all the authors who have ever written.'[5] Other writers, including the Opies (well-known authorities on children's literature) have dismissed the idea, saying that each fairy tale, for example, should not be seen as conforming to a particular basic plot.[6] However, the idea persists and Booker's 700-page tome certainly seems to make a good case.

Booker's seven plots

1. Originally containing real monsters, breathing fire, Man-against-the-Monster stories may now have aliens or more abstract entities, such as government or big business. Movies with a message often have this plot.
2. Rags-to-riches narratives, telling the story of one person's rise from humble beginnings to wealth or power, are very popular in period novels.
3. The Quest is a favourite of the fantasy genre. A person, or perhaps an animal or fictional creature, sets off to find something, encountering obstacles along the way. Obviously, he/she/it succeeds in the end.
4. The fourth basic plot is Voyage and Return. In films, this is the structure of the Road movie, where people are constantly on the move, finding in the end that life is really better at home.
5. Comedies, according to Aristotle, contain a moment when one or more of the characters moves from ignorance to knowledge.[7] The ignorance, shared with the audience, may come from mistaken identity, for example, or a secret. With knowledge comes reconciliation (and with a romantic comedy, a wedding), which is Todorov's return to equilibrium.[8]
6. With Tragedy, the most common narrative force is hubris. The hero becomes more and more ambitious, greedy or arrogant, until finally he/she is cut down.[9] In other words, a fault within the character causes the tragedy.
7. The final plot, Rebirth, is a kind of reversal of Tragedy. The hero gets deeper and deeper into trouble of some sort, but is eventually rescued, by Propp's *princess* or another character, and the restored equilibrium is happy.[10] They all live happily ever after, as all fairy tales end.

When we realize that there are conventional stages, characters, genres and plots, it is hard to understand how we can continue to be entertained by fictional narrative. However, in the hands of a skilful writer, the conventions become a creative force rather than a constraining one.

1. https://moviedistributionfacts.wordpress.com/tag/popular-movie-genres/ retrieved on 15.06.2011
2. http://www.bookmarket.com retrieved on 10.06.2011
3. Bartlett, F. (1932) *Remembering: A Study in Experimental and Social Psychology*, Cambridge: Cambridge University Press
4. Booker, C. (2004) *The Seven Basic Plots*, London: Continuum
5. Ibid., p. 8
6. Opie, P. and Opie, J. (1974) *The Classic Fairy Tales*, Oxford: Oxford University Press
7. Belfiore, E. (2000) 'Narratological plots and Aristotle's mythos', *Arethusa* Vol. 33 pp. 37–70
8. Todorov, T. (1969) *Grammaire du Décameron*, The Hague: Mouton
9. Booker, p. 329
10. Propp quoted in Lacey, N. (2000) *Narrative and Genre*, London: Palgrave Macmillan, pp. 51–52

1 Match the questions and answers. All the words are from Theme 3.

a. What is an *endorsement*?

b. What do you see on a *billboard*?

c. Who has *copyright* of a piece of fiction?

d. What has a *punchline*?

e. Why do supermarkets use *loss-leaders*?

f. What happens in a *reconciliation?*

g. What are some of the *conventions* of narrative fiction?

h. When should you write *(ibid.)*?

i. Where do *aliens* come from, according to fiction?

j. What is a *brand*?

.... A joke – it is the funny ending.

.... A product from a particular maker which many people recognize.

.... An advertisement, often for a film.

.... A statement from a celebrity or personality from sport or television saying they use the product.

.... Conflict, stages, plots, genre, characters.

.... Outer space, or perhaps another dimension.

.... People who were in conflict reach agreement.

.... The writer, because he/she owns the right to reproduce it.

.... To get people into their shop to buy other products.

.... When you are quoting again from the same work.

2 Match the opposites.

a. fiction .... accurate
b. code .... allow
c. villain .... decode
d. good .... deny
e. ignorance .... Earth man
f. antagonist .... evil
g. famous .... hero
h. exaggerated .... knowledge
i. sequel .... live action
j. forgettable .... memorable
k. ban .... non-fiction
l. admit .... prequel
m. alien .... protagonist
n. friend .... stranger
o. CGI .... unknown

3 Match the synonyms.

a. story .... acceptance
b. authorities .... aggression
c. violence .... at first
d. concession .... by the way
e. initially .... catchy tune
f. synopsis .... destroy
g. genre .... do
h. argument .... follow
i. experience .... go through
j. commit .... government
k. eliminate .... meaning
l. conform .... narrative
m. message .... proposition
n. jingle .... summary
o. incidentally .... type

Writing: Reality TV – real or fiction?

3.16 Vocabulary for writing   Drama or reality?

A Activating ideas

1. Find examples of drama and reality TV programmes in the TV schedule on the right.

2. Are you surprised by the percentage of any genre in the pie chart?

B Understanding sentences

Read the text from a media website. One word is missing from each sentence. What is the word, in each case? Where does it go?

Example: This is the clear message from the media authority Nielsen.com in its latest figures.

C Understanding vocabulary in context

Find the words in *italics* in the text.

1. Which word or phrase means ...?

   a. a drama which continues for many months or years

   b. reported

   c. words for actors in a play

   d. competition

   e. programme

   f. to make people feel ashamed of themselves

   g. feeling that you have made a fool of yourself

   h. not in a studio

2. Write a definition for the remaining italicised words, beginning ...
   A person or people who ...
   A place where ...

   Example:
   authority
   a person who knows a lot about a particular field

D Developing critical thinking

Would you like to appear in a reality TV show? If so, which kind? If not, why (not)?

	8.00PM	8.30PM	9.00PM	9.30PM	10.00PM
	Extreme Makeover: Home Edition		Desperate Housewives		Brothers & Sisters
	Viva Laughlin		Cold Case		Shark
	Sunday Night Football				
	The Simpsons	King of the Hill	Family Guy	American Dad	
	Life is Wild		America's Next Top Model		

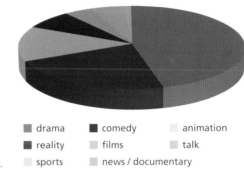

■ drama   ■ comedy   ▨ animation
■ reality   ▨ films   ▨ talk
▨ sports   ▨ news / documentary

Figure 1: *Television audiences by genre (USA, 2010)*[1]

US TV audiences still love drama!

This is the clear message from the media *authority* Nielsen.com in latest figures. During the last year, the largest TV *audiences* were for drama, which took, average, 44 per cent of *viewers*. It seems that the majority of Americans still prefer to watch *actors* rather members of the public. Clearly, drama is a very large genre and contains many sub-genres, such as *soap operas*, crime thrillers and science fiction but all have things in common – actors and a *script*.

In second place in the Nielsen survey is reality TV, up three per cent from the previous year, despite many rude comments *critics*, both inside and outside the television industry. For example, Barry Langberg, a Los Angeles *lawyer*, represented an unhappy couple from a reality *show*, is *cited* as saying:

'Something like this is done for no other reason than to *embarrass* people or humiliate them scare them. The *producers* don't care human feelings ... only care about money.'[2]

The reality genre also has sub-genres with wide variety of *settings*. Some series are filmed *on location*, like a desert island, some filmed at private houses and others take place in a *studio*. But in all cases, the format is similar, with *contestants* from the general public taking part in a *contest* and gradually eliminated, often, as Mr Langberg says, with embarrassment or *humiliation*.

1. adapted from http://blog.nielsen.com/nielsenwire/wp-content/uploads/2010/09/Nielsen-State-of-TV-09232010.pdf
2. http://atheism.about.com/library/FAQs/phil/blphil_eth_realitytv.htm

audience *(n)*
authority *(n)* [= expert in a field]
cite *(v)* [= quote]
contestant *(n)*
convention *(n)* [= rule]
critic *(n)*
documentary *(n)*
dramatic *(adj)*
episodic *(adj)*
escapism *(n)*
film *(v)*
format *(n)*
franchise *(n and v)*
   [= type of programme]
on location
producer *(n)*
psychological need
public *(n)*
quotation *(n)*
reality TV
related *(adj)*
   [= connected]
Schadenfreude
script *(n)*
scripted *(adj)*
serial *(n)* [= story in parts]
setting *(n)*
similarity *(n)*
survival *(n)*
the extent of
the issue of
the relationship
   between
the similarities
   between
TV schedule
viewer *(n)*
viewing *(n)*
villain *(n)*
volume *(n)* [= quantity]
vote *(v)*
voyeurism *(n)*

A   Activating ideas

What is reality TV? Tick the items that are true for this genre.

- ☐ It's scripted.
- ☐ It's dramatic.
- ☐ It's humorous.
- ☐ It has real-life situations.
- ☐ It features ordinary people.
- ☐ It features celebrities.
- ☐ It features professional actors.
- ☐ All the programmes have the same format.
- ☐ It's very popular all around the world.

B   Preparing to write

1. Study the assignment. How does each statistic prove the popularity of reality TV around the world?
2. Read the introduction to the assignment opposite.
   a. Is it a good introduction? Why (not)?
   b. Rewrite the introduction in a better way.

C   Noticing the paragraph structure

1. Study the first page of notes opposite. What will be the main statement in the paragraph?
2. Study the second paragraph of the essay. Mark and number the subsections of the paragraph in order.
   - ☐ Direct quotation
   - ☐ Statement
   - ☐ Supporting evidence
   - ☐ Related statement
   - ☐ Reported speech

D   Preparing to write

Study the second page of notes. Complete these sentences.

1. The main statement here is that … audiences like reality TV because it is similar to fiction.
2. Aristotle said that …
3. Conflict in reality TV comes from …
4. Producers of *Treasure Quest* set up some of the dangers to …
5. 'Stuck-up Stephanie' was the villain …

E   Writing the paragraph

Write the third paragraph of the essay. Use the second page of notes and the paragraph structure from Exercise C.

Media Studies Department

Reality TV

The genre started in the UK and the United States about 20 years ago. It is now extremely popular around the world. One of the first reality programmes in the UK, *Big Brother*, had a regular audience of five million people until recently (channel4.com, 2011). The format is now franchised in more than 50 countries around the world (worldofbigbrother.com, 2010). Over 20 per cent of 50,000 people interviewed in South America said that they watch reality television frequently (zonalatina.com, 2011). About 35,000 20-year-olds audition every year for a chance to participate in MTV's *The Real World* in the USA (latimes.com, 2010).

Assignment:
Outline possible reasons for the worldwide popularity of the reality TV genre.

References
channel4.com (2011), info/press/news retrieved on 26.06.11
worldofbigbrother.com (2010), BB/index.shtml retrieved on 26.06.11
zonalatina.com (2011), realitysurvey retrieved on 26.06.11
latimes.com (2010), showtracker retrieved on 26.06.11

1. volume

reality TV major part of schedules = audience often little choice

RTV = 60% all programmes made around world (www.nielsenmedia.com, 2010)

because TV co.s like RTV = v. cheap to produce

Andrea Gibson, CEO, Wow TV, 'Reality TV requires no actors, no scripts and no expensive settings. Some programmes take place in one studio, made to look like a house or a school.' (Gibson, 2011)

Eric Johannson, Producer, Treasure Quest, 'We flew everyone to an island located in the South Pacific and the whole thing was filmed on location, but even that was much cheaper than making a drama production or a documentary.' (Johannson, 2011)

2. similar to fiction

audiences like reality TV – like fiction, i.e., conventions

based on real life but presents conflict = 'basis of all narrative fiction' – Aristotle (Belfiore, 2000)

conflict in RTV =

1. basic idea, e.g., Treasure Quest (TQ) – struggle against nature

2. through selection of contestants, e.g., Private School (PS)

Miles Morton, TV critic, 'Producers like some binary in the Private School staffroom or on Treasure Quest island. For example, you might get a rich girl and a poor boy, or perhaps a teacher who is a progressive and one who is a reactionary.' (Morton, 2011)

Barbara Hughes, sociologist, Westingham Uni., 'There is often a "villain" in reality TV. The public watch the programme to see him or her destroyed, for example, "Stuck-up Stephanie" in Series 1 of PS.' (Hughes, 2010)

Outline possible reasons for the worldwide popularity of the reality TV genre

Reality TV, which started in the UK and the United States about 20 years ago, has become one of the most popular genres on television around the world. In this essay, I will consider the reasons for this popularity. Firstly, I will consider the volume of reality TV on television around the world. Secondly, I will consider reality TV and narrative fiction. Thirdly, I will consider reality TV and the psychological needs of the audience. Fourthly, I will consider the range of reality TV programmes.

There are a number of reasons for the popularity of reality TV. Firstly, the genre is now a major part of the schedules, so the volume of reality TV means that the audience often has little choice of viewing. Figures from Nielsen Media show that the genre accounts for 60 per cent of all programmes made around the world (nielsenmedia.com, 2010). Television companies make a lot of reality TV because it is very cheap to produce. 'Reality TV requires no actors, no scripts and no expensive settings,' says Wow TV CEO, Andrea Gibson (Gibson, 2011). 'Some programmes take place in one studio, made to look like a house or a school.' Eric Johannson of *Treasure Quest* agrees, pointing out that it does not cost as much to produce reality TV as drama or documentary, even if it involves taking everyone to a remote island and location filming (Johannson, 2011).

Secondly, audiences like reality TV because it is similar to fiction in terms of its conventions. …

A Reviewing vocabulary

Rewrite each sentence, using the words in brackets.

1. In this essay, I will consider reasons for the popularity of reality TV. (why)

   In this essay, I will consider why reality TV is (so) popular.

2. The volume of reality TV means the audience often has little choice of viewing. (because of)
3. Reality TV is cheap to produce so television companies make a lot of programmes. (cost / leads)
4. The genre requires no actors or scripts. (needed)
5. Audiences like reality TV because it is similar to fiction. (similarity)
6. Sometimes the producers create conflict in their selection of contestants. (results in)

B Identifying a key skill

Read the Skills Check. What kind of evidence does the writer in the example give for:

- the statement?
- the related statement?

C Practising a new skill

1. Match each statement with a suitable piece of evidence.

   a Global warming is caused by greenhouse gases.

   b Recruitment of new employees will be easy in Causton.

   c Most decisions for teenagers in my culture are made by their parents.

   d Mobile phones have not had any effect on cultural values in rural areas.

   e Economic performance is linked to geography.

   f Sales dropped to 5 million per annum in 1975.

   1. 93 per cent (writer's survey of ten families)
   2. Graph (The Waterman Pen Company)
   3. Atmospheric CO_2 has risen in line with average world temperatures (World Meteorological Organization)
   4. Official (UNESCO, Africa)
   5. Survey of 150 countries (World Bank)
   6. Unemployment rate in the area is 20 per cent (UK government figures)

2. Write a sentence or a short paragraph for each statement + evidence in C1. Link the two pieces of information in different ways.

Skills Check

Supporting statements with evidence

You must support statements in an academic essay with **evidence**.

The most common types of evidence are:
- statistics, including original research
- quotations
- reported speech / ideas

The evidence must come from authorities in the field.

With these types of evidence, you must:
- put the **source** in brackets after the statement, e.g., (Bartlett, 1928)
- give full details in a **References** section at the end of the essay

Example:

statement	Reality TV is now a major part of the schedules ...
support (from an authority)	Figures from Nielsen Media show ... (nielsenmedia.com, 2010)
related statement	Reality TV is very cheap to produce ...
quotation (from an authority)	'Reality TV requires no actors, no scripts ...', says Wow TV CEO, Andrea Gibson (Gibson, 2011).
reported speech (of an authority)	Eric Johannson of *Treasure Quest* agrees, pointing out .... (Johannson, 2011)

References:
Gibson, A. (2011), *Making reality* ... etc.

Look again at Tables 1 and 2 in 3.14.   ⑮

Look at the sentence on the right and answer the questions.
1. How many clauses are there?
2. What is the subject of each clause?
3. What is the verb of each clause?
4. What form is each verb in?

> We flew everyone to an island located in the South Pacific.

We can use a past participle, e.g., *located* to join a **passive sentence**. The **subject** of the passive sentence is often the same as the **object / complement** of the first sentence.

A Forming the past participle

1. What is the past participle spelling of each regular verb?

a. believe	believed	d. ban		g. offer	
b. describe		e. die		h. stop	
c. play		f. try		i. regret	

2. What must you do before you add the final ~*ed* to each regular verb? Tick the correct rules. Find examples in A2 above.

a. take off final *e*
b. change final *ie* to *y*
c. change final *y* to *ie*
d. with one-syllable verbs, double the final consonant letter after a single vowel letter
e. with multi-syllable verbs, double the final consonant letter after a single vowel letter

B Joining with the past participle

Study each pair of sentences. Rewrite the second sentence in the passive. Then write all the information in one sentence, using a past participle.

1. Shakespeare's first play was called *Henry VI*.	He wrote it in about 1590.
2. This study identifies the key decisions.	People in families take decisions.
3. The study involved 1,000 participants.	We chose participants from six age groups.
4. The company sells computer chips.	Companies in Japan make the chips.
5. Most scientists believe in global warming.	Greenhouse gases in the atmosphere cause it.
6. The pen used a new ink.	Biro's brother, Georg, invented it.

C Completing sentences with past participles

Write a logical ending to each sentence.

1. People in many countries know the tragedy *Romeo and Juliet*, written ... by William Shakespeare / in the 17ᵗʰ century.
2. In the 16ᵗʰ century, colonists began to travel to America, discovered ...
3. The highest mountain on Earth is Everest, conquered ...
4. One of the wonders of the Ancient World is the Great Pyramid of Giza, built ...
5. Long-distance communication was revolutionized by the telephone, invented ...
6. The United Kingdom and France are now linked by a tunnel, drilled ...
7. Learning by doing is a theory, proposed ...
8. The atmosphere releases nitrogen, dissolved ...

A Reviewing sentence and paragraph structure

In this lesson, you are going to complete the essay in 3.17.

1. Read paragraph 1, the introduction, again. Complete the text with one phrase in each space.

the extent of	the issue of	the reasons for	the relation between	the similarities between

Reality TV, which started in the UK and the United States about 20 years ago, has become one of the most popular genres on television around the world. In this essay, I will consider .... this popularity. Firstly, I will look at .... the genre on television around the world. Secondly, I will discuss .... reality TV and narrative fiction. Next, I will consider .... reality TV and the psychological needs of the audience. Finally, I will examine .... the range of reality TV programmes, from popular music contests to survival games.

2. How much can you remember of paragraph 2? What are the statements? What is the supporting evidence? What about paragraph 3? Look again at 3.17 and check your ideas.

B Thinking, organizing and writing

You are going to write the final two paragraphs of the essay.

Para 4:   Reality TV and psychological needs, i.e., escapism, Schadenfreude and voyeurism.

Para 5:   Reality TV and range of sub-genres.

Research information for these two paragraphs. The source material is on pages 162 and 163. Organize the information into two paragraphs. Write statements with supporting evidence. Record the sources that you use (see 3.15).

C Editing and rewriting

1. Exchange drafts with a partner. Check his/her work and mark with *?*, *S*, *G* or *P*.

2. Read your marked essay and correct the points. Write the essay again.

D Writing the references

Make a reference list for the sources you have used.

E Writing a parallel essay

Study the assignment. Do your own research and write the essay.

---

escapism (*n*) /ɪˈskeɪpɪzəm/ the tendency to escape from daily reality or routine by indulging in daydreaming, fantasy or entertainment; psychologists believe that we all have a need for this at certain times; *People watch action films for ~.* [etymology: from *escape*]

Schadenfreude (*n*) /ˈʃɑːdnfrɔɪdə/ satisfaction or pleasure at someone else's misfortune; psychologists say this is a basic human emotion, even if it is not very attractive; *He experienced ~ at his colleague's failure to get promotion.* [etymology: from German – *damage* + *joy*]

voyeurism (*n*) /ˈvɔɪɜːrɪzəm/ the observation of another person from a position of hiding; generally the person concerned would object to being watched if they were aware of the voyeur; psychologists recognize that there are many kinds of voyeurism, including criminal activity; *Reality TV is a kind of ~ although the contestants know we are watching.* [etymology: from French – *one who views*]

Media Studies Department

Soap operas (or soaps)
This name refers to episodic works of fiction, presented in serial format. The name comes from programmes produced for radio in the 1950s by the manufacturers of soaps, i.e., washing powder.

Assignment:
Outline reasons for the popularity of TV soap operas.

Celebrity Big Brother house, UK

If people get embarrassed or humiliated on reality TV programmes, they only have themselves to blame. They shouldn't go on the programme if they are afraid of making fools of themselves.   **(Reality TV contestant)**

We have a duty to ensure that the television companies provide decent programmes. They should not make violent programmes for children and they should not turn the evening schedule into a modern form of freak show from the Middle Ages.   **(Member of Parliament)**

Reality TV

I love reality shows and so do all my friends. They give ordinary people an opportunity to appear on television, and even to become famous. It's great voting for your favourite contestant, or voting off the ones you hate! **(Jenny, 14)**

Reality shows are very popular with every kind of person. Each show has a very clear demographic so we can choose products for each ad break which will appeal to that section of society. There really is something for everyone in the genre.   **(Advertising executive)**

A Activating ideas

Read the opinions above. Decide if you agree or disagree with each one.

B Gathering and recording information

Study the information on the right. Decide whether you are for or against the motion. Think of:

- some points in support of your side
- some counter-arguments

Do research to find quotations supporting your side and/or countering the other side. Record your sources.

C Preparing a presentation

Work with other people on the same side of the debate. Prepare a presentation, including concessions to counter-arguments. Use slides and/or visuals to illustrate your points.

D Listening to a debate

Work in groups. Listen to the debate. Which side has the stronger arguments? Vote and decide who has won the debate.

E Writing

Write an essay with the title:
'To what extent should reality TV programmes be controlled by television regulators?'

> Hadford University
> Debating Society
>
> This house believes that:
>
> *Television programmes
> that involve
> humiliation of contestants
> should be banned*
>
> from 1.00 to 2.00
> in Room C132

Theme 4

Living life to the full

- Life systems

- A sporting life

- Learning for leisure

- Living longer, living better

4.1 Vocabulary for listening — Cells, tissues and organs

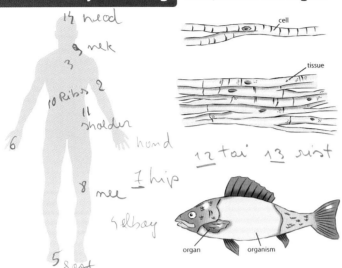

Figure 1: The human organism

Figure 2: Cells, tissues and organs: relationships

A Activating knowledge

Study Figure 1.

1. ◉ 4.1 Listen and write the number of each word in the correct place on the diagram.
   Example: 1. ankle

2. Name each part.
   Example: *Number 1 is the ankle.*

B Understanding new words from illustrations and definitions

Study Figure 2. Number each label according to the definitions below.

1. group of cells which act in a particular way
2. group of molecules; the smallest unit of life
3. group of organs working together to achieve a particular objective, like converting food into energy
4. organ systems working together in one body
5. tissues which perform a particular function, like breaking down food

C Understanding new words in context

1. ◉ 4.2 Listen to part of a lecture about physiology. When the lecturer stops, number the next word.

   Example: *OK. So first, let's look at the levels of organization that make up the human ...*

	breathe.		form.
	cells.		functions.
	digestion.		heart.
	electricity.		purpose.
1	body.		systems.

2. ◉ 4.3 Listen and check your answers.

artery (*n*)
blood stream
bone (*n*)
cell (*n*)
circulation (*n*)
circulatory (*adj*)
compression (*n*)
diaphragm (*n*)
digestion (*n*)
digestive (*adj*)
exchange (*n*)
fracture (*n*)
immune (*adj*)
impulse (*n*) [= electrical]
inflammation (*n*)
injury (*n*)
interface (*v*)
intestines (*n pl*)
joint (*n*)
muscle (*n*)
muscular (*adj*)
nerve (*n*)
nervous (*adj*)
nutrient (*n*)
organ (*n*)
physiology (*n*)
physiotherapy (*n*)
respiration (*n*)
respiratory (*adj*)
skeleton (*n*)
skull (*n*)
spinal (*adj*)
spine (*n*)
sprain (*n*)
strain (*n*)
swelling (*n*)
tissue (*n*)
vein (*n*)

A Activating ideas

Study the diagrams opposite. Read the lecture information and try to answer the questions.

B Understanding an introduction

1. ⊕ 4.4 DVD 4.A Watch the introduction. Tick the words in the box which the lecturer mentions.

> associated   breathing   circulatory
> components   digestion   function   immune
> interrelated   muscular   nutrient   physiology
> reproductive   skeletal   systems

Faculty of
Biological Sciences
Physiology
Core Course Phy 403

Lecture 1: Human body systems
What are the main systems?
What does each system do?
How do the systems work together?

2. Mark the stressed syllable of the ticked items.

3. Complete the information about the lecture below with words from the box above.

> In this lecture, which is part of the core course in _physiology_, the lecturer will talk about six human body _systems_, including the _skeletal_, muscular and _circulatory_ systems. He will describe the _function_ of each system, mention some of the _components_ and explain how the systems are _interrelated_

C Understanding a lecture

1. ⊕ 4.5 DVD 4.B Watch each section of the lecture. Make notes on the function(s) of each system.

2. How are the systems interrelated? Draw arrows to show the following relationships:
   - gives nutrients to
   - gives oxygen to
   - gives nutrients and oxygen to
   - is attached to
   - is controlled by

D Showing comprehension

Make a question about the main body systems for each answer opposite.

1. What is the function of the skeletal system?

E Developing critical thinking

How can you remember the main organs in each system?

1. It supports the body and protects the organs.

2. 206.

3. The shoulder or the hip.

4. A hinge joint.

5. It allows the body to move.

6. Over 600.

7. Because muscles can only contract.

8. It uses electricity.

9. The digestive system.

10. Because the body can't use nutrients without oxygen.

11. William Harvey.

12. Arteries take blood away from the heart, veins take it back to the heart.

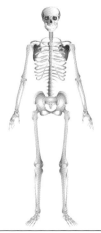

1 | skeletal system
supports body, protects organs

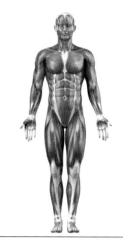

2 | muscular system

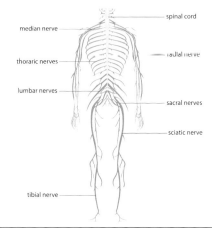

3 | nervous system

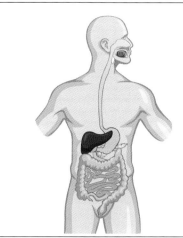

4 | digestive system

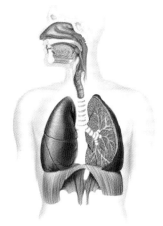

5 | respiratory system

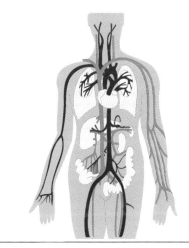

6 | circulatory system

A   Predicting the sound of new words

1. Read the Pronunciation Check.

2. The words below are from the lecture handout in 4.2. They are probably new to you. How do you think they are pronounced? Match each word to a phonemic transcription.

a. bronchi		/ˈb r æ k iː/
b. colon	a	/ˈb r ɒ ŋ k iː/
c. larynx		/s e r ə ˈb e l ə m/
d. nasal		/ˈk əʊ l ə n/
e. sciatic		/ˈl æ r ɪ ŋ k s/
f. pharynx		/ˈn eɪ z l/
g. cerebellum		/ˈf æ r ɪ ŋ k s/
h. trachea		/s aɪ ˈæ t ɪ k/
i. trapezius		/t r ə ˈk iː ə/
j. brachi		/t r ə ˈp iː z iː ə s/

3. ⊙ **4.6** Listen to the correct pronunciation and check your ideas.

B   Identifying a new skill

1. Study these notes from the lecture in 4.2. Why did the student write them like this?

The muscular system
= enables body to move
can only contract
so pairs of muscles (antagonistic)
biceps
triceps ——— diaphragm
abs ←
hamstrings
Achilles

2. Read the Skills Check and check your ideas.

C   Practising a new skill

You are going to hear part of three lectures.

Lecture 1: Studies on the effects of TV violence

Lecture 2: The history of the Internet

Lecture 3: A comparison of Chile and Pakistan

⊙ **4.7** Listen and make notes. Add extra information in the correct place.

Pronunciation Check

Predicting pronunciation

It is good to try to guess the pronunciation of new words on lecture handouts so you recognize them in the lecture. But as you know, English is not pronounced as it is spelt in many cases, so guessing is not always accurate. Use your dictionary to check stress and the sounds of individual phonemes.

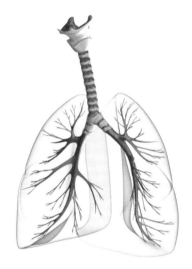

bronchi of respiratory system

Skills Check

Filling in additional information

Lecturers don't always give all the information for one area at the same time. Listen for the following expressions. They warn you that the next piece of information is out of order in some way.

I forgot to say (that) …
Did I mention (that) …?
I should have told you about …
I meant to point out that …
Just going back to X for a minute, …
Can you go back and add …

⊙ **4.8** Listen. What has the lecturer forgotten in each case?

Sometimes speakers begin sentences with *What* ... or *It* ... for emphasis. The tense information sometimes moves in these structures.
Study the examples in each table and find the S, V, O and A (if any) in each case.

⑯

Table 1

What	I'm going to do first is ...	talk about each system.
	the skeletal system does is ...	support the body.
	Harvey did was ...	experiment with fish and snakes.

Table 2

It	will be	next week that we look at sports injuries.
	is	the brain which controls the nervous system.
	was	Harvey who discovered the circulation of the blood.

🎧 **4.9** Listen to the sentences. Does the speaker pause in any of the sentences?

A Recognizing cleft sentences

1. 🎧 **4.10** Listen to the beginning of some questions or statements.
   Is the speaker asking a question (Q) or starting a statement (S) in each case?
   How do you know?
   Examples:
   a. *What is* ...
   b. *What we'll look at* ...

2. 🎧 **4.11** Listen to the whole of each question or statement and check your answers.
   Examples:
   a. *What is the solution?*
   b. *What we'll look at first is the digestive system.*

a.	Q
b.	S
c.	
d.	
e.	
f.	
g.	
h.	
i.	
j.	
k.	
l.	

B Understanding cleft sentences

1. Look at the transcript for Exercise A2 on page 212. Find the statements.
2. Complete the table below with the basic parts of each statement.
   Example: *What we'll look at first is the digestive system.*

	S	V	O	A
b	We	'll look at	the digestive system	first.

C Understanding pseudo-cleft sentences

1. 🎧 **4.12** Listen to the beginning of some pseudo-cleft sentences. Letter the logical way to complete each sentence.
2. 🎧 **4.13** Listen to the whole sentence in each case and check your answers.

	that Bell invented the telephone.
	that the telegraph declined in popularity.
a	that we look at the history of the telephone.
	which began high-speed communication.
	which Bell invented.
	who invented the telephone.

Sports Science Department

1.4: Dealing with sports injuries
Strains and sprains?
Bruises and contusions?
Compression and elevation?

What are the main causes of sports injuries?
How can we deal with them?

A Preparing for a lecture

1. Study the lecture information above and the diagram and slides on the right. How will the lecturer pronounce each of the highlighted words?

2. ● 4.14 DVD 4.C Watch the introduction to the lecture. Check your answers.

B Following a lecture

1. ● 4.15 DVD 4.D Watch the first part of the lecture. Add notes to each section of the first slide on the right. Make sure you go back and add information which the lecturer gives out of order.

2. ● 4.16 DVD 4.E Watch the second part of the lecture. Add notes as before.

3. What is ...
   a. IGF-1?
   b. RSI?
   c. tennis elbow?
   d. an anaesthetic?
   e. a compression bandage?
   f. physiotherapy?

C Developing critical thinking

Imagine you find a lecture difficult to follow.

1. What will you do this time?
   - blame yourself and your poor English?
   - accept that sometimes lecturers do not give perfect lectures?
   - ask to copy someone's notes?
   - discuss the lecture with several other students?
   - ask the lecturer for help?
2. What will you do next time?
   - do more preparation?
   - listen carefully to the introduction?
   - record it and listen several times?

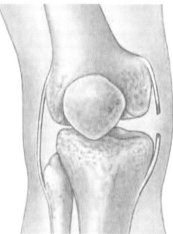

The knee joint

Sports injuries
- types
  - trauma
    - minor
    - major
  - inflammation
  - swelling
- overuse

Sports injuries
- treatment
  - P
  - R
  - I
  - C
  - E
  - physiotherapy

4.6 Vocabulary for speaking Mental and physical conditions

A Activating ideas

What's wrong with the young women in the photographs? What should they do?

B Understanding new vocabulary in context

1. Divide the words and phrases in the box into two groups. Explain your answer.

> anxiety asthma cold depression fatigue flu
> neurosis obsession breathing difficulties

2. ⊚ **4.17** Listen to an interview with a sports psychologist. Check your answers to Exercise A.

3. Complete each sentence with a word from Exercise A.

a. When you **go down with** a cold or ___flu___ , you get tired easily.

b. _____ is a **symptom** of a physical problem.

c. Many sportspeople have _____, which is a respiratory **condition**.

d. During an **attack**, people with asthma experience _____.

e. Top athletes often have an _____ with their sport. They think about it all the time and **train** hard because they are obsessed.

f. Sometimes obsession is bad because it leads to _____ – worrying about your **performance**.

g. Sometimes, you become so obsessive that you **experience** _____.

4. ⊚ **4.18** Listen and check your answers.

5. What does each **bold** word mean in context?

C Understanding new words in context

1. Study the pronunciation of some words from this lesson. Write the number next to the correct word in the list on the right.

1.	/əˈɡreʃn/		9.	/fəˈtiːɡ/
2.	/əˈɡresɪv/		10.	/fəˈtiːɡd/
3.	/æŋˈzaɪətiː/		11.	/njʊəˈrəʊsɪs/
4.	/ˈæŋkʃəs/		12.	/njʊəˈrɒtɪk/
5.	/ˈæsmə/		13.	/əbˈseʃn/
6.	/æsˈmætɪk/		14.	/əbˈsesɪv/
7.	/dɪˈprest/		15.	/ˈbreθ/
8.	/dɪˈpreʃn/		16.	/ˈbriːð/

2. ⊚ **4.19** Listen and check your answers.

3. ⊚ **4.20** Listen again and repeat.

aggression (n)
aggressive (adj)
anxiety (n)
anxious (adj)
asthma (n)
asthmatic (adj)
attack (n) [= physical illness]
authoritative (adj)
breathe (v)
bring on [= cause to start]
cognitive (adj)
condition (n)
control (v) [~ a disease]
controllable (adj)
depressed (adj)
depression (n)
deprive (v)
exertion (n)
fatal (adj)
fatigue (n)
feedback (n)
goal (n) [= target]
injury (n)
intensity (n)
lack of sleep
medication (n)
mental (adj)
neurosis (n)
neurotic (adj)
obsessively (adv)
passionate (adj)
perceive (v)
perception (n)
physical (adj)
psychological (adj)
readiness (n)
respiratory (adj)
sense of self-worth
sensitive (adj)
symptom (n)
tension (n)

A Gathering information

1. Study the assignment. What is your answer to the question?
2. ⊘ **4.21** DVD **4.F** Watch two presentations about physical factors. Which presenter is better? Why? Tick one or more.

   - [ ] he/she doesn't hesitate
   - [ ] he/she introduces the presentation
   - [ ] he/she looks at the audience regularly
   - [ ] he/she introduces the research
   - [ ] he/she makes it easy to understand her sentences
   - [ ] he/she speaks loudly
   - [ ] he/she uses a variety of sentence patterns
   - [ ] he/she uses simple sentences

3. ⊘ **4.21** DVD **4.F** Watch the presentations again. Complete the notes in Table 1.

> Sports Science
> SS 101
>
> **Tutorial assignment**
> What are the main physical factors which affect sporting performance?
>
> Research the factors, then choose one to present at our next tutorial. Make sure you have an authoritative source to support any statements in your presentation.

Table 1: *Factors affecting sporting performance*

factor	symptoms	research	source
fatigue	feeling tired during exe;	exe. after diff. cognitive task = "exe. more diff."	
asthma	inability to breathe properly	certain sports affect asth. more than others – swimming rarely brings on attacks;	

B Practising a model

Study each basic sentence from the first presentation. Practise saying each sentence with the additional information in the correct place. Add extra words as necessary.

1. I looked at fatigue.   (factor / sporting / performance)

   I looked at fatigue as a factor in sporting performance.
2. Fatigue is tiredness.   (feeling / extreme / weakness)
3. The symptom is giving up.   (fatigue / athletes / doing / physical / exercise)
4. The athletes have done a task.   (cognitive / thinking / before / exercising)
5. Researchers looked into the factor.   (three / Marcora, Staiano and Manning)
6. Athletes perceive activity.   (found / completed / difficult, thinking / tasks / physical / harder)
7. The research was reported.   (*Journal / Applied Physiology /* 2009)

C Producing the model

1. Prepare a presentation on **fatigue** or on **asthma**.
   Use the notes in Exercise A. Make sure you refer clearly to the source of the research.
2. Give your presentation in pairs.

When you are presenting, remember:
- speak clearly
- look at your partner
- stress key words

When you are listening, remember:
- show interest
- ask for clarification
- help the speaker if he/she gets lost

A   Activating ideas

Look at the health problems in the box below. What do they have in common?

cold   flu   stress   sore throat   depression   meningitis   tiredness

B   Studying the models

1. Cover the conversations below. 🎧 **4.22** Listen and match each conversation to a photograph above.

2. Write one word in each space.

1
A: What _____ to be the trouble?

B: Well my throat is really sore. And I _____ I've got a temperature.

A: Mm. I'm just going to _____ your glands. Mm. OK. It's nothing too serious. Just strep throat.

B: Oh right. My friend _____ that recently.

A: Yes. It's very infectious. I'_____ write a prescription for some antibiotics.

2
A: Are you _____ alright?

B: Not really. I've _____ a really bad headache. Feel sick too.

A: You _____ terrible. And you're very hot.

B: Yeah? But I can't stop shivering. I really _____ feel too good.

A: OK, I'm _____ to call the health centre.

3
A: What _____ the matter?

B: Nothing really. Just feeling a bit stressed.

A: Oh. Do you want to _____ about it?

B: Well, my student loan hasn't _____ yet. I've got two essays to finish and I can't _____.

A: OK ... well ... let's _____ and get some fresh air. Then you can _____ me all about it.

4
A: _____ you ever had TB?

B: I _____ think so. What is it?

A: Tuberculosis. It's a respiratory disease.

B: Oh, right. No, I _____ never had it.

A: Are you currently _____ any medication?

C   Practising the models

1. Add a few more lines to each conversation above.

2. Practise the conversations.

3. How can each problem be treated? How can each be prevented?

D   Building vocabulary

Complete these sentence patterns with words from the box.

1. I've got (a/n) ...ache.

2. I've got a pain in my ...

3. I've got (a/n) ...

4. I've ... myself.

5. I'm feeling ...

arm   back   better   burnt   cold   cut   dizzy
head   hot   hurt   ill   indigestion   leg   neck
sick   sore throat   temperature   exhausted   tooth

A Using sense groups

1. Read the Pronunciation Check.
2. Divide this part of the asthma talk in 4.7 into sense groups and sentences. Practise saying sentences with pauses and correct intonation.

> It's possible that certain sports affect asthmatics more than others. For example, Fitch and Godfrey (1976), writing in the *Journal of the American Medical Association*, found that swimming very rarely brings on an asthma attack.

B Identifying a new skill

1. ● **4.23** Listen to three extracts from the discussion in 4.7. What is the male speaker doing in each sentence? How does the female speaker respond in each case?
2. Read the Skills Check and check your ideas.

C Practising the new skill

Study the example below. Then have more conversations with the prompts on pages 171, 176 and 180.

BOGOF (Theme 3)

> **Student 1**
> BOGOF = Buy One Get One Free
>
> **Student 2**
> BOGOF = ½ price

S1: BOGOF stands for Buy One Get One Free.

S2: So what you're saying is, BOGOF is the same as half price?

S1: Yes, that's right.

　　OR

　　Well, to some extent. But you have to buy two of the same product.

　　OR

　　No, that's not really the point. The word *free* is more powerful than the words *half price*.

Pronunciation Check

Sense groups

We must divide long sentences into groups of words which make sense, and put short pauses (/) between 'sense groups'. Put a longer pause (//) at the end of each sentence. Your voice should rise slightly at short pauses, and fall at longer pauses.

Example:

I researched asthma / which is an illness /

of the respiratory system. // One of the

symptoms of asthma / is an inability /

to breathe properly. // In severe cases /

the illness / can be fatal. //

● **4.24** Listen and repeat.

Skills Check

Summarizing

We often want to summarize a speaker's words, to check that we have understood. Speakers can confirm, partly confirm or reject summaries.

Summarizing
So what you're saying is ...?
Are you saying that ...?
In other words, ...

Reacting to summaries
Yes, that's right.
Well, to some extent.
No, that's not really the point. The point is ...

● **4.25** Listen and repeat the expressions above. Copy the stress and intonation.

4.9 Grammar for speaking Review of modals

We use modals to give special meanings to verbs. ⑰
Study the sentences in the table. Which sentence says the following?

- It's a small possibility. ☐
- It's not necessary. ☐
- It's a positive law or rule. ☐
- It's a negative law or rule. ☐
- This is good advice. ☐
- It's a possibility. ☐

S	V		other information
	modal	infinitive (without *to*)	
1 We	must	support	statements in essays.
2 People's ideas	mustn't	be quoted	without a reference.
3 Asthma	can	be	fatal.
4 People with flu	should	avoid	exercise.
5 Asthmatics	don't have to	stop	all sport.
6 Fatigue	might	be caused	by lack of sleep.

🔊 **4.26** Listen to the sentences in the table. Which part of the verb is stressed in each case?

A Changing statements to laws or rules

1. Make each statement into a rule with *must* or *mustn't*.
   a. Academic essays include a list of references.
   b. References follow conventions, for example, brackets for dates.
   c. You don't include other people's words without a reference.
   d. Page numbers are given for direct quotes.
   e. In most cases, personal opinions aren't included.
   f. Wikipedia is not used as a source.
2. 🔊 **4.27** Listen and check your answers. How does the speaker say the modal in each case?
3. 🔊 **4.28** Listen again and practise.

Table 1: Infinitives with *must*

active	passive
must(n't) be /mʌs(n)biː/	*must(n't)* be done
must(n't) do /mʌs(n)duː/	

B Talking about possibility

1. Study the first statement below. 🔊 **4.29** Listen and repeat the examples.
2. Work in pairs. Take it in turns to make the statements and reply with modals of possibility. Give an alternative possibility (in brackets) in each case.
   a. Nuclear power is the future for energy supply. (solar)
   b. Lack of food is the greatest world problem. (clean water)
   c. Global warming is caused by human activity. (natural cycle)
   d. Economic progress is driven by technology. (good government)
   e. Children become violent because of television programmes. (violent parents)
   f. Poor countries need aid from other countries. (trade)
   g. Crime is the result of drug addiction. (poverty)
   h. Road accidents are caused by bad driving. (road design)

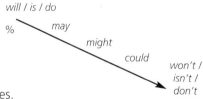

will / is / do
%   may
    might
      could
        won't /
        isn't /
        don't

Figure 1: Degrees of possibility

> *Nuclear power is the future for energy supply.*

> *Well, it **might be** the future. But more solar energy **could be used**, instead.*

> *I think we should use more renewable energy, like wind power.*

C Giving advice

What do you think we should do about some of the problems in Exercise B?

A   Preparing to research

Do you agree or disagree with each statement?

1. Listening to music can help athletes to reduce tension.
2. Top male athletes are often aggressive.
3. Exercise can reduce levels of anxiety.
4. Athletes need to be focused on a specific goal in order to be successful.
5. Athletes do not need feedback on their performance because they know how they performed.
6. Athletes often become neurotic about small aspects of their training.

B   Researching information

1. Study the assignment. Research one of the factors and make notes – see file card.
2. Practise sentences to explain your research. Make sure you include full information about the source.

C   Presenting and discussing

Work in groups with at least one person for each factor.

Remember, when you are presenting:

- Use sense groups and the correct intonation.
- Refer to sources clearly.
- Be prepared to explain any words or ideas in your research information if you are asked.
- Respond to summaries of your research using expressions from the Skills Check in 4.8.

Remember, when you are listening:

- Make notes of the research – see file card.
- Try to summarize points using expressions from the Skills Check in 4.8.

Sports Science
SS 101

Tutorial assignment
What are the main **psychological** factors which affect sporting performance?

Research one of the factors below to present at our next tutorial.

- tension   page 172
- neurosis   page 174
- aggression   page 176
- feedback   page 167
- mental preparation   page 171

Factor:
Research:

Source:

4.11 Vocabulary for reading — Shorter working week, longer life!

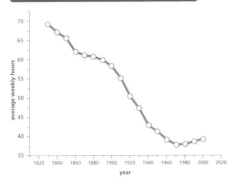

Figure 1: *Average weekly hours (US) 1820–2000*
Source: Vandenbroucke, G. (2006) A Model of the Trends in Hours Retrieved on 13.06.2011 from http://dornsife.usc.edu/IEPR/Publications/Working_Papers05.shtml#4

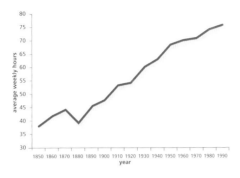

Figure 2: *Life expectancy (US) 1850–1990*
Source: Retrieved on 21.06.2011 from http://perfecthealthdiet.com/?p=2308

A — Reading line graphs

1. What trend does each graph show?
2. Suggest reasons for each trend.
3. What will the figures be by 2050 if each trend continues?

B — Understanding new vocabulary in context

1. Complete the paragraphs from a social studies article with a word from the mini-dictionary below for each space. Make any necessary changes.
2. What is the main point of each paragraph?

abolish (v) 7	remove, e.g., a law
campaign (v) 2	work strongly for
impetus (n) 1	force in a direction
longevity (n)	duration of a life
indication (n)	sign
radical (adj) 8	new, very unusual
reflect (v) 5	show
retire (v) 6	stop working
sedentary (adj) 4	sitting down
significant (adj)	important, e.g., in statistical terms
state (n) 3	government

C — Developing critical thinking

1. What are the social and economic implications of the trends in the figures?
2. Do you have any *radical proposals* to deal with the issues around increased longevity?

Figures show that average working hours in developed countries have fallen steadily for the last 200 years (Figure 1). The *impetus* for this change has mainly been the rise in power of the working class in these countries, *abolish* throughout the period. Many countries now have *radical* controlled hours which provide considerable leisure time in a week. Most people in the developed world now work a maximum of 40 hours a week, largely in *sedentary* office jobs. However, there are *indications* that the trend may be changing. Research shows a slight increase in working hours in recent years.

...

Many countries now provide for retirement after a particular age with state pensions, paid for by contributions from the current labour force. However, the official retirement age in many countries does not *reflect* the recent rise in *sign*, particularly in the developed world (see Figure 2). In the 1950s, people only had two or three years of life expectancy after *state* 6, so pensions were only paid for a short period. Nowadays, on average, a person will receive an old-age pension for about 20 years. This raises the question of how society will cope. Very few people suggest *retire* state pension payments, but *longevity* proposals *are* needed to take into account the *sedentary* rise in life expectancy.

a good case
abandon (v)
abolish (v)
abstract (adj) [= opp. of concrete]
campaign
citizen (n)
citizenship (n)
class (n) [= social division]
concrete (adj) [= opp. of abstract]
curriculum (n) [pl. = curricula]
educationalist (n)
educator (n)
entrepreneur (n)
flexible (adj)
foster (v) [= encourage]
furthermore
humanities (n pl)
impetus (n)
labour force
leisure (n)
lifelong (adj)
literacy (n)
longevity (n)
numeracy (n)
personal education
positive thinking
proposal (n)
provision (n)
radical (n)
raise the question
reflect (v) [= be related to]
retire (v)
retirement (n)
sedentary (n)
self-starter (n)
social education
state (n) [= government]
supposition (n)
take into account
working class(es)

A Preparing to read

Study the assignment.

1. Think of good research questions.
2. What sources can help you research the assignment?
3. Make a spidergram of your ideas about state education.

B Understanding the text

1. Imagine you are researching the state education system in the UK. Read the article. What are the main points? Complete each sentence.

   a. State education in Britain may have started because ...
      the working class had poor literacy and numeracy.
   b. Some people say that obedience, learnt at school, prepared people for ... *literocy ond numerocy*
   c. It could be argued that long, boring schooldays prepared people for ...
   d. After 1944, state education followed in some ways Plato's ideas of ...
   e. The national curriculum since 1988 has concentrated on ...
   f. Gough thinks that state education based on the national curriculum ...
   g. Gough thinks state education should produce ...

2. Which of the points above are useful to you for the assignment?

C Understanding vocabulary in context

Find an informal word or phrase in the box for each formal verb from the text.

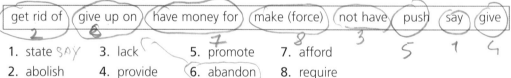

| get rid of | give up on | have money for | make (force) | not have | push | say | give |

    2   6   7   8   3   5   1   4

1. state *say*   3. lack   5. promote   7. afford
2. abolish   4. provide   6. abandon   8. require

D Developing critical thinking

What would Gough's ideal school be like, in terms of curriculum, timetable, teaching and buildings?

State education in the UK: Preparing children for the 21ˢᵗ century ... or the 19ᵗʰ?

The vast majority of countries in the world have a compulsory education system, paid for by the state. But what is the purpose of education provided by a government? Life is very different now from 100 years ago, or even 20, but does compulsory education equip people for the modern world? In this article, we look at state education in Britain since 1870 and ask: What is it preparing children for?

In the UK, the Forsters Education Act (1870) was the first step towards state education in Britain. It stated that all parts of the country should provide schools (UK Parliament, 2011). However, there was no requirement in the Act for the schools to be free. Therefore, the working classes could still not afford to send their children to school and, for the most part, children continued to work from an early age. However, in 1891, fees for state schools were abolished and therefore education became available to all (UK Parliament, 2011). Some argue that the government decided to provide free education for the working classes because Britain was falling behind other countries. They think that the government believed workers lacked obedience, literacy and numeracy skills (Lowe, 2007; Mitchell, 1996). Carr and Hartnett describe the 'historic role'

Social Studies Faculty

Around the world, some educationalists argue that state education should create obedient citizens, others believe it should produce useful workers, and a small number think it should make well-balanced people.

Assignment

How does compulsory education in your country prepare children for the 21ˢᵗ century?

of education as 'producing a labour force which had respect for ... authority' (Carr and Hartnett, 1996; p. 124).

So it would seem that state schools were designed to be places to prepare working-class children for lives in factories and, if required, the army. The state school day involved exercises which promoted patriotism and obedience to authority (BBC, 2011). Children sat in rows, in silence, copying work from the board. In later life, they sat in rows, in silence, working in a factory. Furthermore, the learning did not involve thinking but simply following instructions, in the same way that factory work also involved little mental activity during long working days. Most factory workers were on a 5.5-day week (Mitchell, 1996).

Passed in 1944, the Education Act made *secondary school* education compulsory for all children. The previous acts had only introduced *primary* education. However, this Act went further, detailing the introduction of different types of schools which would reflect the types of work people would do in later life. The supposition, in the Spens Report and later the Norwood Report, was that there are three kinds of children. Some can deal with abstract concepts, some need more concrete explanations and the majority prefer to do practical activities (Board of Education, 1943). Tawney explains: 'Secondary schools would be various in type, and not all children would pass to the same kind of school' (Tawney, as cited in McCulloch, 1998; p. 49).

It is possible that the 1944 Act was strongly influenced by the ideas of Plato, 3,000 years before (McCulloch, 1998; Carr and Hartnett, 1996). Plato stated that people can be divided into three classes, gold, silver and copper. Each class was best suited to a particular job in society: 'God as he was fashioning you, put gold in those of you who are capable of ruling ..., silver in the auxiliaries, and ... copper in the farmers and other craftsmen' (Plato, 1995; p. 98). This, as McCulloch and others suggest, would appear to be very similar to the different types of school created by the 1944 Education Act. However, the system was abandoned in the 1970s, for several reasons, and Britain moved to a system of secondary schools called *comprehensives*, which take children of all levels of ability.

Since 1988, all state schools have been required to follow a national curriculum. Many theorists have argued that this curriculum is strikingly similar to the curricula of state schools in the early 19th century (Chitty, 2008). Lawton says that 'a national curriculum was produced which was based simply on the list of subjects that education ministers ... had

presumably studied at school' (Lawton, 1992; p. 49). The subjects are history, the sciences, the arts, languages, and morality. Chitty argues that there is 'no mention of integrated subjects like humanities or environmental studies, or of ... personal and social education, or of "newer" subjects like psychology, sociology, politics and economics' (Chitty, 1989; p. 209). Furthermore, the curriculum is based on ideas about education that could be said to suit Victorian factory-worker life, with little leisure time or thinking for yourself. Gough argues that:

> A compulsory education, to a rigidly prescribed curriculum, in a classroom of 30 in a school of hundreds, at set hours, Monday to Friday, is splendid preparation for life as a 19th-century factory hand. But it is precisely, almost brilliantly, wrong for creating self-starters, entrepreneurs, free thinkers, risk-takers, leaders, visionaries, inventors, innovators, flexible employees, creative artists or anyone Britain actually needs. We no longer force adults to work in Victorian workhouses. So why do we force children to learn in Victorian schools?
>
> (Gough, 2011)

Seemingly, then, the education system in Britain has continually tried to prepared children for later life. There is a good argument that the Victorian 'factory-preparing' and 'soldier-building' system was highly effective. However, it would appear that the current UK national curriculum does little to prepare the nation's young people for 21st-century life.

© Lucy Phillips, 2011, University of Winchester, UK

References

BBC (2011) *Primary History: Victorian Britain*, http://www.bbc.co.uk/schools/primaryhistory/victorian_britain/victorian_schools/ (retrieved 12.06.2011).

Board of Education (1943) *Curriculum and Examinations in Secondary Schools*, London: HMSO.

Carr, W. and Hartnett, A. (1996) *Education and the Struggle for Democracy*, Buckingham: Open University Press.

Chitty, C. (1989) *Towards a New Education System: The Victory of the New Right?* London: Falmer Press.

Chitty, C. (2008) The UK National Curriculum: an historical perspective, *Forum*, 50.

Gough, J. (2011) If I Ruled the World, *Prospect*, http://www.prospectmagazine.co.uk/tag/victorian-schools/ (retrieved 12.06.2011).

Lawton, D. (1992) *Education and Politics in the 1990s: Conflict or Consensus?* London: Falmer Press.

Lawton, D. (1994) *The Tory Mind on Education 1979–94*, London: Falmer Press.

Lowe, R. (2007) *The Death of Progressive Education: How Teachers Lost Control of the Classroom*, London: Routledge.

McCulloch, G. (1998) *Failing the Ordinary Child*, Buckingham: Open University Press.

Mitchell, S. (1996) *Daily Life in Victorian England*, Westport: Greenwood Press.

Plato (1995) *The Republic*, London: Everyman.

UK Parliament (2011) *The 1870 Education Act*, http://www.parliament.uk/about/living-heritage/transformingsociety/livinglearning/school/overview/1870educationact/ (retrieved 12.06.2011).

A Reviewing vocabulary

Complete the final word in each sentence.

1. Some people say that a major role for schools is to teach children ob_____.

2. We should continually review the subjects on the cu_____.

3. Some children can do abstract subjects and some cannot. This was the su_____.

4. After some years, this idea of different types of school was ab_____.

5. UK state education is not suited to the needs of the modern world, according to some ed_____.

6. Many theorists believe that it is the 21st-century world that school subjects should re_____.

7. The first aim of any education system should be li_____.

8. The second aim should be nu_____.

9. There is a sensible argument that schools should try to produce good ci_____.

10. Many people now work less and have far more le_____.

11. Medical advances are responsible for the huge increase in lo_____.

12. Every country in the world is going to have to look again at the official age of re_____.

B Identifying and practising a new skill (1)

1. Read Skills Check 1.

2. Look again at the text in 4.12. What, in your opinion, are the key words or sentences in each paragraph?

C Identifying and practising a new skill (2)

1. Read Skills Check 2.

2. Look at the key words and sentences you have highlighted from Exercise B2. Which of these words and sentences will help you to complete the assignment in 4.12? Underline the items. Then find the source of the ideas or information in each case. Highlight each source in a different colour. Highlight it also in the list of references at the end.

Twenty-three per cent of children leave school unable to read or write

Why don't children know maths anymore? asks industry leader

Politician calls for return of army service for 18-year-olds

Children don't know about their own country, says government minister

Skills Check 1

Recognizing the key points

You must recognize the key point(s) of each paragraph. Highlight key words/sentence(s). The topic sentence will guide you.

Examples:

topic = national curriculum	Since 1988, all state schools have been required to follow a national curriculum.
key point = similar to early C19	Many theorists have argued that this curriculum is strikingly similar to the curricula of state schools in the early 19th century (Chitty, 2008).

Skills Check 2

Recording sources (2)

You must record sources that you want to cite (see 3.13). Highlight the sources of key information in a different colour.

Example:

	... similar to the curricula of state schools in the early 19th century (Chitty, 2008).

In many cases, key points come from the writer of the text. In this case, put the name and date of publication in the margin.

Example:

Phillips, 2011	the education system in Britain has continually tried to prepare children for later life.

Academic texts often state **facts**. It is usually clear when a writer is stating a fact. Be careful, though! Sometimes 'facts' are only facts according to the writer. Which fact below is in this category? ⑱

S	V	other information
The Education Act	stated	that all parts of the country should provide schools.
There	was	no requirement for the schools to be free.
All state schools	have been required	to follow a national curriculum since 1988.
The subjects	are	history, the sciences, the arts, languages, etc.
The system	does not prepare	children for life in the 21st century.

However, many sentences in academic texts tell you that the statement is an idea, a theory or a piece of research. These are *possibilities*, so the writer **hedges** the statement in some way.

Notes:
* Each sentence below contains **two parts** – a **hedging device** and a **statement**.
* The **hedging device** is usually in the **present** while the **statement** can be in **any tense**.

hedging device	statement		
	S	V	extra information
It **seems** that	the curriculum	does not prepare	children for 21st century life.
It is **possible** that	the 1944 Act	was influenced	by the ideas of Plato.
Seemingly,	the state system	has tried to prepare	children for later life.
There is **a good argument** that	the Victorian system	was	highly effective.

A Distinguishing between facts and possibilities

Find each statement below in the text in 4.12. Does the writer state it as a fact, or hedge it in some way? If it is stated as a fact, do you think it is actually the writer's opinion?

1. The working classes could still not afford to send their children to school. *Opinion*
2. In 1891, fees for state schools were abolished. *Fact*
3. State schools were designed to prepare children for lives in factories. *Opinion*
4. The state school day promoted patriotism and obedience. *Opinion*
5. Leisure time was very limited. *Opinion*
6. There are some children who can deal with abstract concepts. *Opinion*
7. The national curriculum was a list of subjects that education ministers had studied at school. *Opinion*

B Recognizing hedging devices

Which words from the box can replace each **bold** word to complete the hedging devices?

arguably	argue	belief	likely	maintain	probable
seem	seemingly	suggested	supposition	think	

1. Some theorists **believe** / *think* that ...
2. Many educationalists have **argued** / *suggested* that ...
3. The **assumption** / *supposition / belief* is that ...
4. It would **appear** / *seem* that ...
5. It is **possible** / *probable* that ...
6. **Presumably,** / *seemingly / arguably* this is the reason for ...

A Preparing to read

Read the assignment. What's your reaction to the question?

B Understanding a text

Read the essay. Highlight the key points in each paragraph. Record the sources of information you want to quote.

C Checking understanding

Which of these statements does the writer believe strongly? Which are hedged in the article? Decide, then look again at the text to check your memory.

1. We should continue to teach world knowledge at school.
2. People should learn key skills like literacy, numeracy and IT.
3. Children should be taught to deal with money.
4. Children should be taught to be creative.
5. If you do not look after your body, you will suffer in later life.
6. Healthy living should be part of the school curriculum.
7. Schools should teach children positive thinking.
8. School curricula should contain all the subjects, 'old' and 'new'.
9. Education should happen throughout life.
10. Governments should provide opportunities for lifelong learning.
11. Teachers should educate children in the need to continue learning.
12. Demand for lifelong learning will result in state provision.

D Developing critical thinking

Which points from Exercise C do you agree with? Which should schools do? Which should be left to universities or later learning opportunities?

Faculty of Social Studies

'Anyone who stops learning is old, whether at 20 or 80. Anyone who keeps learning stays young.'
Henry Ford

Assignment

How can state education help people to live with the extra free time of the 21st century?

How can state education help people live with more free time?

As some educationalists see it, the 'historic role of education' is 'producing a labour force' (Carr and Hartnett, 1996; p. 124). However, this role may be changing, with a significant increase in free time during a lifetime. In this essay, I consider how governments can deal with this issue while continuing to meet the basic needs of state education.

There was a good argument for educating for work in the 19th century, when people spent the vast majority of their lives working. In 1900, for example, the average person in the UK and the US worked a 60-hour week, usually involving hard physical labour on low pay. When they were not at work, people had neither the energy nor the money to spend on leisure (Vandenbroucke, 2006). However, nowadays, the average adult in the UK works just over 41 hours a week (BBC, 2008), leaving nearly 127 hours per week for other activities. Removing time spent sleeping – seven hours a night on average (BBC, 2007) – leaves us with nearly 80 hours' free time. In other words, the average person has twice as much free time as work time during a working week.

This issue becomes even more important when we take into account the average retirement age in the developed countries of around 64.5 for men and 62 for women (Age UK, 2011), compared with the current life expectancy of around 85 (ONS, 2010). Not only will people spend most of their 'working life' actually at leisure but they will also have, roughly, 20 years after they retire to do as they wish. These changes in the structure of the work:leisure ratio raise the question of how governments can prepare people for 21st-century lives.

There is a good case for continuing to teach at school the world knowledge involved in traditional subjects like history, geography and science. People presumably need to know about the world they live in. There must also remain considerable focus on key skills which are related to work, such as literacy and numeracy. New skills for work, such as using IT, are also evidently of value. However, there are other subjects which may be valuable during free time or in retirement. One of these is dealing with money. It could be argued that state education should teach people to understand personal finance in general, and saving for retirement in particular, in order to ensure that they can enjoy their free time. Furthermore, it is arguable that creativity should be fostered in schools, in order for people to find things to spend their free time on.

Some theorists also believe that, in this age of sedentary occupations in offices, we need to teach people the value of exercise, or perhaps more importantly, the harmful effects of not exercising, particularly with increased longevity (NHS, 2011). The dangers of ill-treating your body may catch up with you if you live until your 80s, whereas they may not have appeared if you had died earlier. Although government campaigns such as *Change 4 Life* (NHS, ibid.) have reflected concerns about teaching healthy living, it could be argued that the topic needs to be an integral part of a 21st-century curriculum. It is not enough simply to make children exercise for an hour a week at school. We must also teach them why they are doing it and why they should continue to do it after leaving school.

Perhaps the most radical proposal at the moment is that schools should teach children to be happy throughout their lives. According to Professor Martin Seligman, studies have shown that psychological training 'could save the state millions of pounds dealing with problems later in life' (Woolf, 2011). Seligman, who is a former president of the American Psychological Association, reports studies in British schools which found that 'kids who ... did positive thinking had more social skills and more zest for learning' (ibid.).

The supposition behind the arguments above is that the school curriculum needs to accommodate traditional subjects *plus* all the additional ones. But there is another solution. I believe that we should stop looking at education as something which largely or wholly happens between the ages of 5 and 18 (or 21 if you go on to university). Clearly, education is now something which should continue throughout a person's life, with additional input as it is required at every stage.

It is true that many local authorities and other bodies provide night-school classes in craft skills such as woodwork, or aerobics, or modern languages and so on. But all of these have to be paid for by the participants, so uptake is small. It is now time for Ministries of Education around the world to fund lifelong learning. Modern society must ensure that people can benefit from the huge amount of additional leisure which they enjoy, from better working practices and increased longevity.

Some theorists believe, however, that the impetus for change should come, not from the suppliers of lifelong learning, but from the consumers. Christopher Day, Emeritus Professor in the Faculty of Social Sciences at the University of Nottingham, believes that one of the main tasks of teachers is to get students interested in the idea of lifelong learning (Day, 1999). If teachers at schools can achieve this, it is likely that people will demand state provision throughout their lives. Perhaps this demand will ensure that the state provides what is required free of charge.

Tanmay Mukherjee, 2011, Edinburgh University

References

Age UK (2011) *Average Retirement Age on the Rise*, retrieved on 13.07.2011 from http://www.ageuk.org.uk/latest-news/archive/average-retirement-age-on-the-rise/
BBC (2007) *Why Should We Have Eight Hours' Sleep?*, retrieved on 13.07.2011 from http://news.bbc.co.uk/1/hi/magazine/6546209.stm
BBC (2008) *UK Work Week Among EU's Longest*, retrieved on 13.07.2011 from http://news.bbc.co.uk/1/hi/7598467.stm
Carr, W. and Hartnett, A. (1996) *Education and the Struggle for Democracy*, Buckingham: Open University Press
Day, C. (1999) *Developing Teachers: The Challengers of Lifelong Learning* London: Routledge Farmer
NHS (2011) *Change 4 Life*, retrieved on 13.07.2011 from http://www.nhs.uk/change4life/Pages/change-for-life.aspx
Office for National Statistics (ONS) (2010) *Life Expectancy*, retrieved on 13.07.2011 from http://www.statistics.gov.uk/cci/nugget.asp?id=168
Vandenbroucke, G. (2006) *A Model of the Trends in Hours* (Working Paper 05.40), retrieved on 13.07.2011 from http://dornsife.usc.edu/IEPR/Publications/Working_Papers05.shtml#40
Woolf, M. (2011) *Sit still, children: today we're going to learn to be happy*, The Sunday Times, No 9, 750 July 17, 2011

1 Cover the final column. Try to answer each question.

1. What is a *tissue*, in biology?	a teacher, a sports coach or a manager
2. What can *muscle tissue* do?	about 85
3. What does the *digestive system* do?	being able to read and write
4. Which system does the *spine* belong to?	contract but not expand
5. Which system is *asthma* a problem of?	converts food into nutrients
6. What did the English physician, *William Harvey*, discover in the 17th century?	1 a group of cells with the same function
7. How does the *nervous system* send messages around the body?	high temperature, severe aches and pains in joints and muscles, headache, fatigue
8. Where is the *Achilles tendon*?	in a school or university
9. What are some of the *symptoms* of flu?	in the heel
10. What is the difference between a bruise and a *contusion*?	it has more than doubled
11. When do you take *medication*?	it uses electricity
12. How do you behave if you are *neurotic*?	people in offices or professional drivers
13. What is the average *life expectancy* nowadays in the developed world?	something you think is true
14. What has happened to *longevity* in the last 150 years?	the circulation of the blood
15. What kinds of workers have *sedentary* jobs?	the respiratory system
16. What is a *supposition*?	the skeletal system
17. What is *literacy*?	there is none – one is the common term, the other is the medical term
18. If you provide the *impetus* for something, what do you do?	when you have an illness or a disease
19. Where do you find a *curriculum*?	you push people in a particular direction
20. What sort of person gives *feedback*?	you worry about everything

2 Uncover the final column. Match the questions and answers above.

3 Cover the first column. Make a good question for each answer.

4.16 Vocabulary for writing The changing beehive

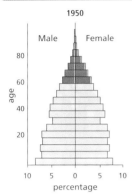

1950

Figure 1

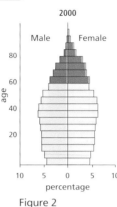

2000

Figure 2

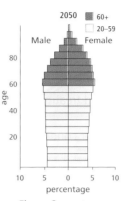

2050 ■ 60+ □ 20–59

Figure 3   (Source: UN, 2002)

accelerate (*v*)
ageing (*adj*)
beehive diagram
benefit (*n* and *v*)
child-bearing age
contribute (*v*)
decide against (*v*)
decline (*n* and *v*)
dependency ratio
dependent (*adj*)
developed (*adj*)
   [~ countries]
elderly (*adj*)
fertility (*n*)
health care
incidence (*n*)
labour force
life expectancy
link (*n* and *v*)
longevity (*n*)
medical innovation
population ageing
postpone (*v*)
pregnancy (*n*)
proportion (*n*)
prosperity (*n*)
provider (*n*)
put pressure on (*v*)
rise / rose / risen (*v*)
seemingly (*adv*)
significantly (*adv*)
social security benefit
spouse (*n*)
stability (*n*)
support (*n* and *v*)
trend (*n*)
urbanization (*n*)
variation (*n*)

A   Activating ideas

Study the figures above. What do they show?

B   Understanding new vocabulary in context

1. Complete the definitions of the key terms with a word or phrase from the list on the right.
2. How can each definition continue? Choose from below.

a   *Fertility* may continue until well after 45, for example, women have recently had successful *pregnancies* above the age of 60.

b   Nowadays, with increased *longevity*, the term is used more for people over 70 or even 80.

c   The number of dependents compared to the number in the labour force is called the *dependency ratio*.

d   These people are the main *providers* of state funds, in the form of income tax.

e   We can see from this kind of diagram the *proportion* of men and women in the population, as well as the *ratio* of, for example, children and old people.

Key terms

A graph which shows the *demographic* structure of a population is called a ⎁beehive⎁ diagram, because it is shaped like an artificial home for bees.   □

Women between 15 and 45 are considered to be of _____, although medical *innovations* mean birth can occur much later in life nowadays.   □

The definition of _____ has changed in the last 50 years. In the 1950s, this life period started at 60.   □

Officially, people between 15 and 65 are considered to be in the _____, even if they are *unemployed*.   □

People below 15 and above 65 are considered to be _____, because they usually receive *support* from the state, for example, child *benefit* to parents or old age *pension* after *retirement*. These people, by definition, are not in the labour force.   □

C   Describing a beehive diagram

1. Study Figure 1 and write an answer to each question in a full sentence. In 1950, approximately what percentage …

    a. of women were of child-bearing age?
    b. of people were considered to be elderly?
    c. of men were in the labour force?
    d. of people were dependent?

2. Write sentences describing some key features of Figure 3.

A Reviewing sentence patterns

Rewrite each sentence, beginning with the words given.

1. The average is lower than in 1990. The average was _____

2. The average is lower than 20 years ago. The average has

3. The trend continues at present. The average is _____

4. There is a possibility that the average will fall further in the next five years. The average might

5. It is probable that the average will rise again in ten years' time. The average will

Faculty of Health Sciences
Public Health Department

'Population ageing all over the world means there will be too many dependents and too few workers in the future. The number of persons over 65 will rise to a level which cannot be supported by the working population in terms of social security benefits.'

Assignment
To what extent is population ageing a world-wide problem?

B Thinking and organizing

1. Read the assignment. Why might population ageing lead to:
   • more dependents?
   • fewer workers?
   • higher social security benefits?

2. Study the figures. Which area of the world will population ageing affect the most? Which area will have more working people over 65?

3. Study the notes below. Which notes show that population ageing is happening all over the world? Which notes show that it may not be such a big problem?

   a. 'Age-distribution changes in less developed regions have been slow, but will accelerate over the next 50 years' (p. 15)
   UN (2002) *World Population Ageing* retrieved on 22.07.2011 from www.un.org/esa/population/publications/worldageing19502050

   b. 'Not all young and old persons require support ...'
   Taeuber, C. (1992) *Sixty-five plus in America*, US Bureau of the Census, Current Population Reports, Special Studies, pp. 23–178 RV Washington cited in UN 2002

   c. '... older persons in many societies are providers of support to their adult children ...'
   Morgan, D., Schuster, T., & Butler, E. (1991) 'Role reversals in the exchange of social support', *Journal of Gerontology*, 46, S278

C Writing, editing and rewriting

1. Write the essay. Remember:
   • Describe significant features of the graphs.
   • Support statements with evidence.
   • Give the source of supporting evidence.
   • Paraphrase research notes OR quote direct.
   • Hedge statements if necessary.
   • List the references at the end of the essay.

2. Exchange drafts and check your partner's work.

3. Write the essay again.

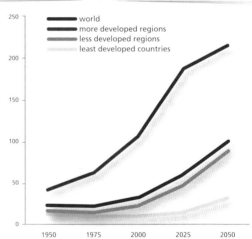

Figure 1: Number of persons 65+ per 100 children

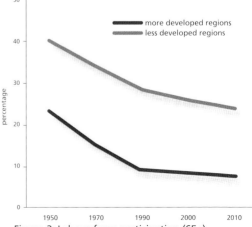

Figure 2: Labour force participation (65+)

The positive and negative aspects of ageing populations

   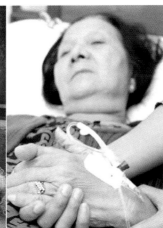

A Activating ideas

1. What different aspects of being elderly do the photographs show?
2. Complete each bold word in the table. Be careful with spelling.

Table 1: Possible positive and negative aspects of an ageing population

positive aspects	negative aspects
They make a significant **con**tribution to certain parts of the leisure industry because many take more holidays than younger people.	They sometimes need a great deal of **he**_____ care because body systems fail or organs develop illnesses, like cancer.
They have learnt a huge number of **sk**_____ which they can still use if given the opportunity.	They usually receive social **se**_____ payments, e.g., old-age pensions.
They have acquired a vast amount of **kn**_____ which they can share with the next generation.	They may suffer from **lo**_____ because they have lost spouses, friends and relatives.
They often provide **ch**_____ for their grandchildren.	They may experience **bo**_____ because they don't know how to cope with leisure.
Some are financially **ind**_____, with their own homes and savings.	They may feel they have nothing further to **con**_____ to society, so nothing to live for.

B Taking part in a discussion

1. What are the typical stereotypes of elderly people, in the media and in society in general?
2. What are the dangers of these stereotypes?
3. How can we avoid stereotyping?

C Gathering information

Study the assignment. Choose one of the topics.

1. Find evidence in the research on pages 128–129 and do additional research. Make notes, recording the sources.
2. Write the assignment.
3. Exchange the draft with a partner for editing, then write a final version.

Sociology Department

'Older Americans ... are seen by many people as being feeble in mind and body and ... economic burdens on society. It is often believed that they have little to contribute once they reach their sixties. ...This stereotype exists not just in the United States, but in other nations as well.'
Falk, U., and Falk, G. (1997) *Ageism, the Aged and Aging in America*, Charles C. Thomas, Springfield: USA

Assignment
Write an essay on ONE of the following:
1. Discuss the positive and negative aspects of an ageing population, with particular reference to your country.
2. How can we help people who are living longer to live better?

1

'The World Bank concludes that the issues related to population ageing in Latin America can only be countered by crafting a new social agenda for Latin America.' (P & D Network, 2011)

'Population ageing will be the most dominant demographic challenge confronting the European Union in the 21ˢᵗ century and will affect everybody. Sustained low fertility and increasing longevity will speed up population ageing in the coming decades.' (Rychtaríková, 2011)

'... population ageing is rapidly becoming one of the most serious concerns for Japan and other developed countries in the first half of the 21ˢᵗ century.' (Takayama, 2001)

References
Pension and Development Network (2011) *Population ageing in Latin America* retrieved on 15.07.11 from www.pensiondevelopment.org/578/population-ageing-latin-america.htm
Rychtaríková, J. (2011) *Population ageing: A common challenge for Europe* retrieved on 15.07.11 from www.geographischerundschau.de/international/content_current_issue.php?bestellnr=23311003
Takayama, N. (2001) *Pension arrangements in the oldest country: The Japanese case* retrieved on 15.07.11 from www.ier.hit-u.ac.jp/pie/English/homepage/appendix.html

2

Tom Kirkwood, Professor of Medicine at Newcastle University, states that our current view of ageing is that it is inevitable and, furthermore, that our bodies have an expiry date. He says that people believe 'we age because in some fundamental sense we cannot survive for longer, or that we are programmed to die because this is necessary to make way for the next generation.' However, Kirkwood suggests that this view is completely incorrect. Instead, he argues that our bodies are designed to survive, not die, and that eventually, through advances in science and technology, we will be able to live much, much longer.

Kirkwood, T. (2001) *Lecture 1: Brave Old World*, retrieved on 14.07.11 from http://www.bbc.co.uk/radio4/reith2001/lecture1.shtml

3

One problem with ageing is the increased susceptibility to illnesses. In particular, illnesses such as cancer, Parkinson's disease, arthritis, osteoporosis and heart disease are much more common in the elderly. Not only does ageing make each of these diseases more likely individually, but you are also more likely to experience a multiplicity of conditions.

Kirkwood, T. (2001) *Lecture 1: Brave Old World*, retrieved on 14.07.11 from http://www.bbc.co.uk/radio4/reith2001/lecture1.shtml

4

According to Tom Kirkwood, there are far too many people who like to dwell on the dangers inherent in the longevity revolution without celebrating the progress that has opened these new horizons. He says that the majority of people hold extremely negative stereotypes of the ageing process.

Kirkwood, T. (2001) *Lecture 1: Brave Old World*, retrieved on 14.07.11 from http://www.bbc.co.uk/radio4/reith2001/lecture1.shtml

5

Cancer is a disease that affects the cells of the body. The cells become abnormal but continue to multiply. There are approximately 200 different types of cancer and many different possible causes. These include contact with carcinogens (substances that cause cancer, such as cigarette smoke), genes, immune system, weight, diet and physical activity, environment, viruses, bacteria and age. Age is a key cause, as many types of cancer become a lot more common as a person ages. This is because the cells have more time to develop abnormal characteristics and reproduce these in future cells.

Cancer Research UK (2010) *What Causes Cancer?*, retrieved on 14.07.11 from http://cancerhelp.cancerresearchuk.org/about-cancer/causes-symptoms/causes/what-causes-cancer

6

While the populations of more developed countries have been ageing for well over a century, this process began recently in most less developed countries, and it is being compressed into a few decades. (p. 5)

Kinsella, K. and Phillips, D., (2005) 'The challenge of global ageing', *Population Bulletin*, 60

7

Population ageing will have a profound impact on the workforce as countries try to fill the shortage whilst still providing jobs for young people. Furthermore, this will result in retirement ages being raised. In previous years, older workers have needed to retire in order to make way for the younger generation, who cost employers less.

Bloom, D. E., Canning, D. and Fink, G. (2011) *Implications of Population Ageing for Economic Growth* (Working Paper 16705), retrieved on 14.07.11 from http://www.nber.org/papers/w16705

8

Population ageing has occurred rapidly in developing countries and, as a result, these countries are completely unprepared. They do not have the infrastructure in place, in terms of access to health care, to cope with an elderly majority.

Hayutin, A. (2007) *Global Ageing: The New New Thing – The Big Picture of Population Change in Asia*, Stanford Centre of Longevity, retrieved on 14.07.11 from http://longevity.stanford.edu/blog/2011/06/global-aging-the-new-new-thing-the-big-picture-of-population-change-in-asia/

9

An increased proportion of elderly people leads us to an urgent need to examine problems in Western society. These include access to health care and the general population's perception of the elderly.

The amount of resources old people can access in terms of health care is determined by a number of factors such as locality, age, gender and class.

Henrard, J. C. (1996) 'Cultural problems of ageing especially regarding gender and intergenerational equality', *Social Science and Medicine*, 43.

10

There are many perceived, or, in many cases, actual, benefits of elderly people. These include their skills and knowledge, which tend to be traditional, their security with regards to owning their own property, their political power and their contributions to society through certain services such as child care.

Hooyman, N. R. and Kiyak, H. A. (2011) *Social Gerontology: A Multidisciplinary Perspective*, Boston: Pearson Education.

11

It is arguable that, previously, there has been a cultural divide between the ways different countries view their elders. In developing countries, older people have tended to be revered and looked after in the same home as the younger generations. However, in developing countries, the younger generation are now more educated than their elders, and so do not view their elderly as wise and knowledgeable. Furthermore, many elderly people in India, for example, do not live with their family, and reports from young people in China have suggested they feel more responsibility towards their jobs than their parents or grandparents. However, this is not the case in Japan, where 'the majority of middle-aged persons still believe that the care of older parents is the children's responsibility' (p. 56).

Hooyman, N. R. and Kiyak, H. A. (2011) *Social Gerontology: A Multidisciplinary Perspective*, Boston: Pearson Education.

12

The media have begun to call the current older generation 'SKI-ers', not because they go skiing a lot, although many of them do, but because they are Spending the Kids' Inheritance. 'The stereotype of grandparents sitting at home with a blanket over their knees could not be further from the truth.' The over-50s are responsible for 40 per cent of spending on leisure in the UK which amounts to around £240 billion a year.

BBC (2004) *Spending Parents Leave Little Inheritance*, BBC News, retrieved on 15.07.11 from http://news.bbc.co.uk/1/hi/business/3493641.stm

Theme 5

The past, present and future of food

- Agriculture through history

- Interfering with nature?

- Should man be a herbivore?

- GM: The future or the end?

5.1 Vocabulary for listening Producing and protecting

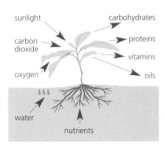

A Activating knowledge

What do food crops need to grow well?

19.00–19.30
Talking point
The future of farming ... or the past?
In today's programme, we meet Malcolm Arnold. He farms five hectares in the east of England. Malcolm is not convinced that modern methods of farming are better than old ones. In fact, he fears that modern methods may destroy us all.

B Understanding vocabulary in context

1. Study the radio programme listing. Why do you think Malcolm fears modern methods of farming?

2. ⊕ **5.1** Listen to the first part of Malcolm's talk.

   a. What kind of farming is he in favour of?

   b. Why could we call this kind of farming 'the future or the past'?

3. Complete each sentence from Malcolm's talk with a word from the list on the right.

   a. At one time, all farmers were .organic.

   b. We know, of course, that plants need sunlight and water, but plants need ...., too.

   c. Nutrients exist naturally in ....

   d. Eventually, the soil becomes ....

   e. At one time, farmers put nutrients back organically, with animal
   ...., ...

   f. ... particularly .... from the cows and horses on the farm.

   g. Farmers must protect their crops from ...., like birds, insects and bacteria.

   h. From the earliest times, farmers have used natural ...., like sulphur, to destroy pests.

   i. Pests have been responsible for ...., with farms producing few or no food crops.

4. ⊕ **5.2** Listen to the final part of Malcolm's talk. When he stops, number the next word or phrase.

	environment.		laboratory.
	farming.		past.
	fish.		pesticides.
	future.		rivers.
	health.	1	simple.

C Developing critical thinking

What is your view? Should farming return to organic methods?

agriculturalist (n)
artificial (adj)
berry (n)
breeding (n)
cereal (n)
crop (n)
digress (v)
digression (n)
domesticated (adj)
edible (adj)
famine (n)
fertile (adj)
fertilizer (n)
grind (v)
harvest (v)
hunter-gatherer (n)
indigenous (adj)
manure (n)
mechanization (n)
mechanize (v)
nitrogen (N) (n)
nutrient (n)
organic (adj)
pest (n)
pesticide (n)
phosphorus (P) (n)
planting (v)
plough (n and v)
potassium (K) (n)
preserve (v)
protection (n)
rear (v)
revolutionize (v)
starvation (n)
sulphur (S) (n)
tame (adj)
tractor (n)
waste (n)
wheat (n)
wild (adj)
yield (n)

A Activating ideas

1. Study the information about a lecture. What does the quote mean? Choose the best paraphrase.

   a. Before agriculture, each area could only support a small number of people.

   b. Before agriculture, people fought about land.

2. Find the caption below for each illustration opposite. Look up any new words in a dictionary.

A feast	
A watering hole	
A watermill	
Crop rotation	
Domesticated animals	
Domesticated wheat	
Hilly flanks (sides)	
Hunter-gatherers	1
Planting rice	
Ploughing with a horse	
The Fertile Crescent	
Wild grass	

3. What is the link between the illustrations and civilization?

B Understanding a lecture

1. ⊕ **5.3** DVD **5.A** Watch the introduction. What is the best way to take notes for each part of the lecture?

2. ⊕ **5.4** DVD **5.B** Watch the first half of the lecture. Complete the handout on page 179. Add extra notes to the basic information. Remember! The lecturer may not give all the information in order.

3. ⊕ **5.5** DVD **5.C** Watch the second half of the lecture. Complete the handout on page 166 with key points, including the lecturer's attitude to each theory.

C Showing comprehension

Use your notes from the lecture. Answer the questions about the history of agriculture.

1. How did hunter-gatherers survive?

2. Where were wild grasses first harvested, according to some sources?

3. Which animals were first domesticated in Pakistan?

4. Where was the plough invented?

5. Who invented the seed drill?

6. Why was 'miracle rice' so valuable?

D Developing critical thinking

Which theory for the origins of agriculture do you think is most likely? Explain your answer.

Faculty of Agriculture and Animal Husbandry
Core course: The history of agriculture

'Before the discovery of agriculture, mankind was everywhere so divided, the size of each group being determined by the natural fertility of its locality.' Arthur Keith

According to many agronomists, civilization could not start until agriculture was developed over 14,000 years ago. In the present day, agriculture is responsible for maintaining civilization by feeding an ever-growing population. In this lecture, we look at the history of agriculture and examine some of the theories of how it started.

A Reviewing vocabulary

1. Mark the stressed syllable in each word from the lecture in 5.2.

> agriculture agricultural climate
> cultivate domesticated edible famine
> fertile harvest indigenous irrigate
> irrigation machine mechanize preserve
> resource starvation tractor

2. ⊙ **5.6** Listen and check your ideas.

3. What is the vowel sound in the stressed syllable? Choose from the phonemic key in the Pronunciation Check.

   Example: 'agriculture – /æ/

B Identifying a new skill

1. Study this part of the lecture from 5.2. What is the lecturer doing in the part in *italics*?

> The plough appeared in about 4000 BCE in the area we now call Iraq. *That reminds me. I was in a village on the southern edge of the Sahara and I saw camels pulling ploughs. They are still using animals because tractors break down too often in the sand, and you can't get the spare parts. Anyway, where was I?* Ah, yes. 5000 BCE. Over the next 5,000 years, there were a lot of small improvements to agriculture, including irrigation and power supply.

2. Read the Skills Check and check your ideas.

C Practising the new skill

You are going to hear four extracts from different lectures.

1 **The development of Qatar and Lebanon**

2 **Long-distance communication: semaphore**

3 **Children and violence on television**

4 **The central nervous system**

⊙ **5.7** Listen and make notes. When the lecturer digresses, write one or two words to help you remember. Ask other students about the digression at the end of each extract.

Pronunciation Check

Understanding phonemic symbols

Learn to identify the phonemic symbols for the main vowel sounds. Then you can check the pronunciation of new words in a dictionary. This will help you predict the sound in speech.

/æ/	pat	'agriculture,
/e/	pet	
/ɪ/	pit	
/ʌ/	but	
/ɑ:/	part	
/ɜ:/	per	
/iː/	Pete	
/ɔ:/	port	
/eɪ/	pay	
/aɪ/	pie	

Skills Check

Recognizing and dealing with digression

Lecturers sometimes digress during a lecture. This means they go away from the main point. Sometimes they tell a personal story, or a joke. Sometimes they talk about a related point.

Digressions usually begin with:
That / Which reminds me … (of a funny story …)
I remember … (once / when I was …)

They usually end with:
Anyway … (Where was I? What was I saying?)
Getting back to (the point) …
That's enough of that.

Digressions are often very hard to understand in a foreign language. You must learn to recognize the start and the end of the digression. Then you can ignore it during the lecture. But make a note …

story about camels?

… and ask other students after the lecture.
Why did she tell the story about the camels? What was the point of the camel story?

Don't worry if they can't explain. Digressions are … digressions! They are not the main point of a lecture.

Complex sentences contain two clauses.
- The **main clause** gives the main information. The **subordinate clause** gives other information.
- An **adverb** in the subordinate clause gives the **relationship** between the two clauses.
  Either the main clause or the subordinate clause can come first.

㉑

subordinate clause				main clause		
adverb	subject	verb	other	subject	verb	other
When	I	was	young	I	used to pick	wild grass.
If	the animals	migrate		you	must follow	them.
Because	the population	was rising	fast	agriculturalists	were	afraid of famine.
Although	this theory	could be	correct	scientists	have found	no evidence.

🔊 **5.8** Listen to the examples. Where does the speaker pause in each case?
Give the same information, beginning with the main clause. Make any necessary changes.

A Identifying parts of complex sentences

Mark the main clause (M), and the subordinate clause (S) in each sentence.

1.　S　　　　　　　　　M
   If you follow animals / you cannot establish towns.

2. Although the seed drill was invented in 1701 it wasn't used widely until the 1850s.

3. I saw camels pulling ploughs in a town south of the Sahara when I worked there.

4. Many areas need irrigation because there is not enough natural water.

B Predicting from the adverb and subordinate clause

1. 🔊 **5.9** Listen to the first clause of some complex sentences.
   Find a suitable ending.

   Example:　a. *When you are a hunter-gatherer,* …

	it imports from countries in the region.
	the host is ashamed.
	they could send a letter.
	they started to plant seeds.
	we must retain rainfall in reservoirs.
	you begin to protect it.
a	you spend all day hunting and gathering.

2. 🔊 **5.10** Listen and check your answers.

C Predicting from the main clause and adverb

1. 🔊 **5.11** Listen to the main clause of some complex sentences.
   How could the speaker finish each one?

2. 🔊 **5.12** Listen and check your ideas.

D Predicting the main or the subordinate clause

1. 🔊 **5.13** Listen to the first clause of some sentences. When
   the speaker pauses, discuss possible endings to the sentence.

2. 🔊 **5.14** Listen and check your ideas.

nerves

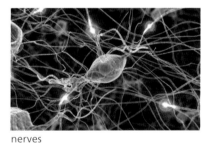

muscles

Sumerian writing

A Activating knowledge

Study the assignment and the title slide from a student presentation. What are *uniform food products*? Why do supermarkets want them?

B Studying a model

1. Study the slides from the presentation on page 175. What points does each slide make? Discuss.

2. 🔊 **5.19** DVD **5.E** Watch the student's presentation. Make notes of extra points on the slides.

3. Work in groups. Take it in turns to present the information.

C Revising discussion skills

1. 🔊 **5.20** Listen to extracts from the presentation and discussion. Complete each phrase or sentence with one word in the space.

a. _Did_ you say the website was called Waste 2?	5
b. Where _it was_ I?	
c. You were _Talking_ about selective ... something. _Changes_	
d. _These_ selective breeding change the genetic code of the plants?	
e. So what you're saying _is_ plant breeding is the same as GM.	
f. No, not _at_ all.	
g. I don't know _if_ this is relevant, but GM crops are banned in my country.	
h. But, as I said just _now_, plant breeding is not the same as GM.	
i. I've _forgot_ what I was going to say.	
j. You were _about_ to give us some disadvantages.	
k. Are you _saying_ that it raises the cost of the products?	
l. Yes, that's _exactly_ right.	
m. Do you _mean_ *millions* of tons?	
n. Yes, sorry. I _meant_ to say *millions*.	

2. 🔊 **5.21** Listen and check your answers.

3. What is the function of each sentence above? Study the functions in the box below and write the correct number after each phrase or sentence. You can use the same number more than once.

a
c
G

1. checking information	G 4. linking to a previous contribution	ʄ 7. summarizing
2. helping a speaker		ℓ 8. expressing uncertainty about relevance
3. saying you are lost	ß 5. asking for clarification	
	6. reacting to a summary	d 9. clarifying

4. 🔊 **5.22** Listen to the phrases and sentences in C1 and copy the stress and intonation.

D Taking part in a discussion

Do customers really want uniform food products?
How can we reduce food waste from rejected produce?

Business Studies Faculty

Supermarkets and farmers
Supermarkets make many decisions which affect farmers and farming. Research an area in which supermarkets use their buying power, and present a point for discussion at the next tutorial.

Who wants
uniform food products?

A Activating ideas

What is a formal equivalent for each informal sentence?

1. Hiya. Good morning / afternoon / evening.
2. You alright there?
3. Want a hand with that?
4. Give me the receipt.
5. Cheers.
6. No problem.
7. Here you go.
8. See you later.

B Studying the models

1. Cover the conversations. How could each question continue in a supermarket?

2. Choose a question phrase for each space in the conversations. You can use the same question form more than once.

Are you ...?	Could you ...?	Do you ...?	Is there ...?
Can I ...?	Did I ...?	Have you ...?	Shall I ...?
Can you ...?	Did you ...?	Is it ...?	Would you ...?

3. 🎧 **5.23** Listen and check your ideas.

1
A: Hiya. _____ put the basket on here?
B: Sure.
A: _____ need a bag? They're 5p.
B: Er, no thanks. I can manage.

2
A: That's £14.50. _____ got a loyalty card?
B: No, I haven't.
A: _____ paying by cash or card?
B: Um, card. _____ put it in the machine?
A: Yes, please and check the amount.
B: Um. _____ working?
A: Other way round.
B: Oh, yeah. Oh, and _____ have cashback?
A: How much _____ like?
B: £10, please.
A: OK. Enter your PIN number, please.

3
A: I'm sorry. _____ go to the next checkout?
B: Why? What's the problem?
A: This checkout is 'baskets only'.
B: Oh, OK. I didn't see the sign.

4
A: Hi. You alright there?
B: Well, _____ return this shirt? It's in this bag.
A: _____ anything wrong with it?
B: No, it's just too small.
A: _____ want to change it for a bigger size?
B: No, thanks. I'd like a refund.
A: OK. _____ got your receipt?
B: Um, oh dear. _____ leave it in the bag?
A: Yes, here you go. _____ pay by card?
B: Yes, here you are.
A: Cheers.

C Practising the model

1. Practise the conversations above.

2. Choose one of these faulty items to return to the supermarket. Write a conversation like #4 at the customer service desk.

3. Practise the conversation with a partner.

a. a jacket with a button missing
b. a DVD that doesn't play
c. a leaking carton of juice
d. a cracked glass
e. a jumper with a hole in it

cloning

intensive farming

A Previewing vocabulary

Study the photographs above. 🔊 **5.29** Listen to some sentences. Which photograph is each sentence related to?

Examples:
Chemicals are used to improve growth. intensive farming
Each animal is an exact copy in genetic terms. cloning

B Researching information

1. Study the assignment. What ethical issues does each of the areas raise?

2. Choose one of the topics then look at some student notes:
   Cloning   page 173
   Intensive farming   page 168

3. Work with other people with the same area. Practise making sentences from the notes.
   - Use a range of ways of giving the source. Be careful about choosing quoting verbs and subject–verb agreement.
   - Make some complex sentences.

C Presenting and discussing

Work in groups with two or three people from each area.

Remember, when you are presenting:
- use sense groups and the correct intonation
- be prepared to explain any words or ideas in your research information if you are asked
- respond to summaries of your research

Remember, when you are listening:
- make notes of the research
- try to summarize points

D Developing critical thinking

Do you agree with each quotation on the right? Why (not)?

Faculty of Philosophy

The ethics of farming
Everyone agrees that the world needs a plentiful supply of cheap food. Cloning and intensive farming are two methods of meeting this need. But what ethical issues do these practices raise?

Research
EITHER   cloning
OR   intensive farming

Present the issues for discussion at the next tutorial.

One of the issues I've had all along with cloning is that just because we *can* do something scientifically doesn't mean we *should* do it.

Greg Jaffe,
Director of the Project on Biotechnology for the
Center for Science in the Public Interest

The question is not, 'Can animals *reason*?' nor, 'Can animals *talk*?' but rather, 'Can animals *suffer*?'

Jeremy Bentham (1748–1832),
English lawyer, philosopher and social reformer

Reading: Should man be a herbivore?

5.11 Vocabulary for reading — Types of diet

A Activating knowledge

What is the connection between the photographs?

B Understanding sentence development

Number in order the lines in each paragraph from an online encyclopedia article.

— □ X

Animals and diet

☐ and cows, which only eat plants are called <u>herbivores</u>. Animals, like lions
☐ and killer whales, which only eat meat are <u>carnivores</u>. Herbivores are at
☐ cases, carnivores then eat these animals. The third kind of animal includes humans,
☐ most bears and some birds. They are omnivores, eating both animals and plants.
☐ plant like the fruit or berries, and convert them into energy. In many
☐ the bottom of <u>food chains</u>. They eat plants, such as grass, or parts of a
☐1 There are three main kinds of animal in terms of <u>diet</u>. Animals, like sheep

☐ as cows and sheep, and <u>livestock rearing</u> for food became common.
☐ been quite rare at this time because animals were hard to catch and kill.
☐ <u>gatherers</u>. In other words, they <u>followed</u> a way of life which involved
☐ However, around 7000 BCE, people began to domesticate animals, such
☐ hunting animals and gathering fruit and berries. <u>Meat-eating</u> may have
☐ There is some evidence that humans have been omnivorous since <u>Neolithic</u>
☐ or Stone Age times (c9500 BCE). It is believed that early humans were <u>hunter-</u>

☐ animals for food. Nowadays, some people support vegetarianism for
☐ eat meat for <u>ethical</u> reasons. They believe that humans should not kill
☐ eating anymore. Others point to the health dangers of meat, including
☐ <u>environmental</u> reasons, believing that the planet cannot support meat-
☐ <u>hazardous</u> chemicals in fish, especially those which are farmed.
☐ the high percentages of <u>saturated fat</u> in red meat and the levels of
☐ Throughout history, some humans have become <u>vegetarians</u>, refusing to

---

C Understanding new vocabulary

What's the difference between each pair of words? Discuss, then check with a dictionary.

1. *herbivore* and *carnivore*
2. *fruit* and *berry*
3. *food* and *diet*
4. *animals* and *livestock*
5. *grow* and *rear*
6. *ethical* and *legal*
7. *endangered* and *extinct*
8. *hunter* and *gatherer*
9. *vegetarian* and *vegetarianism*
10. *hazardous* and *poisonous*

Vocabulary list

advocate (*v*)
berry (*n*)
carnivore (*n*)
carnivorous (*adj*)
complete (*adj*)
congregation (*n*)
contemporary (*n*)
cruel (*adj*)
dental (*adj*)
diet (*n*) [= normal food]
domesticate (*v*)
endangered species
environmental (*adj*)
ethical (*adj*)
follow a way of life
food chain
gather (*v*)
hazardous chemical
herbivore (*n*)
herbivorous (*adj*)
heretic (*n*)
hunt (*v*)
hunter-gatherer
intensive farming
kill (*v*)
livestock rearing
Neolithic (*adj*)
omnivore (*n*)
omnivorous (*adj*)
outbreak (*n*)
partial (*adj*)
pesticide (*n*)
ration (*n*)
recommended daily intake
renowned (*adj*)
saturated fat
sect (*n*)
sustainable (*adj*)
topsoil (*n*)
vegetarian (*n* and *adj*)
vegetarianism (*n*)

A Activating ideas

Read the assignment. What is your view of vegetarianism?

B Understanding the text

Read the text from a popular science magazine.

1. Complete the student's table of notes.
2. Which is the strongest reason for vegetarianism, in your view?

Faculty of Social Studies

The sociology of food
Topic 3: Vegetarianism

In some parts of the world, vegetarians are seen as cranks – people with unusual ideas about the world. However, it may be that vegetarianism is not a strange practice, but the future of food on this planet.

Research the reasons for partial or complete vegetarianism throughout history and today.

people	period	reasons	source
a. early men	Stone Age	because not able to catch many animals	Piperno & Dillehay, 2008; Humphries, 1994
b. Pythagoras			
c. Buddhists			
d. poor people in the Middle Ages			
e. Leonardo da Vinci			
f. people in World War II			
g. people in recent times			
h. people today			

C Developing critical thinking

Discuss these questions.

1. Has the article changed your views on vegetarianism?
2. Why might vegetarianism increase in the future?

Why vegetarianism?

Andrew Ellison

Early men are usually described as hunter-gatherers. They hunted small animals and gathered fruit and nuts from trees and bushes. This view accepts that, from earliest times, man was an omnivore, although it is not clear which tribes began the practice of hunting. However, there is evidence to indicate early human diets were vegetarian. The dental remains of an ancient civilization in Peru are typical. Although researchers could not determine if the people were completely vegetarian, their diet certainly consisted mostly of plants (Piperno and Dillehay, 2008). This implies that Neolithic men were more *gatherers* than *hunters*. Jared Diamond provides evidence for this. He visited a tribe that still follows the Stone Age way of life. They showed him what they got from a day's 'hunting' – 'two baby birds, a few frogs, and a lot of mushrooms.' When questioned, the tribesmen admitted that large animal killings were rare (Diamond, 1991, as cited in Humphries, 1994). This kind of research gives some evidence of how long ago vegetarianism started.

According to the Vegetarian Society (2011), the renowned mathematician Pythagoras, who lived in the sixth century BCE, was vegetarian. In fact, for centuries, vegetarians in some societies were called 'pythagoreans'. Pythagoras had strong views on how animals should be treated, writing that they should not be killed for food or clothing. He also thought a vegetarian diet was healthier (ibid.). During the same period in history, several religions in Asia, including Hinduism, Brahmanism and Buddhism, were teaching their followers not to eat meat. Non-violence and respect for all life forms is what these faiths teach (ibid.). The Vegetarian Society notes that Buddha and Pythagoras were almost exact contemporaries, although we don't know whether Buddhist teachings influenced the Greek thinker (ibid.). Early Christian sects also practised vegetarianism, but they were largely rejected as heretics by the main body of the church (ibid.).

During the Middle Ages, from the 5th to the 15th century CE, meat was very expensive. Only the rich could afford to eat it. Poor people, who were the majority of the population, ate a vegetarian diet, though not out of choice. At this time, it seems that few people were vegetarian for ethical reasons. However, by the time of the Renaissance, there were some famous supporters of animal welfare. The artist Leonardo da Vinci is known to have refused to eat meat (Vegetarian Society, 2011). Gradually, vegetarianism grew in popularity, especially as members of the Christian church began to advocate it. For example, Reverend William Cowherd created a vegetarian congregation in Manchester in 1809. We know who used the term *vegetarian* first. It was used in England at the first meeting of the Vegetarian Society in 1847. By 1910, there were many vegetarian restaurants in London, highlighting the growing popularity (ibid.).

The Second World War contributed greatly to the spread of vegetarianism. In many countries, meat was not available, on ration, or extremely expensive for the duration of the conflict (Vegetarian Society, 2011). 'In 1945 ... there were about 100,000 vegetarians in the UK' (ibid.).

Vegetarianism was given a boost during recent times. The 'meat scares' of the 1990s, including the appearance of CJD ('mad cow disease') and outbreaks of Listeria and Salmonella, made many people concerned about where meat came from (Vegetarian Society, 2011). A significant number of people stopped eating meat. They were afraid of what diseases it might contain. At about the same time, organizations such as Compassion in World Farming started to make people aware of how some meat is produced (CIWF, 2011). The cruelty of many intensive farming practices was revealed and some, like the export of live animals for slaughter, were banned in the next few years.

So, as we have seen, there are a number of reasons why people have become vegetarians throughout history. All of these reasons still exist today, to a greater or lesser extent. In view of this, it is perhaps surprising how few people are vegetarians, at least in the West. Only about three per cent of people in both the UK and the US presently follow a vegetarian way of life (Vegetarian Society, 2011a; Vegetarian Resource Group, 2009). It seems that religion, ethics and price are not enough to turn people from meat-eating.

However, there is another reason for turning to vegetarianism. Every time energy passes through an animal, 90 per cent of it is used to keep the animal alive (see Figure 1). So livestock rearing is a very inefficient way of using food energy. The livestock population of the United States today consumes enough grain and soya beans to feed over five times the human population of the country. These animals consume over 80 per cent of the corn and over 95 per cent of the oats (Robbins, 1987).

At the moment, we clearly have a choice about vegetarianism, but by 2025, with a world population of eight billion, vegetarianism may become a necessity.

© 2011
For References, see page 168.

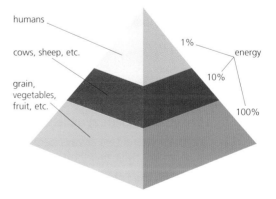

Figure 1: Energy transfer in food chains

A Reviewing vocabulary

Match words from each column to make phrases from the text in 5.12.

1. hunt		a person
2. gather		a way of life
3. provide	I	animals
4. practise		life forms
5. cite		evidence
6. follow		fruit
7. influence		research
8. respect		vegetarianism

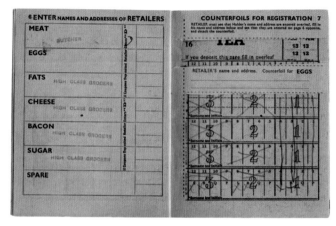

War-time ration book

B Identifying a new skill

1. How do writers show relationships between consecutive sentences?

2. Read the Skills Check and check your ideas.

C Practising the new skill

1. Look at the highlighted pairs of sentences or parts of sentences in the text in 5.12. What is the relationship between each pair, 1 and 2? Choose from:
   - 2 is the reason for 1
   - 2 is the result of 1
   - 2 is an example of 1

2. Read each sentence below. What do you expect to come in the next sentence, **reason** (rea), **result** (res), **example** (e.g.) or **explanation** (exp)?

3. Find the sentence in the relevant text (in brackets) and check your ideas.

   a. There are many sites of historical interest in Tunisia. (1.12)   *e.g.*

   b. Cyprus has three languages. (1.14)

   c. In 1862, the teenage Edison saved a little boy from being hit by a train. (2.12)

   d. Edison's invention of the electrical vote recorder was not successful. (2.12)

   e. Edison decided to make things which people wanted. (2.12)

   f. While she was crossing the Atlantic, Hedwig met an important Hollywood producer. (2.15)

   g. In the middle of the Second World War, Hedy Lamarr had an idea. (2.15)

   h. Humans are experts at understanding fictional narrative even though it is written in code. (3.12)

   i. The main characters always begin in a stable situation, married happily, successful at work or enjoying an idyllic childhood, then something happens. (3.12)

   j. In the UK, the Forsters Education Act was the first step towards state education in Britain. (4.12)

   k. There are other subjects that may be valuable during free time or in retirement. (4.15)

Skills Check

Understanding sentence relationships

Relationships between consecutive sentences are often clearly marked.

Example:
... vegetarianism grew in popularity, especially as members of the Christian church began to advocate it. **For example,** *Reverend Cowherd created a vegetarian congregation in Manchester in 1809.*

However, sometimes you must work out the relationship between sentences.

Example:
Early men are usually described as hunter-gatherers. They hunted small animals and gathered fruit and nuts ...

In this case, the second sentence is **the reason** for the first sentence.

While you are reading, keep asking:
What is the relationship between this sentence and the last sentence?

Sentences sometimes contain a **main clause** and an **interrogative clause**. Work out the 'hidden question' in ㉓ the interrogative clause. This question is sometimes answered somewhere else in the text.

main clause			interrogative clause			
Research	cannot determine		**if**	they	were	vegetarian.
We	do not know		**whether**	Buddha	influenced	Pythagoras.
Pythagoras	had	strong views on	**how**	animals	should be treated.	
People	became	concerned about	**where**	meat	came from.	

'Hidden questions':

	Were	they (the tribes)			vegetarian?
	Did	Buddha		**influence**	Pythagoras?
How	**should**	animals		**be treated?**	
Where	**does**	meat		**come from?**	

A   Working out the 'hidden question'

What is the 'hidden question' in each of these sentences or parts of sentences from the text in 5.12?

1. ... it is not clear which tribes began the practice of hunting.
    Which tribes began the practice of hunting?
2. They showed him (Diamond) what they got from a day's hunting.
3. This kind of research gives some evidence of how long ago vegetarianism started.
4. ... Compassion in World Farming started to make people aware of how some meat is produced.
5. There are a number of reasons why people have become vegetarians throughout history.
6. Given these reasons, it is perhaps surprising how few people are vegetarians in the West today.

B   Looking for the answer to a hidden question

Look at your questions in Exercise A. Try to find the answer in the text.

Example: *1. not answered in text*

The relative pronouns *who* and *which* can be part of interrogative clauses.   ㉔
*We know **who** used the term 'vegetarianism' for the first time.*
*It is not clear **which** tribes began the practice of hunting.*

But they can also give more information about a noun or noun phrase.
*The poor people, **who** were a majority of the population, could not afford meat.*
*Three per cent of the UK population is vegetarian, **which** amounts to 1.8 million people.*

C   Recognizing interrogative clauses

What are the words *who* and *which* doing in these sentences? Letter the word in each sentence:
a = introducing an interrogative clause   *b* = giving more information about a noun / noun phrase

1. There is an increasing number of people in many countries who do not eat meat.
2. The practice of vegetarianism which is advocated in many eastern religions is widespread in Asia.
3. Vegans are very strict vegetarians who do not use any animal products, including wool and honey.
4. It is hard to know which country has the highest percentage of vegetarians.
5. Most countries in the world have a compulsory education system which is paid for by the state.
6. Although many people believe that the Wright Brothers made the first powered flight, historians argue about who was really first.

A   Previewing vocabulary

Choose a word on the right (a or b) to follow each word or phrase on the left.

	a	b
1. livestock	rearing	growing
2. arable	food	farming
3. endangered	organism	species
4. greenhouse gas	emission	production
5. recommended daily	intake	food
6. intensive	agriculture	farming
7. hazardous	chemical	element
8. saturated	protein	fat

College of Agricultural Science

Agroecology Department

Assignment

To what extent is meat-eating sustainable in the future? Research the following factors involved in livestock rearing:

    a. economic

    b. environmental

    c. ethical

    d. health

B   Understanding a text

1. Read the assignment. Why might meat-eating become *unsustainable*?

2. Work in groups, 1 to 4. Each group researches one factor. Find relevant information in the sources opposite and make a list of points relating to your factor.

3. Work in new groups of four, one person for each factor. Share your research. How can you answer the question in the assignment?

C   Using key skills

1. Use the new skills and grammar points from 5.13 and 5.14 to help you with these tasks. Find evidence in the research to prove or disprove each statement below.

   a. Animals are often treated badly in intensive farming.
     T – cramped conditions; small birth crates; animals can't turn round, forage for food; crowded sheds; stress

   b. Humans must eat meat to get the protein they need.

   c. A vegetarian diet is healthier than one involving meat-eating.

   d. Bottom-trawling is a method of fishing.

   e. Crop-rearing does not involve cutting down trees.

   f. Wild salmon are low in their food chain.

   g. Dolphins are not normally caught for food.

   h. Fish-eating has not led to any environmental damage to oceans.

   i. Kangaroos do not produce greenhouse gas emissions.

2. Complete Table 1 with information from the research.

D   Developing critical thinking

1. What counter-arguments are made for the livestock industry in the research?

2. What other points could meat-eaters say in support of their diet?

Table 1: Some effects of livestock rearing

water use	12 × food crops
land use	
pesticide contents	
calories per hectare	
greenhouse gases	
effect on topsoil	

A study by the Vegetarian Society indicates how much water is consumed in the process of livestock rearing (Vegetarian Society, 2011). The amount is far greater than required to raise crops on the same land. In a separate study, Robbins found that it takes 12 times more water to produce food for meat-eaters than to produce food for vegetarians (Robbins, 1987). Since there is a global shortage of fresh water, it is clear how significant this finding is.

…

Robbins quotes the authority on pesticides, Lewis Regenstein, as saying 'Meat contains approximately 14 times more pesticides than do plant foods (Robbins, 1987). Thus, by eating foods of animal origin, one ingests greatly concentrated amounts of hazardous chemicals.' Fish are often highly polluted although it is generally safe to eat species from low down the food chain. Wild salmon are particularly recommended (Gudmundson and Sweet, 2011).

Fish-eating has a massive effect on the environment, as over-fishing has resulted in endangered fish species (Vegetarian Society, 2011). Ocean food chains are threatened. Furthermore, fishing often results in unwanted species being caught in the nets (ibid.). Whales and dolphins are often snared by mistake. Peta argues that bottom-trawling is as destructive to the seabed as deforestation is on land (Peta, 2011).

Given the world's ever-increasing population, there is a constant need to find new places where people can live. Currently '30 per cent of the earth's entire land surface is used for rearing farm animals' (Vegetarian Society, 2011). Raising livestock for meat uses 2.5 times the amount of land needed for a vegetarian diet (ibid.). Preparing land for any kind of agricultural enterprise often involves deforestation. However, animals that are farmed extensively require far more space than crop-rearing (Vegetarian Society, 2011b).

More and more people are becoming aware of how animals raised for meat are treated. The Vegetarian Society states that the majority of animals reared in the UK are farmed intensively (Vegetarian Society, 2011). Many live their whole lives indoors without being able to move around freely. These animals cannot do what they normally do, such as forage and build nests. Observers are always shocked at how small birth crates often are. The mothers cannot turn round or feed their young. Fish are also subjected to intensive farming, which causes them stress and increases their susceptibility to disease (ibid.).

According to the Vegetarian Society, 'one study estimated that the farming of animals caused more emissions (18 per cent of world total) than the world's entire transport system (13.5 per cent)'. Some of these emissions are from the animals themselves, and some from the transportation of animals for slaughter and their meat to market (Vegetarian Society, 2011). However, not all livestock produce greenhouse gas emissions. Kangaroos could replace cows and sheep if their meat was more widely accepted by consumers (Gates, 2011).

People who support the livestock industry often explain why meat-eating is essential. They maintain that people must eat meat to get sufficient protein in their diet. This claim ignores how much protein is contained in cereals and vegetables. Wheat is 17 per cent protein and cabbage is 22 per cent, for example. In fact, if you ate only potatoes, which are 11 per cent protein, you would reach your minimum daily intake of protein (Robbins, 1987). They also claim that meat is the primary source of iron and zinc in the human diet. Dieticians accept that pregnant women and teenagers in particular need these elements (Institute of Medicine, 2006).

Robbins cites the US Soil Conservation Service as reporting that over four million acres of topsoil are lost to erosion in the US every year. Of this loss, 85 per cent is directly associated with livestock-grazing (Robbins, 1987).

The Vegetarian Society states that 'A balanced vegetarian diet is low in fat (especially saturated fat), high in complex carbohydrates and packed with a variety of vitamins and minerals; just as the government and the medical profession recommend' (Vegetarian Society, 2011).

Thousands of communities around the world depend on livestock rearing. In the UK alone, 315,000 people work in the industry, producing 11 million tons of leather and 2 million tons of food, in addition to meat (Holmes, 2010). Manure from livestock contributes 15 per cent of fertilizing nitrogen. Without that, organic farming would disappear. Grazing land that supports animals often does not support arable farming (ibid.).

For References, see page 178.

1 Try to answer each question.

2 Find the information in the relevant reading text (in brackets).

1. Which countries border Tunisia? (1.12)	
2. Which civilization first made Tunisia an important area? (1.12)	
3. Where is Cyprus located? (1.15)	
4. When was Cyprus divided into Greek and Turkish areas? (1.15)	
5. How many tourists visit Cyprus every year? (1.15)	
6. When was Edison born? (2.12)	
7. What was the first device that Edison patented? (2.12)	
8. What was Edison's favourite invention? (2.12)	
9. How did Hedwig Kiesler become Hedy Lamarr? (2.15)	
10. Who did Hedwig Kiesler collaborate with to produce her invention? (2.15)	
11. What did Levi-Strauss believe about all narrative fiction? (3.12)	
12. Who stated that narratives conventionally follow a structure of three stages? (3.12)	
13. What are the characters in narrative fiction, according to Propp? (3.12)	
14. What is the basic plot of a rags-to-riches story? (3.15)	
15. What is the most common force in a Tragedy, according to Booker? (3.15)	
16. When were state schools first established in Britain? (4.12)	
17. What were Plato's three classes of people? (4.12)	
18. How long, according to the BBC, does the average adult in Britain spend at work? (4.15)	
19. What is the current (2010) life expectancy in the developed world? (4.15)	
20. Who believes that the state should teach children to be happy throughout their lives? (4.15)	
21. What were vegetarians called in Europe until 1847? (5.12)	
22. Which faiths advocate vegetarianism? (5.12)	
23. How many people in the United States are vegetarian, according to a 2009 study? (5.12)	
24. How much of the world's land surface is used for livestock rearing? (5.15)	
25. What nutrient is 11 per cent of potatoes? (5.15)	

5.16 Vocabulary for writing   **The principles of GM**

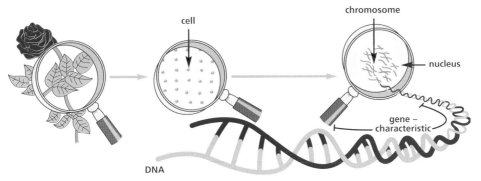

Figure 1: DNA in plants

A Activating knowledge

Complete the first paragraph from a web encyclopedia article with words from Figure 1.

B Building sentences

Write more sentences for the web article. Use each group of words, symbols and abbreviations below. Do not change the order or items or the form of any word.

1. GM = 'genetic modification' / 'genetically modified'.
   GM stands for 'genetic modification' or 'genetically modified'.

2. form of biotechnology.

3. Biotechnologists now able modify genes of plant produce new variety / even new species.

4. 1. biotech scientists identify gene for particular characteristic.

5. e.g., existing plant resistant to particular pest? / produce bigger yield?

6. 2. gene for pest resistance / higher yield removed from plant.

7. 3. gene inserted into cell belonging to different plant.

8. genetics of plant modified

9. new variety now has characteristic.

10. 4. seeds gathered – farmers supplied with new variety

C Using new vocabulary

Find pairs of words in the list on the right. Explain the connection.
Examples:

biotechnology, biotechnologist = different forms of the same word
modify + genes = collocation
maintain, sustainability = both have 'ai'

GM

Inside every plant, there are millions of _____. Each cell has a _____, which contains _____ which, in turn, are made up of _____. The DNA in a particular plant can be divided into about 20,000 sections. Each section is called a _____. Each gene carries the information for a particular _____.

additional (*adj*)
because of (*adv*)
biotech (*n*)
biotechnology (*n*)
come to pass
compelling (*adj*)
  [= very strong]
conventional (*adj*)
despite (*adv*)
discriminate (*v*)
equivalent (*n*)
extension (*n*) [= next step]
gene (*n*)
genetic modification
  (GM)
genetics (*n*)
harm (*n*)
harmful (*adj*)
infectious (*adj*)
maintain (*v*) [= say is true]
migrate (*v*)
migration (*n*)
modification (*n*)
modify (*v*)
mutate (*v*)
mutation (*n*)
nutrient (*n*)
nutrition (*n*)
outsell (*v*)
outweigh (*v*)
pest (*n*)
potentially (*adv*)
precise (*adj*)
relative (*adj*) [= compared
  to something else]
relinquish (*v*)
resistant (*adj*)
risk (*n*)
seed (*n*)
selective breeding
shelf-life (*n*)
sustainability (*n*)
turn your back on
vaccine (*n*)
yield (*n*)

A Activating ideas

Study the quote in the assignment.

1. What does the green movement think about GM crops, according to the professor?
2. What does the professor think about them?
3. Why might he take that view?

B Preparing to write

Study the questions in the assignment. Work in pairs.

1. Answer the questions from your own knowledge.
2. Find answers to the questions in the research notes on page 177.
3. Look at the spidergram. How many paragraphs is the student going to write?

C Recognizing the essay type

1. What kind of essay do you have to write?
   - ☐ Argument
   - ☐ research report
   - ☐ For and against
   - ☐ Description
2. What is the hidden thesis in the assignment?

D Reviewing, quoting and citing

You learnt in 3.18 about quoting from authorities and giving research sources. Complete each paragraph of the essay opposite with a quoting verb or phrase from the box in each space. You can use some verbs and phrases more than once.

according to	claims	concluded	finding	go
have found	maintain	maintains	points	quotes
saying	says	seems	states	support	supports

E Noticing the discourse structure

Study three paragraphs from the essay opposite.

1. How has the writer organized the research information into paragraphs?
2. What are the main elements of each paragraph?
3. How will the essay continue?

F Completing the essay

Look again at the research notes on page 177.

1. Write five more paragraphs for the essay opposite. Vary the way you write the topic sentence for each one.
2. Write an introduction.
3. Write a conclusion.

Department of Biotechnology

Assignment 3:

GM crops – the road to feeding the world?

Those in the green movement may have their hearts in the right place, but there is very little knowledge [of GM technology]. The debate is low-grade and alarmist. Our aim is to get more production on less land, which means that less land is used for agriculture. Any ecologist will tell you that conventional agriculture has a larger negative impact on the world than anything else.

Dr Ray Bressan,
a professor at Purdue University and academic with biotech company FuturaGene

Many people have made up their minds about GM crops already, coming down either in favour or, in most cases, against. But biotechnologists are calling for a proper debate about the issue. In this assignment, you must research the issue and discuss the benefits of genetically modified crops.

Consider these questions:
- Do farmers understand GM crops?
- Are GM foods safe?
- Do they cost more than conventional food crops?
- Do they grow more quickly?
- Do they produce higher yields?
- Are they more nutritious?
- Are they more resistant to pests and diseases?
- Do they last longer?
- Do they help farming to be sustainable?

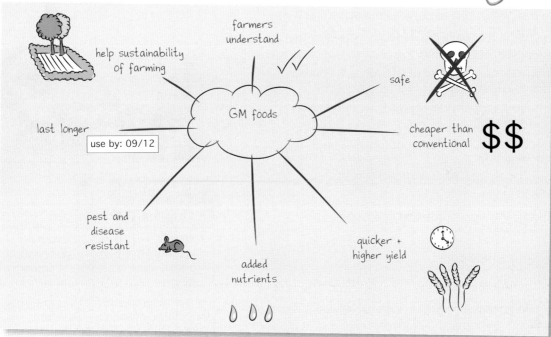

Discuss the benefits of genetically modified foods.

The first point in favour of GM foods is that farmers understand the basic idea. They are a logical extension of selective breeding. For thousands of years, farmers have been selectively breeding plants, which changes the genetics of the plants. _____ American Public Media, 'Genetic engineering is just the latest form of biotechnology – the most precise method yet' (American Public Media, 2011).

A second argument for producing GM crops relates to safety. Several authors _____ the idea that GM foods are safe. A BBC journalist _____ that 'there is no evidence that modified crops cause illness in humans'. Another journalist _____ 'GM crops are no more harmful to the environment than conventional plant varieties' (Black, 2004). Finally, scientific studies _____ evidence to support their safety. For example, a University of Queensland PhD study _____ that GM crops are worth growing despite the risks. It _____ out that the benefits of GM food outweigh the dangers, _____ 'no compelling evidence of harm to humans from GM plants' (Science Alert, 2008). A GM food producing company, ArgEvo, _____ that GM foods are actually safer than non-GM foods because of additional testing (BBC, 2009b; BBC, 2006).

Thirdly, there is the question of cost. It _____ that GM crops can be cheaper than non-genetically modified foods (BBC, 2006). A Chinese professor _____ that people have been eating GM foods in China since 2000, because of their relative cheapness (Juan, 2010). Krebs (2000) _____ this view, _____ that 'GM tomato paste, which is slightly cheaper than non-GM paste, is outselling its conventional equivalent in J. Sainsbury plc' (Krebs, 2000). Some people _____ further, maintaining that GM foods are the future of cheap food. The *Times* _____ a scientist as _____ that resistance to GM foods may mean the end of cheap food (Henderson, 2007). 'If we turn our backs on the technology which scientific learning can offer, then the end of cheap food can come to pass' (ibid.).

A   Reviewing grammar

Find the mistake in each sentence and correct it.

1. In this essay, I look at the advantages for GM foods.
2. I consider the ability of GM foods increasing the sustainability of farming.
3. The first point in favour of GM foods they are a logical extension of selective breeding.
4. For thousands of years, farmers are selectively breeding plants.
5. A second argument for producing GM foods relate to safety.
6. Scientific studies find evidence to support the safety of GM crops.
7. Thirdly, there is the question of costing.

B   Identifying a new skill

1. How could you improve these two paragraphs?

    a. GM crops can be grown more quickly than non-GM crops. GM crops can produce a higher yield than conventional crops. Biotechnology can produce more crops. It can develop better crops. This is important because there is a need to increase food crops as world population rises.

    b. Biotechnologists can add nutrients to GM foods to make them even healthier than normal crops. Biotech researchers have added beta-carotene to rice. It may even be possible to add vaccines to crops. If scientists can add vaccines, GM foods could protect humans from infectious diseases.

> **Skills Check**
>
> **Using lexical cohesion**
>
> It is bad style in English to repeat the same word many times in one paragraph. You can avoid repetition of **nouns** by using:
>
> - a **different noun** for the same item
> - a **different sentence structure**
> - a **pronoun** instead of a noun
>
> You can avoid repetition of **verbs** by using:
>
> - a **different verb** for the same action
> - a **different part of speech** formed from the verb
> - the verb **do** as a replacement verb
>
> Don't worry about repeating nouns and verbs in the first draft of your essay. But make a note of repetition during editing and make changes in the final version.

2. Read the Skills Check. Then rewrite the two paragraphs above.

C   Practising the new skill

Rewrite each sentence below in two different ways, using the words in brackets.

1. It costs a lot of money.	expensive	high
It is very expensive. The cost is very high.		
2. They are cheap.	expensive	cost
3. They last longer.	long-lasting	bad
4. Some scientists take a different view.	opinion	see
5. There are risks in the experiment.	risky	dangerous
6. They are not harmful.	harm	danger
7. It seems that they are safe.	apparently	appear
8. There are many tests on them.	tested	conducted
9. Firstly, I consider price.	issue	relates
10. The results were difficult to interpret.	It was hard	interpretation

5.19 Grammar for writing *although / because vs. despite / because of*

The structure of a **subordinate clause** depends on the introductory **adverb**. (25)
Study the examples in the table. What structure do we use ...
• after *although* and *because?* • after *despite* and *because of?*

main clause				subordinate clause / phrase	
GM crops	may be	worth growing		although	there are risks.
				despite	the risks.
GM foods	are said to be	safer	than non-GM foods	because	they are tested more.
				because of	additional testing.

Remember! We can also begin a sentence with a subordinate clause.

A Changing sentences into noun phrases

Change these sentences into noun phrases which could be used after *because of / despite*.

1. There are risks.	the risks
2. They are tested more.	
3. It doesn't cost very much.	
4. It is very fast.	
5. It takes a long time.	
6. It is very difficult.	
7. It is very profitable.	
8. The company was sold.	

B Choosing the correct adverb

Complete each sentence with *although / despite / because* or *because of.*

1. Reality TV is popular with TV companies because it is cheap to make.
2. .... population ageing started later in developing countries, it is now happening faster.
3. Sales of fountain pens continued to decline .... the significant price reduction.
4. Sales of fountain pens increased later .... the manufacturers rebranded their product.
5. .... its location in Western Europe, the UK does not suffer from tropical diseases.
6. .... Switzerland is land-locked, it is still extremely successful economically.
7. Most parts of Italy have easy access to seaports .... it is a peninsula.
8. .... the thickness of the new ink in Biro's invention, it did not flow properly.

C Using clauses and phrases after subordinating adverbs

Complete each sentence in four ways, using *although*, *despite*, *because* and *because of.*

1. Organic food is gaining in popularity in Britain ...
   - although it is more expensive than conventional food.
   - despite costing more than conventional food.
   - because many people are becoming worried about intensive farming methods.
   - because of growing concern about intensive farming methods.
2. Many biotechnologists support GM foods ...
3. Audiences like reality TV ...
4. Population ageing is a worldwide problem ...
5. Some countries are successful economically ...

A Reviewing vocabulary

What is the opposite of each word or phrase?

1. GM foods	conventional foods
2. natural	
3. benefit	
4. harmful	
5. precise	
6. drawbacks	
7. support (an idea)	
8. much more	
9. add	
10. long-lasting	

B Reviewing vocabulary

Study the assignment.

1. What does the professor think about GM crops?
2. Find words in the questions which mean:

a. not on purpose	accidentally
b. tell the difference between	
c. go from one place to another	
d. change in a bad way	
e. possibly	
f. give away	
g. owned by	

3. Can you answer any of the questions now?
4. What is the hidden thesis in this Argument essay?
5. Complete the introduction to the essay on page 164.

C The TOWER of Writing

1. Research the assignment on the Internet. Type *GM* + each of the questions in the assignment. Make a note of points from one or two sources for each question. Record the sources.

2. Organize the information into sections. Use the assignment questions and the introduction to help you organize. Write one or more paragraphs for each section.

3. Write the first draft. Don't worry about lexical cohesion! Try to use *because of* and *despite* correctly a few times.

4. Exchange drafts with a partner. Mark your partner's work in the normal way. In addition, on this occasion, write *R* next to any repetition of nouns or verbs.

5. Write the essay again.

Department of Biotechnology

Assignment 4: GM crops – the road to disaster?

There are a lot of people in Europe in favour of biotechnology [in GM crops], who are prepared to take risks, but a considerable number are resistant and see no benefits. Many people see biotech taking us into the realm of unknown dangers.

George Gaskell,
Professor of Social Psychology at the London School of Economics

In the last assignment, you considered the benefits of GM crops. This time, you must look at the other side of the debate and discuss the dangers.

Consider these questions:
- Can genes mutate with harmful effects?
- Can genes be modified accidentally?
- Can genes migrate to modify other species?
- Are GM crops potentially harmful to birds and insects?
- Is it possible accurately to discriminate GM products from conventional products on supermarket shelves?
- Do farmers relinquish control of seed production to biotech companies?
- Do new species become the property of biotechnology companies?

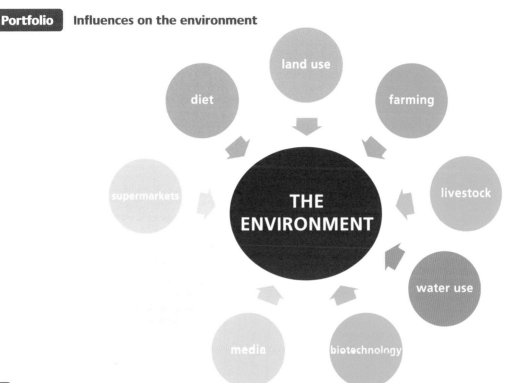

A Activating ideas

Study the diagram above. Which area(s) do you associate each word or phrase below with?

aquifer   audience   carnivore   cells   characteristic   cloning   crop rotation   deforestation

aquifer   audience   carnivore   cells   characteristic   cloning   crop rotation   deforestation
desalination   DNA   documentary   education   emissions   food miles   genetics
growth hormone   manure   modify   pesticide   pollution   research   reservoir   saturated fat
soil erosion   stress   taste   uniformity   vegetarianism   waste   yield

B Taking part in a discussion

Work in groups.

1. What dangers do some of the areas hold for the environment?
2. What benefits can some of the areas bring to the environment?

C Gathering and recording information

Choose one of the areas in the diagram. What effects does this area have on the environment?
Research positive and negative points, from information in this Course Book and on the Internet.

D Preparing a presentation

Prepare to give a talk about your research. Use slides and/or visuals to illustrate your points.

E Listening to a presentation

Work in groups. Make notes about the positive and negative points about each area that is presented.

F Writing

Choose one of the following:

1. Write an essay about the area that you researched in Exercise C.
2. Make a poster presentation of all the areas in the diagram above.

The central thesis in this paper is that individuals may be distinguished by their attitude toward thinking ...The easiest way for individuals to escape this pressure to think is by watching TV. Thus, individuals will watch more TV when they have a lower need for cognition. Results of a survey study show that the concept of escapism proves to be useful in explaining TV use.

Henning, B. and Vorderer, P. (2001) 'Psychological escapism: Predicting the amount of television viewing by need for cognition', *Journal of Communication*, 51:1, pp. 100–120, March 2001

It is largely accepted that escapism can help people more ably interact within reality and cope with some of the stresses of modern life (Scott, 2007).

Scott, V. (2007) *What is escapism?* EzineArticles, http://EzineArticles.com/897426 retrieved on 28.06.11

http://www.weblogmusings.com/realitytv.html

Reality TV is certainly one very popular form of escapism nowadays. It has replaced movies and soap operas for people who just want to lose themselves in a form of entertainment. As Bryant and Vorderer observe, '... people regularly turn to media content in an attempt to escape the stress that they encounter in their daily lives' (Bryant and Vorderer, 2006). However, there is an interesting debate about escapism with regard to reality TV programmes. Audience participation in many reality programmes means that the audience is encouraged to make judgments on the people, or 'characters' in the shows. Bryant and Vorderer ask, 'Does exercising moral judgment in a passive environment constitute a part of escapism? Or does vigorous moral reasoning about characters actually detract from escapism?' (ibid.).

Bryant, J. and Vorderer, P. (2006) *Psychology of Entertainment*, London: Routledge

http://www.tellme.com/voyeurisminrealitytv.htm

There is a weak form of voyeurism involved in watching reality TV. This may meet a psychological need in people. When we see someone on a reality TV show struggling with a problem – parenting, cooking, coping with danger – which we have experienced, we can feel better about ourselves. Of course, another emotion is possible. If we dislike the person with the problem, we may experience schadenfreude. It is not clear whether this is positive or destructive in psychological terms, but it is certainly a basic human emotion (Heider, 1958).

Heider, F. (1958) *The Psychology of Interpersonal Relations*, New York: Wiley

'I watch television for escapism (to release tension)': 20.9% to 25.6% (depending on town or village)

Abstract of results from a survey of Malaysian youths

Osman, M. 'The impact of television programmes on the mindset and attitudes of youths in the rural areas', *Human Communication*, 13: 3, pp. 217– 232

Voyeurism was not identified as a primary motivation for seeking reality content.

Nabi., L., Biely, N., Morgan, J. & Stitt, R. (2003) 'Reality-based television programming and the psychology of its appeal', *Media Psychology*, 5, 303–330

Media Mania Pennsylvania

This blog is published by students in COM 499 Media and Society class at West Chester University of Pennsylvania.

'Because the contestants are regular people just like me, it makes me feel like I could be one of them' (Gardyn 193). Irma Zandl further explained in the article that 'reality TV-driven desire for fame and attention create messages that promise the possibility of overnight success' (Gardyn 193). Reality TV is creating this 'new world' for people. They see these people on television becoming instant celebrities just for being everyday people. This is catching on and chaining out into America because everyone dreams to one day be famous. Another interview within the journal article stated, 'People who watch reality TV, like myself, have some deep desire to go on some great adventure, but maybe they just never had the opportunity or resources to do it themselves' (196).

The list of genres is endless: dating shows, survival shows, home improvement shows, cooking shows, dancing or singing shows, the possibilities never end. There is pretty much a show for everyone's interest.

Gardyn, R. (2001) 'The tribe has spoken', *Interpreting Television*, 189–199 quoted in Papachariassi, Z. and Mendelson, A. (2007) 'An exploratory study of reality appeal: Uses and gratifications of reality TV shows', *Journal of Broadcasting and Electronic Media*, 44:2, 175–199

There are several types of documentary television shows such as the special-living environment where the participants, who could be strangers or couples, are placed in an artificial living environment and certain traits are tested.

Poniewozik, J. (2003) 'Why reality TV is good for us', *Time* February 12, 2003. http://www.time.com/time/magazine/article/0,9171,1101030217-421047,00.html

---

The game show, or competition, is another subgenre of reality television shows where participants are made to live as a group in confined environments as they compete to win a grand prize. The participants are eliminated in the course of the game show through voting by viewers and colleagues who are participants in the reality show.

The other subgenre is made up of self-improvement reality television shows where the individual in need of a make-over presents their problem. The reality television team then introduces the individual to a team of experts who direct the person in the entire process of improving their present situation.

Russell, M. (2010) 'Reality TV – Why all the fuss?' retrieved on 26.11.2010 from www.realitytvtoday.com/.../Reality-TV/Reality-TV—Why-The-Fuss.html 2010

Job searches are often conducted via the reality television shows, where contestants are interviewed for a certain skill then those who are shortlisted are subjected to a series of tasks based on the skills. Usually the job-related competition involves a team of experts in the field as the judges who evaluate the skills possessed by the contestants which are vital for the job in question. The contestants are eliminated over time until the best is left and they are rewarded with a monetary gift, as well as a job in the same profession.

Hill, A. (2005) *Reality TV: Audiences and Popular Factual Television*. New York: Routledge

---

About NRTA

National Reality TV Awards is set to become one of the biggest worldwide television award shows specifically targeting the different sub-genres that make up reality TV.

NRTA (National Reality TV Awards) will be launched in London, UK on 6th July 2011 while the US version of the awards ceremony will be held in Los Angeles on 1st December 2011.

The start of 2011 saw our official website (www.realitytvawards.co.uk) receive over 775,000 nominations from the public for all 15 categories, including docusoaps, competitions / gameshows, job search, self-improvement / makeover and social experiment.

competition on the product (handwritten)

Discuss the _____ of genetically modified foods.

In this essay, I look at the dangers of genetically modified or *cupon to a prize* (handwritten) consider a range of points, including mutation and accidental modification of _____, and escape of genes to other _____. I also discuss harm to birds and _____, and the difficulty of accurate identification of GM products in _____. Finally, I look at the control of seed _____ and ownership of new _____.

Theme 3: Speaking 3.7

the method	the contents of the ad	the science behind the ad	current TV example
the bribe (= money or gifts to persuade someone to do something)	it might be a free gift in/on the package or an entry coupon to a prize competition on the product	people want something for nothing; people believe they will win, even if the chances are tiny	

Theme 3: Speaking 3.10

method	definition	details
viral	uncontrolled spread of information on the Internet, like a virus	the film company puts the trailer online, e.g., YouTube and hopes that it will become a viral hit

---

Theme 1: Speaking 1.10

Mexico City

Mexico City is sinking. The city is one of the most populous in the world. In the distant past, it was an area of lakes. Mexico City takes 80 per cent of its water from an underground reservoir. As a result, the ground has dried out and the city has sunk nine metres in the last 20 years. The city is going to buy its water from other areas of Mexico. The water will be delivered to the city by lorries.

Theme 1: Speaking 1.8

1

I think governments should make water very expensive.

Theme 2: Speaking 2.9

E

In 1895, a German physicist, Wilhelm Roentgen, was exploring the path of electrical rays through various materials. He noticed that the rays passed through his hand but showed the bones. His discovery was X-rays.

problem	solution
plants need sunlight	agriculture started in sunny areas
very little fresh water	
must get water to plants	
plants need nutrients (N, P, K)	
can't establish towns	

problem	solution
only 2/3 of land productive	
can't divide up large farms	
no animal fertilizer	
crops can't absorb fertilizer	
chemicals wash into rivers	

problem	solution
organic products more expensive	
pests destroy crops	
DDT 'causes cancer', etc.	
malaria increases, etc.	

Origins of agriculture – theories

1. **Oasis**
   - Pompelly, 1908 in Rosen, 2007
   - climate change
     - drier climate, people move to oases, animals accept humans = domestication

2. **Hilly flanks**

3. **Feasting**

4. **Demographic**

5. **Evolutionary**

6. **Domestication**

India

There is a problem with fresh water supply in many parts of India. For example, in the capital, New Delhi, 36 million cubic metres of water is needed each day to meet demand. However, only 30 million cubic metres is supplied and only about 17 million cubic metres reaches consumers because a great deal of the water leaks out. The World Bank is supporting a proposal to privatize water supply in India. They say that private companies will be able to supply the whole of India with clean water, although they admit that the price will be higher than at present.

Group B

Speech synthesis

Wolfgang von Kempelen
- 1734   b. Hungary
- studies law and philosophy
- 1769-1791   works on a wooden machine with bellows (for lungs), mouth, nose, reed (for vocal chords)
- 1772   invents typewriter for blind
- 1779   Kratzenstein (Ger. sci.) invents machine — also uses bellows and reed, makes five long vowel sounds — von K. does not know about this!
- 1789   publishes book on speech synthesis — wants other people to improve the design
- 1791   demonstrates machine — makes whole words and short sentences
- 1790s   loses support of the Austrian Emperor
- 1804   d. Vienna in poverty
- 1837   Charles Wheatstone (Eng. sci.) reconstructs K's machine and improves it
- 1930s   people realize not good idea to copy human vocal system
- 1939   Bell Company produces first electronic speech synthesizer

---

method	definition	details
the review	comments by critics in newspapers, etc.; the advertisers choose the best ones, or take 'good' quotes from 'bad' reviews	good reviews can make a film a success; bad reviews can kill a film, although some people go to see if the reviewer is right

---

F

According to the company Nestlé, a lady called Ruth Wakefield was making chocolate cookies (or biscuits) in 1924 but ran out of baker's chocolate, so used broken pieces of semi-sweet chocolate. She thought the pieces would melt in the cooking process, but they didn't. She invented chocolate chip cookies.

---

factor	research	source
feedback – commenting on performance	specific feedback, e.g., 'improve by 40 seconds', is more effective than general feedback, e.g., 'do your best'; feedback during the exercise is more effective than feedback after the exercise	Hall, K., Weinberg, R., and Jackson, A. (1987) 'Effects of goal specificity, goal difficulty, and information feedback on endurance performance', *Journal of Sport Psychology*, 9 (1)

Student B

> <u>Intensive farming</u>
>
> intensive farming =
>
> - keeping animals very close together (battery farming)
> - using chemicals to improve growth
>
> Animals kept in very cramped conditions → diseases and stress.
> Battery farming due to be banned by EU 2012.
> Some supermarkets in UK already stopped selling battery eggs.
> BBC (2008) Battery Farm Eggs Banned by 2012, BBC News, retrieved on 26.07.2011 from
> http://news.bbc.co.uk/1/hi/uk/7180018.stm
>
> Pesticides can harm ecosystem, killing fish, birds, 'good' insects like bees.
> Growth hormone can also get into water system and harm humans.
>
> Statistics show increase in cancer from harmful chemicals in food.
>
> Pillai, M. (2011) Advantages and Disadvantages of Intensive Farming, Buzzle, retrieved on 26.07.2011
> from http://www.buzzle.com/articles/advantages-and-disadvantages-for-intensive-farming.html
>
> Ethical issues: Should we treat animals as units of production?
>   Should we interfere with nature?

References

CIWF (2011) 'Compassion in world farming', retrieved on 4.08.2011 from www.ciwf.org.uk/your_ food

Diamond, J. (1991) *The Rise and Fall of the Third Chimpanzee*, as cited in Humphries, B. (1994) 'What did our ancestors eat?', International Vegetarian Union, retrieved on 1.08.2011 from http://www.ivu.org/history/early/ancestors.html

Piperno, D. and Dillehay, T. (2008) 'Starch grains on human teeth reveal early broad crop diet in Northern Peru', *Proceedings of the National Academy of Sciences*, 105

Robbins, J. (1987) 'Diet for a new America', retrieved on 1.09.2011 from http://michaelbluejay.com/veg/books/dietamerica.html

Vegetarian Resource Group (2009) 'How many vegetarians are there?', retrieved on 4.08.2011 from http://www.vrg.org/press/2009poll.htm

Vegetarian Society (2011) 'World history of vegetarianism', retrieved on 3.08.2011 from http://www.vegsoc.org/page.aspx?pid=830

Vegetarian Society (2011a) 'Statistics', retrieved on 4.08.2011 from http://www.vegsoc.org/page.aspx?pid=750

---

the method	the contents of the ad	the science behind the ad	current TV example
the punch line (= joke or scene with a funny ending)	there is a set-up which prepares the audience for a particular ending, then they are hit with the punchline	people tell funny things to other people, so they spread the name; someone may put the video online and then it might go viral	

D

Art Fry was working for the engineering company 3M, in the 1970s, when he discovered a mild adhesive. He didn't see any value to it. Then he was singing in a choir and he wanted a bookmark that would not damage the song book. He realized that he could make a bookmark with the adhesive, and so invented Post-Its.

....

Theme 2: Speaking 2.8

Student A

While he was studying at the school, he learnt the *Hauy System.*
Hauy System
• developed at NIB by founder, Valentin Hauy
• raised letters of the alphabet
• the letters were very big letters so books were very long and heavy (up to 45 kg!)
• needed several fingers to read each letter
• blind people could read with the system but they couldn't write

....

Theme 1: Speaking 1.10

Southern China

The south of China floods most years while the north of the country suffers from drought. In the north, water for irrigation is reducing underground supplies by more than 30 cubic kilometres per year. If this continues, China will have to reduce the production of grain and will rely on imported crops. The government has begun the largest-ever construction project in China. They plan to divert billions of cubic metres of water from the Yangtze River to refill the Yellow River.

....

Theme 3: Speaking 3.7

the method	the contents of the ad	the science behind the ad	current TV example
the big name (= a personality of some sort – a movie star, sportsperson or television personality)	this person endorses the product; says 'I use/drive/ wear this, etc.'	people want to be special, to use products that famous people use; people trust big names – they think they are telling the truth	

....

Theme 3: Speaking 3.10

method	definition	details
the billboard	advertisements for the film on large boards in towns and cities	eye-catching colour image(s) from the film with the star(s) and the tag line

Sheep, rabbits and foxes in the marketplace

Some researchers in marketing compare interactions in the commercial market with interactions in the animal kingdom. Sometimes two or more products compete for the same market, like sheep and rabbits compete for grass. Sometimes one product kills another product, in the way that foxes eat rabbits. Sometimes two products live side by side, but do not compete, like sheep and foxes, which only very occasionally kill ☑ In this article, we look at competitive interactions in the modern commercial market, according to Smitalova and Sujan (1991).

New products usually enter an old market. For example, a new type of mobile phone, Product A, must compete in the *existing* mobile phone market, which already contains ☐ So Product A needs to take *market share* from the existing products. In this situation, each product loses some sales to the others. Even the new product *suffers* because it loses *potential* sales, that is sales which are lost ☐ According to the 1991 paper, this is Type 1 competition. In this type, each company has a similar *marketing strategy* which is simply ☐ If a company *brands* its existing product with different benefits, e.g., cheaper or faster, it may be able to *recover* lost sales.

Sometimes, a new product offers much better benefits than existing ones, which leads to ☐ This happened with CDs, which very quickly replaced ☐ In the 1991 *analysis*, this is Type 5 competition. The cassette companies could not *react* to the competition, which led to ☐ Sometimes, the *manufacturers* of competing products adopt a new marketing strategy. They say to customers, in effect, 'We do something different.' In other words, they *rebrand* their product as, for example, a luxury item rather than something which is used ☐ As a result, the product does not compete anymore, which to some extent happened ☐ CD sales *declined* rapidly after MP3 players became widely available. However, CDs were rebranded as quality items. They are still popular with some people because of their sound reproduction, which is ☐ This, according to Smitalova and Sujan, is Type 6 competition. The two products compete at first, and then one moves into a different market.

The 1991 paper lists three other types of competition but these are the most common types – see Table 1.

Smitalova, K. and Sujan, S. (1991) *A Mathematical Treatment of Dynamical Models in Biological Science*, London: Prentice Hall.

Student B

	research information	source
5	Money which is spent in independent shops tends to stay in the local economy but supermarkets take money out of the area and give it, as profits, to shareholders in other areas, or even other countries.	Emerson and Hughes, 2001, *Supermarkets: Who Profits?*
6	Because supermarket produce travels long distances, it has to be packaged very carefully. Much of the packaging is multi-material (e.g., cardboard which is stuck to foil which is wrapped in plastic) and therefore impossible to recycle.	Alderton, 2010, *Waste Management*
7	There are 2,300 apple varieties in the National Fruit Collection of Britain, but only about ten varieties of apple are actually sold in supermarkets. This is because the supermarkets only buy from industrial-size farms.	Cornwell, Mills and Pearce, 1995, *Do Supermarkets Really Offer Customers Choice?*
8	A large-scale customer survey suggests that food from supermarkets does not taste as good as food from local markets. 'It doesn't have the same flavour,' said many shoppers. Some researchers believe that the cause is the supermarkets' insistence on uniform size and shape.	Consumer research review, 2011, retrieved on 5.09.2011 from www.foodcouncil.com//supermarkets-and-taste.html

---

7

People should be put in prison for wasting water.

Theme 1: Speaking 1.8

4

The government should stop people digging wells.

Theme 3: Speaking 3.7

the method	the contents of the ad	the science behind the ad	current TV example
the jingle (= catchy tune)	it usually appears several times in the ad and has the name of the product in it	people remember tunes, and if they remember the tune, they remember the product, so they might buy it	

Theme 2: Speaking 2.9

C

In 1946, Percy LeBaron Spencer was working with radar waves when the radiation melted the bar of chocolate in his pocket. He went on to invent the microwave.

Theme 4: Speaking 4.10

factor	research	source
mental preparation – e.g., goal setting	imagining achievement of goals can help prepare the athlete for competition; there is a direct correlation between an athlete's perceived mental readiness and their final Olympic ranking	Orlick, T., and Partington, J. (1988) 'Mental links to excellence', *The Sport Psychologist*, 2

Theme 4: Speaking 4.8

BOGOF (Theme 3)

	Student 1	Student 2
1.	BOGOF = Buy One Get One Free	BOGOF = same as ½ price
2.	lots of companies use BOGOF to promote new products	BOGOF = only method of promotion
3.	BOGOF = often used for loss-leaders	BOGOF = way of selling bad products

Theme 1: Speaking 1.10

Southern Australia

Australia has the lowest rainfall of all the continents, with the exception of Antarctica. One of the largest rivers, the Murray, is drying out. As a result, salt has risen to the surface and destroyed agricultural land. The government is going to limit the extraction of water from the Murray.

the method	the contents of the ad	the science behind the ad	current TV example
the tag line (= a slogan)	it usually appears several times in the ad and has the name of the product in it	people remember slogans, and if they remember the slogan, they remember the product, so they might buy it	

Theme 1: Speaking 1.8

5

We should make people recycle water in their own homes.

Theme 2: Speaking 2.9

B

There is a story that as a child, in about 1745, the Scottish engineer James Watt was watching a kettle boil when he realized the power of steam. Later, he built a steam engine. The story is not true. Steam was already in use as a power source when Watt was a child.

Theme 4: Speaking 4.10

factor	research	source
tension – people feel tense while exercising; muscles feel tight	listening to music can decrease people's perception of effort while exercising; music can make exercising a more pleasurable experience	Szmedra, L., and Bacharach, D. (1998) 'Effect of music on perceived exertion, plasma lactate, norepinephrine and cardiovascular hemodynamics during treadmill running', *International Journal of Sports Medication*, 19

Theme 2: Speaking 2.8

Student B
A soldier came to the NIB in 1821 and introduced him to *night writing*.
Night writing
• developed by Charles Barbier, ex-soldier in the French army, for Napoleon's troops
• 12 raised dots and some dashes
• soldiers could share secret information in battle in the dark and without speaking
• rejected by Napoleon because it was too complex
• Braille didn't really understand it but saw that a code was better than raised letters

method	definition	details
the CGI	computer-generated imagery = life-like cartoon made by computers	film companies use CGI to achieve effects which would be impossible with live action, e.g., *Avatar*

Theme 5: Speaking 5.10

Student A

Cloning

cloning = making an exact copy of a living organism

Scientists take a cell from animal.

Then stimulate with chemicals or electricity – make it divide and therefore grow.

Devolder, K. (2008) Cloning, Stanford Encyclopedia of Philosophy, retrieved on 2.08.2011 from http://plato.stanford.edu/entries/cloning/

Scientists able to grow cloned cells into animals.

Most successful = sheep (Dolly), lived 6 yrs.

Cloned animals often have genetic defects, die young.

Human Genome Project (2009) Cloning Fact Sheet, retrieved on 2.08.2011 from http://www.ornl.gov/sci/techresources/Human_Genome/elsi/cloning.shtml

'farms should be given over to the rearing of fast-growing, well-muscled and higher-producing off-spring of cloned animals' – Keith Campbell, Director of Animal Bioscience, Nottingham University

cloning = useful extension of existing selective breeding

Watts, A. (2007) Cloning is the future for meat production, retrieved on 10.09.11 from http://www.fwi.co.uk/Articles/2007/07/11/105046

Ethical issue: Should scientists create life in the laboratory?
Should we interfere with nature?

Theme 5: Speaking 5.8

Student A

	research information	source
1	The average item of food purchased from a supermarket travels over 1,000 miles; by lorry or plane, from the producer to the store, and then from the store to the customer's home, usually by car. This amount is sometimes called *food miles / kilometres*.	Collins et al., 2005, *Food on the Move*
2	Sixty to seventy per cent of all food in Britain now passes through four supermarkets. This leads to a dangerous concentration of buying power in the hands of a small number of people.	Marshall and Simpson, 2010, *The Rise of Supermarketing*
3	Only large farms can afford to sell produce to supermarkets. This has led to small farmers going out of business and large agribusinesses getting bigger and bigger.	Alberts, 2009, *Farming or Agribusiness?*
4	New supermarkets mean new jobs, but every new supermarket results in a net *loss* of 200 to 300 jobs because a whole network of local shops and their suppliers is destroyed.	Bertolli et al., 2008, *Losing your Local Shop*

2

Water companies should restrict the amount of water each family can use.

Theme 3: Speaking 3.10

method	definition	details
the tag line	a short phrase or sentence	the words should sum up the main idea of the film, e.g., *See our family – and feel better about yours* (*The Simpsons Movie*); the tagline appears on billboards and in the trailer

---

Theme 1: Speaking 1.10

Southeastern Spain

The southeastern coast of Spain receives a reasonable amount of rainfall every year, but needs to meet a huge demand, mainly from the tourism industry. The government announced a 4.2 billion euro plan to divert water from the River Ebro in the north of the country, but it was stopped when a large number of people objected. The government is going to build several desalination plants to provide fresh water for the southeastern coast.

Theme 4: Speaking 4.10

factor	research	source
neurosis – anxiety, depression, low sense of self-worth	top-class male athletes are more neurotic than less successful ones, whereas top-class female athletes are less neurotic than less successful ones	Kirkcaldy, B. (1982) 'Personality profiles at various levels of athletic participation', *Personality and Individual Differences*, 3 (3)

Theme 2: Speaking 2.9

A

The world-famous physicist, Albert Einstein, was travelling to work one day on a tram in 1905 when he thought about riding on a beam of light. He later invented his theory of relativity.

Theme 2: Speaking 2.8

Student C

Braille developed a system which used six dots in a *binary code*.
Binary code
- *binary* means 'two' – it is the basis of all digital devices
- in a binary code, there are two possible values for each position
- in Braille, the two values are flat or raised
- Braille's system uses two columns of three dots
- you can read Braille letters with one fingertip so reading is easier and quicker

Who wants
uniform food products?

Who wants uniform food?

supermarkets
buy output
of farming   **so**   can control way
farmers operate
e.g., uniform produce

[handwritten:] informing and farming ↓
50% / 2011 uniform produce
80% / west2.com.uk

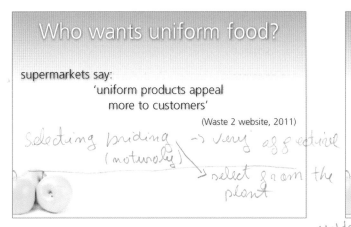

Who wants uniform food?

supermarkets say:
    'uniform products appeal
    more to customers'
(Waste 2 website, 2011)

[handwritten:] Selecting briding → very effective (naturally) → select from the plant

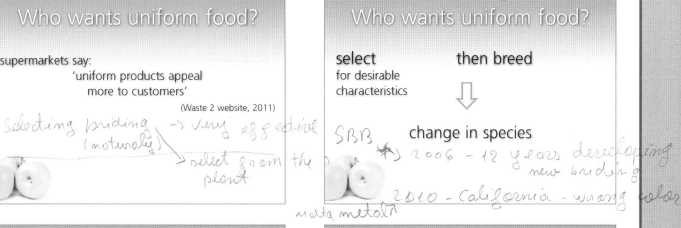

Who wants uniform food?

select   **then breed**
for desirable
characteristics

⇩

change in species

[handwritten:] SBB
2006 - 12 years developing new briding
2010 - California - wrong color
nata metal?

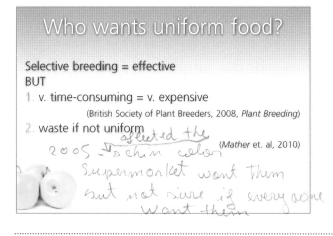

Who wants uniform food?

Selective breeding = effective
BUT
1. v. time-consuming = v. expensive
(British Society of Plant Breeders, 2008, *Plant Breeding*)
2. waste if not uniform
(Mather et. al, 2010)

[handwritten:] selected the
2005 - skin color
Supermarket want them
but not sure if everyone
want them

Who wants uniform food?

3. inferior produce
e.g.,
    Italians pay more for potatoes
    with silver scurf (disease affecting skin colour)
    = crispier when baked
(Duffy, 2005)

Egypt

The Nile River rises in Uganda but flows north through Sudan and Egypt to the Mediterranean. The river is the only real source of fresh water for the majority of the population of Egypt. Several countries south of Egypt, including Tanzania and Ethiopia, have plans to extract water from the Nile. The government of Egypt has threatened to use force against any country that takes Nile water without Egypt's permission.

Theme 1: Speaking 1.8

It should be illegal to have baths. Showers are much better.

Theme 3: Speaking 3.10

method	definition	details
the megastar	a famous actor, male or female	the film company tries to persuade one or more famous actors to star in the film because they know that audiences come to see stars; they believe that people don't want to see an unknown actor

Theme 4: Speaking 4.10

factor	research	source
aggression – reacting with violence in words or actions	athletes who were classed as 'obsessively passionate' about their sport score higher on an aggression scale than participants who are classed as less passionate	Donahue, E., Rip, B., and Vallerand, R. (2009) 'When winning is everything: On passion, identity and aggression in sport', *Psychology of Sport and Exercise*, 10

Theme 2: Speaking 2.9

I

In 1890, the German chemist Friedrich Kekule told the story of his great discovery which happened 25 years earlier. In 1865, he said, he was studying the structure of carbon compounds. One day, he had a day-dream of a snake with its own tail in its mouth. He realized that the structure of benzene was a ring of carbon atoms.

Theme 3: Speaking 3.7

the method	the contents of the ad	the science behind the ad	current TV example
the narrative (= a story)	it is usually a love story with different 'episodes' over a number of weeks, months or even years	people are interested in people so they become interested in the ad; someone may put the video online and then it might go viral	

Theme 4: Speaking 4.8

Braille (Theme 2)

	Student 1	Student 2
4.	Braille hurt l. eye, infected, blind in both eyes	infection spread to r.
5.	Braille invented new system / not allowed to teach	old system better
6.	Braille system = dots	not alphabet

1. <u>farmers understand basic idea</u>
   - logical extension of selective breeding — farmers doing it for thousands of years
   - selective breeding = changes genetics just like GM
   - 'Genetic engineering is just the latest form of biotechnology — the most precise method yet' (American Public Media, 2011)

2. <u>safety</u>
   - 'no evidence that modified crops cause illness in humans', GM crops no more harmful to environment than conventional plant varieties (Black, 2004 in BBC, 2009b)
   - worth doing despite risks — benefits outweigh risks
   - 'no compelling evidence of harm to humans from GM plants' (University of Queensland PhD study cited in Science Alert, 2008)
   - GM foods actually safer than non-GM foods because of additional checking (ArgEvo — food-producing co. — quoted in BBC, 2006)

3. <u>price</u>
   - 'people have been eating GM foods in China since 2000 because of their relative cheapness' (Chinese professor quoted in Juan, 2010)
   - GM tomato paste (slightly cheaper than non-GM) outselling conventional equivalent in Sainsbury's (Krebs, 2000)
   - future of cheap food? 'If we turn our backs on the technology which scientific learning can offer, then the end of cheap food can come to pass' (scientist in Henderson, 2007 in The Times of London)

4. <u>speed / yield</u>
   - food more readily available to people (BBC, 2006)
   - 'Agricultural biotechnology has tremendous potential as a tool for producing more and better foods on existing farmland' (Alliance for Better Foods, 2011)
   - important! — 'need to double food supply by 2025 due to population increases, changes in diets and natural disasters' (BBC, 2009b)

5. <u>nutrients</u>
   - can add = 'even healthier than normal crops (BBC, 1999, BBC, 2006)
   - 'Biotech researchers ... are field-testing rice enhanced with beta-carotene ... — important because rice = primary diet staple in developing world' (Alliance for Better Foods, 2011)
   - produce crops with vaccines against human infectious diseases?? (Human Genome Project, 2008)

6. <u>resistance</u>
   - make resistant to pests and diseases = fewer chemicals / more crops survive (Guardian, 2003), important for developing countries — need big crop yields + good for environment — GM crops need less fuel / water / labour time (Alliance for Better Foods, 2011)
   - can also make crops resistant to weedkillers = farmers can spray chemicals, kill all unwanted plants — no fear of damaging food crops (Guardian, 2003)
   - companies developing biodegradable weedkillers = do not stay in the soil (BBC, 2009b)
   - 'in those countries that have adopted these new crops, farmers and growers are reporting a reduction in the amount of pesticide being used' (ArgEvo on BBC, 2009b)
   - plants that poison any pests themselves! (Guardian, 2003)

7. <u>keep for longer</u>
   - can have longer shelf-life (Alliance for Better Foods, 2011)
   - in developing countries currently, 'as much as 40 per cent of harvested fruit can be wasted because it ripens too quickly' (Devlin, 2010)
   - tomato stayed firm for 1.5 months (Devlin, 2010)
   - hardier?? = able to withstand 'heat, drought, soil toxicity, salinity and flooding' = more reliable crop yields = important for poorer countries (Alliance for Better Foods, 2011)

8. <u>sustainability</u>
   - 'certain biotech varieties of cotton and soya beans require less tilling, preserving precious topsoil and helping to reduce sediment run-off into rivers and streams' (Alliance for Better Foods, 2011)

Theme 1: Speaking 1.8

We should close all car washes.

Theme 1: Speaking 1.10

Turkey

Turkey is reasonably well supplied by natural fresh water. In fact, it sells water from the Manavgat River to other countries in the region. However, it still suffers from water shortages from time to time. The government plans to build 22 dams on the Tigris and Euphrates rivers, but this will have a very bad effect on water supplies downstream, in Syria and Iraq.

Theme 3: Speaking 3.10

method	definition	details
the franchise	a series of films about the same character or set of characters	originally involved a sequel to a successful film, such as *Rocky*, i.e., *Rocky II*, *Rocky III*; then film companies started to make prequels – films about the life of the character before the first film, e.g., *Batman Begins*

Theme 2: Speaking 2.9

H

In 1928, the Scottish scientist Sir Alexander Fleming was studying bacteria that cause food poisoning. He left some slides overnight and found there were no bacteria on some of them. He realized that a mould was growing on the slides. The mould was penicillium and it was eventually made into the drug *penicillin*, which has saved millions of lives since its discovery.

Theme 5: Reading 5.15

References

Gates, S. (2011) http://www.bbc.co.uk/blogs/food/2011/05/is-meat-eating-good-for-the-pl.shtml retrieved on 5.09.2011

Gudmundson, B. and Sweet, M. (2011) http://www.desirefish.com/farmed.html retrieved on 5.09.2011

Holmes, B. (2010) http://www.newscientist.com/article/mg20727691.200-veggieworld-why-eating-greens-wont-save-the-planet.html retrieved on 5.09.2011

Institute of Medicine (2006) *Dietary Reference Intakes: The Essential Guide to Nutrient Requirements* Washington DC: National Academies Press

PETA (2011) 'Is commercial fishing bad for the environment?' retrieved on 5.08.2011 from http://www.peta.org/about/faq/ls-commercial-fishing-bad-for-the-environment.aspx

Robbins, J. (1987) 'Diet for a new America' retrieved on 1.09.2011 from http://michaelbluejay.com/veg/books/dietamerica.html

Vegetarian Society (2011) 'Why going vegetarian is good for the environment' retrieved on 4.08.2011 from http://www.vegsoc.org/page.aspx?pid=520

Vegetarian Society (2011b) 'Reduce your carbon footprint' retrieved on 9.08.2011 from http://www.vegsoc.org/page.aspx?pid=523

date	event	notes
pre-12 000 BCE	hunter-gatherers	killed animals, gathered berries, etc.
12 000 BCE	wild grasses harvested	
11 500 BCE	rice domesticated	
8 500 BCE	barley, wheat grown	
7 000 BCE	goats, sheep domesticated	
6 000 BCE	cows and chickens domesticated	
5 000 BCE	horses domesticated	
4 000 BCE	plough	
next 5,000 yrs	irrigation power sources	
18th C	Agrarian Revolution	
1701	seed drill	
1786	mechanical threshing machine	
1850	steam plough	
early 1960s	Green Revolution	
1961	Borlaug – miracle rice	

method	definition	details
the genre	a type of film – originally there were only a few, such as war, western and romance	nowadays there are dozens of genres – 'rom com' (romantic comedy), 'sci-fi' (science fiction), 'gross out' (funny in a disgusting way), 'buddy' (two friends)

G

A researcher called Michael Sveda at the University of Illinois was working in the lab on a new medicine in 1937. He was smoking at the same time. He put down his cigarette on his workbench, and when he put it back in his mouth, it tasted sweet. His discovery was cyclamate, which is now in most sugar-free drinks.

Group A

Sign language for the deaf

Abbé Charles–Michel de l'Épée
- 1712   b. near Paris
- c 1730   trains as a priest
  - visits poor people
- c 1750   visits family, two children do not talk to him; notices that they are making signs with their hands to talk to each other = children are deaf
- 1750–1755   learns basic sign language of deaf people of Paris; improves and extends it
- 1755   founds school: National Deaf Dumb School of Paris
- 1756–1776   writes sign language dictionary and reference book: Instruction of the Deaf and Dumb; people in France start calling him 'Father of the deaf'
- 1780   ambassador from Russia comes to congratulate him
- 1782   the Austrian Emperor visits the school
- 1784   publishes book The True Method of Educating the Deaf
- 1789   d. in Paris
- 1791   French govt = 'Deaf people have rights'
- 1791   govt take over his school

Ogallala Aquifer (Theme 1)

	Student 1	Student 2
7.	aquifer formed mya	water = fossil fuel
8.	not fed by rainwater now	dry up
9.	farmers need irrigation to grow some crops	stop growing crops

Theme 1: Speaking 1.8

We should not allow people to water garden flowers.

Theme 3: Reading 3.13

book / journal / Internet	
author(s)	
date	
title	
pub. place	
publisher	
journal	
volume	
page nos	
retrieved	
full URL	

book / journal / Internet	
author(s)	
date	
title	
pub. place	
publisher	
journal	
volume	
page nos	
retrieved	
full URL	

book / journal / Internet	
author(s)	
date	
title	
pub. place	
publisher	
journal	
volume	
page nos	
retrieved	
full URL	

book / journal / Internet	
author(s)	
date	
title	
pub. place	
publisher	
journal	
volume	
page nos	
retrieved	
full URL	

book / journal / Internet	
author(s)	
date	
title	
pub. place	
publisher	
journal	
volume	
page nos	
retrieved	
full URL	

book / journal / Internet	
author(s)	
date	
title	
pub. place	
publisher	
journal	
volume	
page nos	
retrieved	
full URL	

method	definition	details
the trailer	small extracts from the film which are shown in cinemas and on TV before the film is released	a sample of exciting / intriguing / romantic moments from the film; can be up to three minutes

CD
name = Compact Disc
Russell = US, physicist
1ˢᵗ commercial CD = 'The Visitors' by Abba
1ˢᵗ CD player by Sony
'Brothers in Arms' by Dire Straits

MP3 player
name = industry standard for digital recording
Brandenberg = Ger.; maths and electronics specialist
Br. worked with other scientists
mistakes in software almost led to cancellation of project
1ˢᵗ MP3s = MPMan by S. Korean Co.

How it works:
music data stored as digital info. in pits (valleys) on metal disc
- listener chooses track
- disc turns
- laser scans information
- digital info. converted to analogue sound
- plays through speaker(s)

How it works:
music data compressed then stored as digital info. on hard drive
- listener chooses song
- digital data retrieved from hard drive
- decompressed
- digital info. converted to analogue sound
- plays through headphones

Extra info:
compression = not every sound recorded (e.g., song on CD = 30 megabytes, song in MP3 format = 3 mb), compression takes out sounds human ear can't hear, records only the softer of two sounds, etc.

Chad

Lake Chad was once one of the largest lakes in the world. In fact, the word *Chad* means 'large lake' in the local language. The area of the lake has shrunk in the last 50 years from nearly 30,000 km² to less than 1,500 km². This shrinkage is due to less rain and more usage for irrigation. Nine million people now suffer severe water shortages. The government is talking to its neighbours about diverting waters from the Congo River to refill the lake.

1.1

Presenter: **1.1. Theme 1: Geography and the modern world**
Lesson 1.1. Vocabulary for listening: The HDI

Exercise B1. Listen to Extract 1. Check your ideas from Exercise A.

Lecturer: Now, I'd like you to look at this map. And I want you to notice the colours in particular. What do they represent? Well, the map shows human development for every country in the world. We'll look at exactly what we mean by human development later in the lecture. Now every year, the United Nations Development Programme looks at human development in every country in the world. So this UN programme produces an index of human development – the HDI, or Human Development Index.

1.2

Presenter: **1.2. Exercise B2. Listen to Extract 2. What questions does the UN ask about each country?**

Lecturer: According to the UNDP, we can measure human development in a particular country by finding answers to four questions. The first one is this, and it's very simple: *How long, in that country, can people expect to live?* This is called life expectancy. In some countries, life expectancy can be as high as 80 years of age. In the poorest countries of the world, it is only about 40 years old.

Now, the second question. *What percentage of people can read and write?* In other words, what is the level of literacy in the country? Here, in the UK, the literacy rate is 99 per cent. In Afghanistan, however, it is only 28 per cent of the population.

Our third question is linked to the second question about literacy. *How many years of education do children receive?* The important thing here is the enrolment rate at each level. What percentage of children complete primary, secondary and tertiary education?

And finally, the fourth question. Any ideas what it is? No? Well, it's this. *What is the average income per person?* We call this the standard of living. It is measured by dividing the total income of the country by the total population. The total income is sometimes called Gross Domestic Product or GDP. When we divide by the population, we get GDP per person, or per capita, as we say.

So our four questions are about life expectancy, literacy, education and income, or standard of living.

1.3

Presenter: **1.3. Exercise B3. Listen to Extract 3. Why does the lecturer mention the following: a) Canada, b) Norway, c) Sierra Leone, d) natural resources, e) location, f) freshwater?**

Lecturer: Now, at the beginning of this lecture, I asked you to notice the colours on the map. Let's think about what they represent. Countries with the highest human development achieve scores of around .9, or 90 per cent. Examples include the USA and Canada and several countries in Northern Europe. In fact, Norway is number 1 in the world on the HDI. So these are the dark green countries on the map. Countries with very low development score only .3 or .4 – 30 to 40 per cent. Several countries in Africa are in this category, including Sierra Leone, which in 2010 was ranked 177 in the world. As you can see, these countries are coloured red, orange or brown.

So what are the similarities between the dark green countries, the ones with the high HDI? Is it their location in the world and their climate? Is it their natural resources? Is it their style of government? And what about the poorest countries in the world? What factors do they have in common? It could be population, poor agricultural land or a lack of fresh water. I want you to consider these ideas and ...

1.4 DVD **1.A**

Presenter: **Lesson 1.2. Real-time listening: Qatar and Lebanon**

Lecturer: Right, so, today we are looking at the effect of geography on human development. I'm going to focus on two small countries in the Middle East. Next time, by the way, we'll look at two large countries. This week, the two countries are Qatar and Lebanon. First, I'll explain how we can divide the main information about a country, like location, etc., into subheadings. Then I'll compare the two countries in terms of each subheading. Finally, I'm going to tell you the rating of each country on the United Nations Human Development Index, and I'm going to ask you to consider this question: Does the geography of each country affect the human development of its population? There are many similarities between the countries but there are also some differences. Perhaps these differences affect human development.

Lecturer: Now, I've given you a handout to fill in today. Can you get that out? Right. As you can see, I'm going to look at five key headings for each country. Together, these points give us a picture of the country. The key points are location, population, land, climate and natural resources. We can divide each of these headings into subheadings. I'd like you to fill in the subheadings.

So under *location*, we have *region* and *borders*. We could have *latitude* and *longitude* as well, but *region* and *borders* is fine for us today.

Secondly, *population*. Under this heading, we look at three points: the *total population*, the *density* and the *urban:rural split*. I just want to make sure that you understand the special terms in this section. *Density* means the average number of people per square kilometre. Some countries have a very high density: small countries with a large population, for example. Some countries have a very low population density. *Urban* means 'living in a town', and *rural* means 'living in the country'. The urban:rural split, therefore, is the percentage of people who live in towns compared with the percentage who live in the country.

Thirdly, *land*. Obviously we need to know the area, but more important really is the amount of agricultural land. That's a percentage, of course. Some countries have a lot of agricultural land, but some have deserts or mountains so the amount is very small. Finally in this section, fresh water – that is, lakes and rivers. This last one is particularly important, because of the global shortage of water nowadays.

Next ... ah, yes, climate. Well, we start with *type*. As you know, there are a number of main types, like temperate or desert. Then there's average rainfall – that's an annual figure, usually. And temperature range. You know, from 1 degree Celsius to 24 degrees Celsius, for example.

Finally, natural resources. Some people include things like forests in natural resources – in other words, things *above* the ground. But in this analysis, I am only going to consider resources *under* the ground. There are two main types of underground natural resources. They are fossil fuels and minerals. Fossil fuels are things we can burn, like oil and gas and coal. Minerals are things like iron, gold, copper. Oh, sorry. There is one more section, isn't there? Human Development Index. We'll come to that at the very end.

Lecturer: OK. So, I hope you've got the subheadings now. Now we are going to compare two countries, using these headings and subheadings.

Both countries are located in the Middle East, but Qatar is in the Gulf whereas Lebanon is at the eastern end of the Mediterranean Sea. Qatar is a peninsula, only bordered to the south by Saudi Arabia, while Lebanon is almost completely surrounded by Syria. Has anybody here been to Qatar? No? Well, it is an extremely interesting place. It's a Muslim country, of course, with a very open outlook on the world. Lots of modern buildings and wide roads. Lebanon is also an extremely interesting place. The capital, Beirut, was once called 'the Paris of the East' because it is beautiful and very cosmopolitan – I mean, there are many different nationalities there and many religions. Does the location of these countries affect their human development?

Right, so, population. We're going to look at the total, then the density and finally the urban:rural split. Firstly, the total size. Neither country has a large population but Lebanon's is three times the size of Qatar's. Qatar has 1.5 million people while the Lebanon has around 4.3 million. This difference in population is reflected in density. Qatar has 120 people per square kilometre while Lebanon's is 413 per square kilometre. The people of both countries live mainly in the towns. Ninety-six per cent of Qataris are urban – they live mainly in the capital Doha, whereas the figure for the Lebanese is 87 per cent. Do any of these points about population affect the human development of this country?

Thirdly, land. We've got area in total, and the amount of that land which is agricultural. We also need to consider fresh water – lakes and rivers in each country. So, neither country is large in area. In fact, they are almost the same size. Qatar comprises 11,400 square kilometres while the Lebanon is slightly smaller, at 10,400 square kilometres. Qatar does not have much agricultural land, because most of the country is desert, but Lebanon has a great deal of land for cultivation. Finally, in this category, Qatar has no fresh water. Literally, none. The country relies on desalination – I mean, getting fresh water from salt water. Lebanon, on the other hand, has a water surplus. Do any of these points about land area and usage affect the human development of the country?

Fourthly, climate. Here we are interested in the basic type, in the average rainfall, and in the temperature range. So first, type. One country, Qatar, has a desert climate. This means hot, dry summers and warm, dry winters. By contrast, Lebanon has a Mediterranean climate. This means hot, dry summers and cool, rainy winters. So both countries have hot, dry summers ... but Qatar is also warm and dry in winter whereas Lebanon has cool, rainy winters. Rainfall in Qatar averages less than 75 millimetres per annum, while Lebanon has around 825 millimetres a year. Both countries have a similar temperature range, but Qatar goes from 15 to 40 degrees Celsius while Lebanon's range is 5 to 38, so Qatar is much hotter all year round. Does the climate of either country affect human development?

Finally, natural resources. With regard to fossil fuels, Qatar has fuels but Lebanon has none, although it is said that there is oil offshore. In terms of minerals, the situation is the reverse. Lebanon has minerals, especially limestone and iron ore, which is used to make steel. Qatar, on the other hand, has no minerals. Does the presence or absence of natural resources affect human development?

Lecturer: So we've heard about some of the geographical features of the two countries.
            Now, the key question is: What is the Human Development Index of each of these two countries? As you know, this index is a measure of life expectancy, literacy, education in general and standards of living. The figure for Qatar is very high, at 0.831. For Lebanon, the figure is slightly lower, at 0.739.

            OK. So, I want you to think about the key question for our next tutorial: Does geography affect human development? Both Qatar and Lebanon have quite a high figure – they are both in the top half of the table of world countries. But Qatar's figure is higher than Lebanon's. Why?

🌐 1.8

Presenter: **1.8. Lesson 1.3. Learning new listening skills: Using lecture structure**
            Exercise A2. Listen to some sentences from the lecture and check your ideas.

Lecturer: 1. Some people include things like forests in natural resources.
                2. And temperature range from the coldest to the hottest.
                3. So we've heard about some of the geographical features of the two countries.
                4. Some countries have a very low population density.
                5. Density means the average number of people per square kilometre.
                6. But more important really is the amount of agricultural land.
                7. They are fossil fuels and minerals.

🌐 1.9

Presenter: **1.9. Exercise C1. Listen to the introductions to three lectures.**

            Lecture 1: Time management.

Lecturer 1: OK. So this week I'm going to talk about time management. There are two main topics, or areas, within time management. Firstly, managing people; and secondly, managing things. So that's people and, er, things.

            But under each heading we have several subheadings. So under the heading *people* we have three subheadings: *colleagues*, *employees* and, most important of all, *the boss*! While under the heading *things* we have three more subheadings. They are *work*, *energy*, and, unfortunately, *distractions*.

Presenter: **Lecture 2: Memory.**

Lecturer 2: So, where have we got to? Right, yes. Memory. This week, I want to summarize everything about this subject so far. So, first, I'm going to look at the *process* of remembering, which involves three stages, according to the Multi-stage memory model. We will look at each stage again – that's sensory, short-term and long-term. Then I'm going to go quickly through the *types* of memory. If you remember, there are four main *types* of memory. Firstly, of course, there is autobiographical memory, like name, date of birth, personal holidays. Then, secondly, there is procedural memory, which is how to do things like drive a car. Thirdly, we have stories, like fairy tales. Finally, shocking events – sometimes called flashbulb memory, because it is like a picture of a moment in our heads.

Presenter: **Lecture 3: Desertification.**

Lecturer 3: In today's session, I want to give you an overview of desertification. In the first part of the lecture, I'm going to describe the causes of desertification. We will look at three main causes: climate change, then farming methods, and finally deforestation – that means cutting down trees. Then in the second part of the lecture, I will describe some ways of greening the desert – that is, reversing the process.

🌐 1.10

Presenter: **1.10. Exercise D2. Listen and check your answers.**

            During the lecture.

Voice: OK. So that's climate.
            Now, let's look at natural resources.
            Right. We've heard about fossil fuels. What about minerals?
            Next, natural resources.
            Let's move on to minerals.

Presenter: **After the lecture.**

Voice: I missed the bit about fossil fuels.
            What did she say about climate type?
            Did you get the information for average rainfall?

Presenter: **1.11. Exercise E1. Listen to an introduction to a lecture about communication. Prepare a page for your notes with scientific numbering.**

Lecturer: I want to talk to you today about communication. We communicate … or, perhaps I should say, we *try* to communicate all the time. But communication – real communication – is not easy. So, I'm going to talk about the process of communication.

Firstly, I am going to talk about barriers to communication. There are several main barriers to communication. I'm going to look at five. We have physical barriers: for example, you can't hear me well. Then there are mental barriers: you can't understand my ideas. There are linguistic barriers, of course – if we don't have a common language. Fourthly, emotional barriers. Perhaps you are angry with me. Finally, there are cultural barriers. Perhaps we have a different view of the communication. So, five main barriers, I will look at each one in more detail. Then, in the second half, I will talk about breaking down the barriers. In this section, I'm going to mention two ideas. Firstly, the role of the information giver, and secondly, the role of the information receiver. So that's giver and receiver.

OK. Let's start with barriers …

Presenter: **1.12. Exercise E2. Listen to the first part. Make notes.**

Lecturer: OK. Let's start with barriers to communication. Firstly, physical barriers. This is really quite obvious but sometimes people try to communicate, even quite important messages, in completely the wrong place. For example, a lecturer tries to announce an assignment at the end of a lecture, when the students have already started to get up, walk around, talk. It is better to announce information like this in a quiet room and to make sure that everyone can hear you and everyone is listening. You must remember that people need to be able to hear you and, preferably, to see you as well. Seeing a speaker helps you to understand the words. Secondly, we have mental barriers. There are two possible reasons for mental barriers – me and you. Perhaps you don't understand me because I have not formed my ideas clearly or because I don't express them clearly. Perhaps you don't understand me because you are not paying attention, or you are not knowledgeable enough or clever enough to understand them. We shall see in the second part how to deal with this barrier, whether it starts with the speaker or the listener. Thirdly, there can be linguistic barriers. I'm sure you are very familiar with those so I'm not going to dwell on it. Fourthly, emotional barriers, which can be the worst kind of all. You cannot understand perfectly what someone is saying to you if you are in an emotional state, angry, depressed, worried. Of course, you can't express yourself perfectly in those circumstances, either. Finally, cultural barriers …

Presenter: **1.13. Lesson 1.4. Grammar for listening: *both / neither; and / but; whereas / while***

Grammar box 1.

Voice: Both countries are located in the Middle East.

Both countries have hot, dry summers.

Both countries have a small land area.

Both countries have some natural resources.

Neither country is large in area.

Neither country has a large population.

Neither country has much agricultural land.

Neither country has any mining industries.

Presenter: **1.14. Exercise A. Listen to an extract from a lecture about Singapore and Tonga.**

Lecturer: OK, now we're going to look at two island nations, Singapore and Tonga. Singapore is in southeast Asia and Tonga is in Western Polynesia in the South Pacific. They have some similarities but many differences. One is very successful in economic terms, and very rich. The other is not very successful, economically, and is quite poor. What role has geography played in these differences?

Anyway, let's consider the similarities first.

Obviously, both countries are surrounded by water but Tonga has over 150 beautiful, tropical islands and Singapore has about 60. However, many of Tonga's islands are uninhabited, and, in the case of Singapore, only the large main island is important. Surprisingly, perhaps, tourism is not a major part of the economy in Tonga although the government has plans to develop this industry. Now, my next point: both countries are small in land area and both have small populations. We'll look at the actual figures later. Let's look at climate. As you've probably guessed already, the two countries have a tropical climate and neither has any actual deserts. On the other hand, neither has much rainfall in summer. Unlike desert climates, both countries have high temperatures in summer *and* in winter whereas of course deserts can be cold in winter. And lastly, both countries are very flat and neither has any mountains.

🪙 1.15

Presenter: **1.15. Exercise B. Listen to another extract about Singapore and Tonga.**

Lecturer: So we have seen some of the similarities between Tonga and Singapore. Now let's consider the differences between these island nations. I said that both are small, but there are big differences between them.

Singapore has an area of 660 square kilometres, and Tonga has 748. However, Singapore is much bigger in terms of population. Singapore has over 5 million people and the population density is very high, at over 7,000 per square kilometre. In fact, it is one of the most densely populated, or crowded, countries in the world. Tonga, on the other hand, has a much smaller population, at 122,000, and a much lower density of 165. Many of its islands, in fact, are uninhabited.

Both countries are flat, as we have heard. The highest point in Singapore, Bukit Timah, is at 166 metres against 1,033 metres in Tonga. The area in Tonga has no name, by the way.

What about agricultural land? Well, Singapore only has one per cent agricultural land – yes, that's right, one per cent, whereas nearly half of Tongan land is under cultivation. Forty-eight per cent, to be precise. The wettest month in Singapore is December, which has an average of 288 millimetres, while Tonga's is March, at 210. So there is not a significant difference there.

Now, we heard about the agricultural land in Singapore – well, the lack of agricultural land, I should say. There is no agricultural land because the whole main island is one large city. So most people in Singapore live in the city and the urban:rural split is 100 to 0. But Tonga is very different. Only 25 per cent of people live in towns. Finally, Singapore is a very rich country with a GDP per capita of $57,000, which is third place in the world, while Tonga only has a GDP per capita of $2,900.

OK. What does all this mean for the HDI? Which is higher, do you think? Let's see. The HDI for Singapore is 0.846, which means it is 27th in the world. By contrast, the figure for Tonga is 0.677, which puts it in 85th place.

Why is Singapore higher? Does the remote location of Tonga give it a major disadvantage …?

🪙 1.16

Presenter: **1.16. Lesson 1.5. Applying new listening skills: Pakistan and Chile**

          Exercise A2. Listen and check your answers. Mark the main stressed syllable in each word or phrase.

Voice: *Region* and *borders* come under *Location*.
          Density and *urban:rural split* are concerned with *Population*.
          Area, *agricultural* and *lakes and rivers* describe *Land*.
          Rainfall and *temperature range* are part of *Climate*.
          Fossil fuels and *minerals* come under *Natural resources*.

🪙 1.17 [DVD] 1.E

Lecturer: I'm going to talk today about two large countries. There are many similarities between the countries but there are also some differences. As you know, when we analyze the geography of a country, we look at five areas: location, population, land, climate and natural resources. Then, as before, at the end of the lecture I'm going to give you the Human Development Index number – or HDI – for each country. Like last time, I'm going to ask you to consider this question: *Does geography affect human development in these countries?*

First, then, location. We need to consider region and borders. One country, Pakistan, is in western Asia whereas the other, Chile, is in South America. Pakistan is bordered in the east by India, in the west by Iran and Afghanistan and in the north by China. Chile has borders with Peru in the north, Bolivia in the northeast and Argentina in the east. Chile also has a very long coastline on the South Pacific Ocean.

OK. Let's look at population now. As before, I'm going to look at three sub-areas under this heading: the total population, the density and the urban:rural split. Pakistan has a large population, but Chile's is quite small. The population of Pakistan is 185 million whereas Chile's population is around 10 per cent of that size, at 17.3 million. Pakistan therefore has a much higher density of population than Chile: 177 people per square kilometre against 20 per square kilometre. What about the urban:rural split? Well, the population of Pakistan is more rural than the population of Chile. The split in Pakistan is 34 to 66, whereas in Chile it is 87 to 13.

Thirdly, land. As you know, we consider area, percentage of agricultural land and availability of natural water, that is, lakes and rivers. Both countries are large. In fact, they are almost the same size. Pakistan has an area of 803,000 square kilometres, while Chile is slightly smaller at 756,000 square kilometres. Both countries have quite a high percentage of agricultural land. Pakistan has 30 per cent agricultural land and Chile has 21 per cent. Both countries have permanent lakes and rivers. The most important river of Pakistan is the Indus, while the most important river of Chile is the Loa.

Fourthly, climate. If you remember, in this area we consider the broad type of climate, then we look at average annual rainfall and temperature range. Both countries are very large so they have different climates in different areas. In fact, Chile has every main type of climate, from *desert* through *Mediterranean* to *Arctic* in the extreme south. Both countries have desert regions in the north of the country. The rainfall range in Pakistan is much lower than in Chile. In Pakistan, rainfall ranges from 125 mm, which is very low, to 1,500 mm, which is very high. Meanwhile, in Chile, average rainfall is between 0.2 mm in the north and 2,900 in the south. The temperature range is also wider in Chile. Whereas in Pakistan there is a temperature range throughout the year between 13 degrees Celsius and 34 degrees Celsius, in Chile the range is much bigger, between minus 18 ... that's minus 18 degrees Celsius ... and plus 38 degrees Celsius.

Finally, natural resources. As you know, we can divide natural resources into fossil fuels and minerals. Both countries have coal, but Chile also has a small amount of oil and natural gas. With regard to minerals, both countries have iron ore and copper.

OK. So we have heard about some of the geographical features of the two countries. What are their HDI ratings? They are very different. On the one hand, the HDI for Pakistan is 0.504, which puts it in the bottom half of the world's countries. On the other hand, the HDI for Chile is 0.805, which means Chile is in the top half. Why is there that difference? Is it connected to geography?

🎧 1.18

Presenter:	1.18. Lesson 1.6. Vocabulary for speaking: Water resources
	Exercise A2. Listen to an extract from a lecture about water resources, and check your ideas.
Lecturer:	Now, I want you to study this diagram. It shows a water system in a mountainous area. OK. All the water comes from rainfall in the mountains. You can see small streams ... here. They all join together into one big river ... here. Now, look at the foot of the mountains. There is quite a large dam. It probably holds several billion cubic metres of water. So the dam holds the water for some time and allows it to soak into the ground. What happens next? Well, if you look here, you can see some of the water from the dam goes to an underground aquifer. An aquifer is a kind of underground store of water. People take water from the aquifer through wells. You can see the wells in the diagram just here. OK, let's return to the river. The river then flows past a reservoir. A reservoir is another method of storing water; it's a kind of artificial lake. Some of the water from the river is diverted into the reservoir and, from there, into irrigation channels for the fields. In other words, farmers use water from the reservoir to irrigate their crops. So there you have the complete system, from rain falling in the mountains, to stored water in the dam, aquifer and reservoir.

🎧 1.19

Presenter:	1.19. Exercise B1. Listen and find an answer to each question about the water system in the diagram above.
Tutor:	a. What is the *source* of the water in this system?
	b. What is *upstream* of the town?
	c. Which parts of this water system could *leak*?
	d. How do people *extract* water from this system?
	e. Do the people *divert* any of the water?
	f. What *feeds* the irrigation channels?
	g. What could lead to *flooding* in the town?
	h. What could lead to *shrinkage* of the aquifer?
	i. Does this area need a *desalination* plant?
	j. Do the people of this area ever *run out of* water or suffer from *drought*?

🎧 1.20

Presenter:	1.20. Lesson 1.7. Real-time speaking: Water problems in a developed country
	Exercise A2. Listen, check your answers and repeat each word.
Voice:	aquifer
	divert
	extract
	irrigation
	rainwater
	reservoir
	shrinkage
	underground

Presenter:	**1.21. Exercise B2. Listen to the student giving information to a discussion group.**
Student 4:	OK. So we are talking about water problems and proposed solutions, right? Who wants to start?
Student 1:	OK then, *I* will. I looked at the problems in the United States. Apparently ...
Student 2:	I didn't realize they had problems with water there!
Student 1:	Well, they do. Big problems, apparently. It seems that the central part of the US is running out of underground water. There's an underground reservoir, called the Ogallala Aquifer and ...
Student 3:	The *what* Aquifer?
Student 1:	Ogallala. So, basically, the Ogallala Aquifer provides half of all the water for the United States.
Student 4:	Um ... just a second! Half of all the water?
Student 1:	Sorry. Did I say half? I meant a third.
Student 4:	And do you mean for drinking *and* irrigation?
Student 1:	No, sorry. I mean just for irrigation. Um, yes, irrigation.
Student 2:	No problem. And, er, why is the water running out?
Student 1:	Because the water was formed in the reservoir thousands of years ago, but the reservoir is no longer ... er ... refilled by rainwater.
Student 3:	What? Thousands of years ago? I thought these underground reservoirs were millions of years old.
Student 1:	Oops! Did I say thousands? I meant to say millions
Student 3:	Oh, right, OK. So how serious is the problem?
Student 1:	It's really serious. Research shows that the reservoir is shrinking fast. The level of the water in the reservoir is falling by one metre every year.
Student 3:	Wow!
Student 1:	Er, yes ... so it will dry up within 200 years. Yes, um, 200.
Student 4:	So, what's the proposed solution?
Student 1:	Well, farmers in the area are suffering shortages, er, so they, er, stopped ... um are going to stop, er, growing crops which require irrigation.
Student 2:	But that's not really a solution, is it? Surely we have to continue to irrigate crops? And what about ...
Student 3:	Well, not necessarily. Farmers could grow crops which are local ... er ... to the area. They ... um, the crops ... probably grow without irrigation.

Presenter:	**1.22. Exercise C2. Listen and check your answers.**
Student A:	Basically, the Ogallala Aquifer provides half of all the water for the United States.
Student B:	Just a second. *Half* of all the water?
Student A:	Sorry. Did I say half? I meant a third.
Student B:	And do you mean for drinking *and* irrigation?
Student A:	No, sorry. I mean just for irrigation.
Student A:	The water was formed in the reservoir thousands of years ago.
Student B:	*Thousands* of years ago? I thought these underground aquifers were *millions* of years old.
Student B:	So, what's the proposed solution?
Student A:	Well, the farmers are going to stop growing crops which require irrigation.
Student B:	I'm not sure that's a very *good* solution.
Student A:	Perhaps not, but it solves the problem in the short term.

Presenter:	**1.23. Pronunciation Check. Listen to these sentences.**
Voice:	*Half* of all the water?
	Thousands of years ago?

Presenter:	**1.24. Pronunciation Check. Listen and repeat some more sentences. Copy the stress and intonation.**
Voice:	*Ten* metres a year?
	A *tropical* climate?
	Four *thousand* per square kilometre?
	Thirty degrees centigrade?
	Visual learners or *aural* learners?
	Last *month* or last *year*?

Presenter:	**1.25. Everyday English: Expressing opinions politely; persuading**
	Exercise B1. Listen to the conversation below about the first headline. What do you notice about it?
Voice A:	Did you know that over 20,000 children die every day unnecessarily?
Voice B:	You mean from poverty and hunger and so on?
Voice A:	Yes. Everyone should give money to charities.
Voice B:	The UN should do more.
Voice A:	Ordinary people can't just ignore the problems.
Voice B:	We can't leave it to charities. And we shouldn't just give aid. We should help the people in developing countries to help themselves.
Voice A:	In the long term. But people are dying, including thousands of children. It's terrible. We must do something about that.

🕑 1.26

Presenter:	**1.26. Exercise B2. Listen to a second version of the conversation. What differences do you notice?**
Voice A:	Did you know that over 20,000 children die every day unnecessarily?
Voice B:	You mean from poverty and hunger and so on?
Voice A:	Yes. I think everyone should give money to charities.
Voice B:	I agree, but don't you think the UN should do more?
Voice A:	That's true, but ordinary people can't just ignore the problems. If the UN doesn't do the job, charities have to.
Voice B:	Perhaps, but we can't leave it to charities, can we? And anyway, surely, we shouldn't just give aid. Shouldn't we help the people in developing countries to help themselves?
Voice A:	Well, OK, in the long term. But in the meantime people are dying, including thousands of children. It's terrible. We must do something about that, mustn't we?

🕑 1.27

Presenter:	**1.27. Lesson 1.8. Learning new speaking skills: Contributing to discussion groups**
	Pronunciation Check. Listen and check your answers.
Voice:	It provides a third of all the water for irrigation in the US. The water was formed millions of years ago. The farmers are going to stop growing crops. They could grow crops which are local to the area.

🕑 1.28

Presenter:	**1.28. Skills Check. Listen to some more contributions. Mark the main stressed word in each sentence.**
Voice A:	Do you mean for drinking *and* irrigation?
Voice B:	No, sorry. I mean just for *irrigation*.
Voice A:	Did you say *thousands* of years ago?
Voice B:	Sorry. I meant to say *millions* of years ago.
Voice A:	They are going to *stop* growing crops.
Voice B:	I'm not sure that's a very *good* solution.
Voice A:	No, but it solves the problem in the *short* term.
Voice B:	They could bring water from *another* area.
Voice A:	But that would be very *expensive*.
Voice B:	Yeah.

🕑 1.29

Presenter:	**1.29. Skills Check. Listen again. Copy the polite intonation.**
	[REPEAT OF SCRIPT FROM 🕑 1.28]

🔊 1.30

Presenter: **1.30. Lesson 1.9. Grammar for speaking: Showing surprise with *think* and *realize***

Grammar box 2. Listen to each statement and comment.

Voice A: The aquifers are thousands of years old.
Voice B: I thought they were *millions* of years old.

Voice A: The reservoir provides half of all the water for irrigation.
Voice B: I thought that it provided a *third* of all the water.

🔊 1.31

Presenter: **1.31. Grammar box 3. Listen to each statement and comment.**

Voice A: The aquifer provides a third of all US irrigation water.
Voice B: I didn't realize it provided a *third*.

Voice A: The level is falling by one metre every year.
Voice B: I didn't realize that it was falling by *one metre*.

🔊 2.1

Presenter: **2.1. Theme 2: Communication**

Lesson 2.1. Vocabulary for listening: Communication mediums: benefits and drawbacks

Exercise A1. Listen to some students working with Table 1. Fill in the information for *posted letter*.

Student A: OK. So we've got the example here for a posted letter. It is slow but cheap. What does the next bit mean?
Student B: Well, we have to consider convenience for the sender and for the receiver. It's not the same thing. Posting a letter is not very convenient for the sender …
Student C: Because you have to go find a post box or go to a post office.
Student B: Exactly.
Student A: Ah, right. I see. But it's very convenient for the receiver.
Student B: Well, only if there is postal delivery. In my country, you have to go to a post office to collect your letters.
Student A: Right. So what about letter through a courier. What's a courier? …

🔊 2.2

Presenter: **2.2. Exercise B3. Listen and check your answers.**

Voice: convenience, convenient, inconvenient
security, secure, insecure
expense, expensive, inexpensive
benefit, beneficial, useless
scarcity, scarce, common
complexity, complex, simple

🔊 2.3

Presenter: **2.3. Exercise C. Listen to some sentences. Number the words in the table above.**

1. Mobile phone calls can be very *expensive*.
2. E-mail is very *secure*, even if you don't put your e-mails into code.
3. The postal system is *inconvenient* if there is no home delivery.
4. The speed of e-mail is one of its main *benefits*.
5. The mobile has largely replaced the fixed-line phone because of its *convenience*.
6. Letters are *inexpensive* but very slow, compared with e-mail.
7. Some people don't use e-mail because they think it is too *complex*.
8. You don't see many public phone boxes in some countries now. They are quite *scarce*.

Presenter:	**2.4. Lesson 2.2. Real-time listening: Long-distance communication and business principles**
Lecturer:	Everybody here? Yes? OK. I'm going to talk to you today about communication over long distances. It's quite an interesting subject in its own right, but we are not here to learn about smoke signals or telephones specifically. We are going to look at the history of long-distance communication to see what the modern businessperson can learn from it. History is a very good case study. Who said that? That's right. Me.

OK. So, first, a quick outline of the history of long-distance communication *before* the telephone, then we'll see how basic business principles applied, even in those early days. Finally, we'll look at the development of the telephone in the light of these principles.

So, where do we begin with the history of communication over long distances? Obviously, human beings have been able to communicate over *short* distances since ancient tribes in Africa and wherever first learnt to speak. But unless you can shout very, very loudly, you cannot communicate with someone in the next town or city by using your *voice*. You need another medium of communication. First, we had things like smoke signals, I guess. They must be thousands of years old. People used to bang drums as well, in some areas, I suppose. But this kind of signal only works over a few kilometres. People wanted a way of communicating over much longer distances. They couldn't use *spoken* language – that's the telephone and, of course, that came much later. They had to use *written* language.

As you probably know, the Sumerians invented writing in about 3000 BCE – that's over 5,000 years ago. Once people had a script, they could send a letter. In other words, they could write something down and give it to a messenger, who could take it to someone in another town or even another country. There is some evidence that the Sumerians sent written messages to each other but we need to move on a couple of thousand years to …

… the earliest recorded postal system. That appeared in about 900 BCE. The Chinese invented it. Couriers carried messages around the country, from the national leaders to their local rulers. They were diplomatic messages, in other words, not things like *Having a lovely time. Wish you were here*. The messages didn't travel very fast. The couriers walked, so speed of transmission was about eight kilometres an hour. They weren't very secure either. Thieves could stop a messenger and take the message from him.

In about 150 BCE, the Egyptians started using horses to carry messages more quickly. Horses can go faster than people but they cannot travel for very long carrying a person – and the messages, of course. So the Egyptians set up a system of relay stations for messengers on horseback. Urgent messages now travelled at about 15 kilometres an hour for the next few thousand years. They still weren't secure, of course. *Why is all of this important to the modern businessperson?* I hear you ask. *Why do I need to know all this rubbish?!* Let's go on a bit and then we'll see.

We have to wait a long time for the next big idea. In 1793, a man called Claude Chappe invented the long-distance semaphore in France. The French government built a network of 556 relay stations all over the country. These were houses with arms on the roof. The arms could move to make different symbols. Urgent messages could travel at about 20 miles an hour now – faster and much more secure. It was very difficult to intercept and stop the message from reaching its destination. It was in code, too, so even if you did intercept it, you couldn't understand it. But the system was very expensive, both to build and to maintain. It was very expensive for the customers who wanted to use it, too. But Napoleon used it all the time to send urgent messages about troop movements – you know, how his armies were moving around the country.

Why have we looked at these ancient systems? Well, they demonstrate in a simple way three basic business principles. Firstly, at the centre of any successful business is a benefit. What does that mean? A successful business satisfies a want. Let me explain. A potential customer *wants* to do something. In the case of long-distance communication, people simply wanted to send messages to a distant location. This want did not change, through thousands of years. But it was met in different ways through the generations. The different ways were faster, or more secure, or cheaper, or more convenient. But they always satisfied the basic want.

We can go further. Customers do not buy *products*. They buy *satisfaction of wants*. In other words, they buy *benefits*. Companies sometimes forget this. They try to sell customers products. They give them details of the product. 'It works at three million mega somethings per kilo something.' 'It's got a widget in the thingamabob.' But most customers aren't interested in products. You can't sell customers products. Customers want to enjoy the *benefit* of the product. The Sumerians didn't want *writing*, the Chinese did not want *messengers*, the Egyptians did not want *horse riders* and the French people certainly did not want *semaphore stations* waving their arms all over the place. They simply wanted to send a message over a long distance. So that's the first point. Always think about the customer's wants, about the needs that your product or service satisfies.

Secondly, successful businesses have trained or skilled *personnel*. The Chinese system had men who knew the way to another town or area. The Egyptian system was more complex. It had horse riders and personnel who looked after the horses at each stop. The French system was even more complex. It had skilled operators who worked the semaphore machinery. The Chinese probably didn't teach their couriers the routes – they knew them already. The Egyptians probably didn't train their horse riders. They employed skilled riders. But the French certainly trained their semaphore operators. So here's the second point. A successful business needs skilled personnel. It either employs them *or* teaches them the special skills which the business needs.

So, to recap. A successful business supplies customers with benefits, and employs or trains skilled people. But successful businesses need something else, and this is sometimes out of their control. What is it?

Well, the Chinese system needed a road between A and B. So did the Egyptian system. The French system didn't need roads, but it needed buildings every few kilometres to relay the signal. This is the third key element. Most businesses need an *infrastructure* – a system of roads, railway lines, air routes, sea lanes, plus buildings – shops, offices, warehouses. The Chinese and the Egyptian message businesses didn't build the roads. They were there already. But the French message system needed a new infrastructure system, and the French government agreed to build it. Businesses must work with existing infrastructure or they must be prepared to allocate scarce resources to new infrastructure.

Oh, I nearly forgot. Final very important point. The semaphore system was very expensive to build and to maintain. Of course, you can spread the cost over all messages, but still each message was expensive. But the system was very fast and very secure, so the government was prepared to pay the high cost. In this case, the government was also the customer, but the principle is the same. If you provide higher benefits, some people will be prepared to pay more for the same basic product or service.

Right. So, think about the key principles – benefits, personnel and infrastructure – as we consider the next invention. It's the telegraph. First I'll tell you how it worked and then we'll look at how it met the principles. The name *telegraph* comes from two Greek words: *tele*, which means 'distant', and *graph*, which, in Greek, means 'writing'. How did the telegraph work? One person keyed in letters on a machine. They travelled as electrical signals to another machine, in another town. The second machine printed the letters on strips of paper. Mostly, the system was used by the railways, so there were telegraph wires between all the stations to carry the messages. But there were problems with the telegraph. Firstly, the letters were in code. It was called Morse code, after the inventor, Samuel Morse. Someone had to turn the letters into Morse at one end, and decode the Morse into letters at the other end. Secondly, only one message could travel along the telegraph line at one time. That is like a road between two towns which can only carry one car at a time. Thirdly, you needed wires connecting each telegraph office. However, in terms of speed, the telegraph was a big improvement on semaphore – and, of course, couriers on foot or horseback. The message travelled at the speed of electricity along a wire, which is, of course, the speed of light. In some ways, it was secure, because only a Morse operator could decode the message. But, on the other hand, the operator read the message before delivering it, so in that way it was insecure. So, bearing all that in mind, what benefits did the new system deliver for customers? What problems did it pose for the business, in terms of personnel and infrastructure?

So that's how the telegraph worked. Now, how did it meet the principles? Well, first, benefits. It was faster and more secure than the postal system ... Oh, dear. I see we are running out of time. So let me leave those questions with you. Benefits, personnel and infrastructure for the telegraph. We'll look at the answers next time. Then we'll move on to the telephone and the mobile. Dear me, I didn't get through very much, did I? Well, anyway, you've got the basic principles. Thank you. See you next week.

🔊 2.5

Presenter: **2.5. Lesson 2.3. Learning new listening skills: Taking notes onto handouts**

Exercise A2. Listen and check your answers.

Voice:
   a. electrical device
   b. Morse code
   c. postal system
   d. skilled personnel
   e. successful business
   f. human beings
   g. urgent message

🔊 2.6

Presenter: **2.6. Exercise C2. Listen and add notes to each slide.**

Slide 1.

Lecturer: OK. Let's consider the telephone as a business model. Remember, we need to look at three elements – the benefits of the product or service, the personnel required and the infrastructure. The fixed-line telephone provided lots of benefits over the telegraph. Firstly, it was very fast – in fact, it worked at the speed of light, because that is the speed of electricity. And it went straight from the sender to the receiver – you did not need a person to take down the message and then deliver it. And, of course, because there was no operator, the system was much more secure. It was years before people learnt how to bug, or listen in, to telephone conversations. But, coming onto personnel and infrastructure, there were drawbacks too. First, personnel. Well, of course, when the telephone was invented, there were no trained personnel. In fact, a new word was coined in about 1912, for people who answered telephone calls and connected people – *telephonist*. These people had to be trained. The company also had to train *linesmen* – people who put up the lines between towns and maintained them. They *were* all men then, but times have moved on a little. Finally, there was no infrastructure. The company needed to build telephone *exchanges* – another new term. They had to put up telephone lines to link the system together, and to lay millions of kilometres of telephone cables, including cables under the Atlantic Ocean and even the Pacific. As a result, the telephone developed really slowly.

Presenter: **Slide 2.**

Lecturer: Right, so let's compare the development of fixed-line phones and mobiles. In the process, we will learn an important business principle. First, the fixed-line phone. The device was invented in 1876 by an American, Alexander Graham Bell, but by 1890 there were only 5 million in use, most of them in the US, and even 30 years later, in 1922, there were only 20 million subscribers – that is, people with a telephone. In 1965, the total reached 300 million, doubling to 600 million by 1995 and doubling again to 1.2 billion in the next 20 years. So it took over 130 years to reach this number.

What about the mobile? Well, the device was invented in 1973 by a researcher working for Motorola, Martin Cooper. By 1985, there were 340,000 subscribers, which rose to 33 million by 1995. In 2003, just 30 years after its invention, there were 1.5 billion mobiles in the world, more mobiles than fixed-line phones. The figure stood at 4.6 billion in 2010. That's almost one telephone for every man, woman and child on Earth!

Presenter: **Slide 3.**

Lecturer: How can we explain the differences? Why did the mobile-phone customer base grow so quickly? Was it because of very high benefits to customers? Well, mobile phones certainly have high benefits for customers – for example, you can use them anywhere. You don't call a place anymore, you call a person. But fixed-line telephones probably had higher benefits back in 1876. What about personnel? To what extent did companies need to train personnel? Well, perhaps not as much as the early days of fixed-line telephones because so much of the system is automatic, so there was a saving there. But in terms of infrastructure – the mobile phone towers, for example – the phone companies had to build everything. So, in many ways, mobile phones had a similar business model to fixed-line phones. But there was one big difference. Mobile phone companies learnt an important lesson from the slow development of the fixed-line telephone. Mobile phones cost about $500 to make in the early days, but companies did not try to pass on that cost to customers. They did not charge customers $500 to have a mobile. In many cases, they gave away the handsets in return for a service contract. As a result, the installed customer base grew very quickly. How could the companies afford to give away their products? Well, they got a service contract in return and the customers paid regularly for the calls. If a business has more customers, its unit costs – its cost per customer – usually go down. So the installed customer base grew quickly *and* the mobile phone companies made money.

🎧 2.7

Presenter: **2.7. Pronunciation Check. Listen to the pronunciation of some pairs of words. Can you hear the first consonant?**

Voice:
1. send messages
2. write letters
3. make progress
4. ask questions
5. eat dinner
6. take back
7. lend money
8. find friends

🎧 2.8

Presenter: **2.8. Lesson 2.4. Grammar for listening: Ditransitive verbs; verbs with prepositions**

Grammar box 6. Table 1.

Voice: New businesses should offer customers better products.
Companies give them details of products.
They didn't teach the couriers the routes.

Presenter: **Table 2.**

Voice: New businesses should offer better products to customers.
Companies give details of products to them.
They didn't teach the routes to the couriers.

Presenter: **Table 3.**

Voice: Thieves could steal the messages from the courier.
Successful companies supply customers with benefits.
The machine printed the letters on strips of paper.

🎧 2.9

Presenter: **2.9. Exercise A. Listen to each sentence. Number the two objects you hear in each case.**

Voice:
1. I'm going to ask you a question.
2. Can you send me a message?
3. He took a message for me.
4. They told her the truth.
5. I'll bring the book to school tomorrow.
6. Could you lend us some money?
7. We are going to buy the Social Sciences lecturer a present at the end of term.
8. Telephone companies charged customers a lot of money for calls in the early days.
9. Claude Chappe showed the government his invention.
10. The semaphore stations cost thousands of francs for the government to build.

Presenter:

2.10. Lesson 2.5. Applying new listening skills: The Internet and business principles

Lecturer:

In our last lecture, we heard about three key principles of business development – real benefits for customers, skilled personnel and effective infrastructure. We looked at the case of long-distance communication where businesses began with a want. But there is another way to develop a new business. We can start with *infrastructure* and think – *What customer wants can I satisfy by using this infrastructure? What benefits can I deliver with this infrastructure?* Am I making sense? You can start with a benefit or with an infrastructure. I suppose you can even start with personnel, but that's a bit weird!

So this week, I'm going to talk about the most important infrastructure of the 21ˢᵗ century. No, it's not the M25 or any other road, and it's not Eurostar or any other railway line. It's certainly not British Airways or Ryan Air! It's the international network of computers which now covers the globe – the Internet. First, a brief bit of history, and then we're going to look at the principles of *etailing* – online selling – as opposed to *retailing* – selling on the high street.

Right, so, let's get the history out of the way. The Internet really starts at the end of the Second World War. In 1945, a man called Bush – no, not *that* one, or his father! This one is called Vannevar Bush. He had a dream. 'It must be possible,' he thought, 'to link all information in a library together.' His dream went further. 'Then we could look at the information on a screen. We wouldn't need to go to the actual books or the documents in the library at all.' He was only thinking about all the information in *one* library, but still, for Bush's dream to become a reality, a lot of inventions had to come together. Let's look at five of them quickly.

Firstly, in 1946, scientists who were working for the US Army built the first real computer. It was called ENIAC. That's E-N-I-A-C. It was enormous and it only worked for a few minutes before breaking down, but it was the start of the computer age.

Secondly, in the 1960s, a man called Ted Nelson invented a name for the connection between documents. He called it *hypertext* because *hyper* means 'over', or 'extra'. We'll come back to this important word later.

Thirdly, in 1974, the first personal computer appeared. Several companies claim the credit, including IBM, of course. The personal computer, or PC, brought the world of computing into the small business and the private home. But these PCs were 'stand-alone'. In other words, they only worked with the information on their own hard drive.

But one year later, in 1975, a man called Vincent Cerf, that's Cerf with a C, invented a way for one computer to talk to another computer. Not chatting about the weather. Sending digital data along a wire. The method was called TCP/IP. The P stands for *protocol* – rules. At that time, the two computers had to be in the same place, the same room or the same building.

But just two years later, in 1977, Dennis Hayes invented the PC modem. This connected one computer to another computer in a *different* location. And yes, you've guessed it, the connection was through the telephone lines. The name *modem* means *modulator / demodulator* by the way, if you are a computer nerd, but that's just another way of saying 'encoder' and 'decoder'. Modems put digital information into analogue form for the telephone lines and turn the analogue back into digital at the other end. This was a very important invention. But it was just like the telegraph of 100 years earlier. The connection was like a single road between two towns. Only one car could travel on it at one time. Bush's dream was still some way away.

Still, by the late 70s, we had most of the parts for the Internet. But two important pieces were missing. The big breakthrough came in 1990. Tim Berners-Lee was a British scientist working in Switzerland. He had the same dream as Bush. He wanted all the scientists in his laboratory to be able to look at each other's documents. For research, of course, not to plagiarize them! He realized that every document needed an address so you could find the document on another computer. He knew about Ted Nelson's word *hypertext*. Berners-Lee invented a way of addressing documents. He said – 'Dear document …' No, he didn't. He called the address *http – hypertext transfer protocol*. Berners-Lee also invented a simple program, called a browser. This program allowed the user of one computer to look at documents on another computer. And, hey presto – we had the Internet. You see, Al Gore really didn't invent it at all.

Berners-Lee's inventions changed the *road* from one computer to another into a *web*. This web allowed documents to appear on any computer screen on the Internet. Berners-Lee called it *the worldwide web* – or *WWW* for short. Actually, it's longer but you get the point.

Before Berners-Lee's inventions of the document address and the browser, the growth of the Internet was slow. In 1981, 213 computers could talk to each other around the world. In 1985, that number was 1,961. Just before Berners-Lee's inventions in 1990, the number reached 150,000. After Berners-Lee's inventions, the growth was incredible. By 1991, 300,000 computers could talk to each other. Five years after that, the number of computers communicating with each other was nearly 6 million and by 2000 it was 80 million. Today, it is over 4 billion.

At first, the Internet was not seen as a business opportunity. This is an important point! Write it down! In its early years, it did what Bush and Lee had imagined. It enabled academics to see the information on other computers in universities. But gradually, some businesspeople began to realize that you could market your company on the Internet. It didn't cost a lot of money to have a web presence. It was much cheaper, for example, than renting or buying advertising space in newspapers or on billboards. So, in the second phase of the Internet, it became a marketing tool. People saw a company on the Internet and then went to that shop, or restaurant, or hotel. Finally, some companies began to see the Internet as the shop itself. *Why do we need expensive high street premises?* they asked themselves. Nobody else was listening! Customers can see our products online and buy them online. Can you see the problem for a company which takes this route to developing a successful business?

To answer that question, we first have to think about how a normal retailer of books or clothes or whatever works. The company has a high street presence – a shop. Why do they have a shop in the high street? Because that's where customers go. As they say in business, always be where your customers go. Someone goes into the shop, walks around looking at the goods on display, and sees something they want. They talk to a salesperson, who is usually a skilled employee. They buy the item and pay at the till – nowadays, usually with a card. They take it home. If they don't want it, or if there is something wrong with it, they take it back to the shop and, nowadays, in most cases, they can get a full refund.

How is an online retailer – or etailer – different? Well, firstly, of course, there is no shop, no high street presence. Instead, there is a web presence. This can be a good thing. As we have seen, customers go to the web in huge numbers, but, of course, you have to make sure they come to your site – your e-shop – so perhaps you need to spend some money driving customers onto your site. Secondly, there are no salespeople, no skilled personnel. Again, this may not be a problem if customers can navigate around your e-shop easily. Thirdly, there are no tills. Again, no problem, if you have efficient, secure systems for taking payment. Fourthly, you cannot take the goods home with you. The company has to deliver them. So, although the company is an etailer, using the *virtual* infrastructure of the Internet for marketing, sales and payment, it still needs to use the *real* infrastructure of postal delivery to get the goods to you. Finally, you cannot take the goods back, so the company also needs to use the real infrastructure of courier collection to enable you to return the goods – and, of course, it needs an efficient system of crediting back the payment to you.

OK. I see we have overrun again, so I'm going to ask you to do the next bit. Can you research either Boo.com or Amazon.com and be prepared to talk about the reasons for success or failure at the next tutorial? That's Boo – B-double O, and of course Amazon you know anyway. Thank you.

🌐 2.11

Presenter:	**2.11. Lesson 2.6. Vocabulary for speaking: Living with communication disability**
	Exercise B. Listen to the case studies of Maria, Alfred and Elena from the lecture.
Lecturer:	In this lecture, I'm going to talk about communication disability from the point of view of employment. Can people with communication disabilities work? Of course they can. But society needs to help them in many ways to get into the workplace. We need to make sure employers do not discriminate against people because of their disabilities. I mean, employers mustn't reject people for recruitment or promotion simply because of their disability.
	OK. We're going to consider three cases during this lecture. We'll come back to them on several occasions. Firstly, we have the case of Maria. Maria is 55 now. She can't see but she was not blind from birth. She lost her sight in a car accident. However, she deals with her blindness extremely well. She has learnt Braille so she can read and write again. She has a guide dog. She now works full time in a call centre. Secondly, there is Alfred. He's 28. Alfred can't hear but he wasn't deaf when he was born. He lost his hearing as a result of an illness when he was 18. He deals with his deafness very well. He has learnt lip-reading and sign language. He now works as a signer at the United Nations. He listens to speeches at meetings and signs the information for people who are deaf or hearing-impaired.
	Finally, Elena. Elena is only seven. She can't speak. She has impaired speaking. As you probably know already, it is unacceptable these days to refer to people as *mute* or, even worse, *dumb*. She was born deaf, and deaf people have great difficulty in learning to speak. There is nothing wrong with Elena's speech *organs*, but her deafness means that she does not know how to make speech *sounds*. However, she is working intensively with a speech therapist to help her to produce speech.
	OK. So, those are our three cases. As I said, we will return to them several times …

🌐 2.12

Presenter:	**2.12. Lesson 2.7. Real-time speaking: Braille – reading and writing for the blind**
	Exercise C1. Listen to a student giving information about Braille to a study group. How does she talk about dates, ages and time periods?
Student A:	I'm going to tell you about the inventor of Braille. In fact, he gave his name to the system – I mean, he was called Braille – Louis Braille. He was born in 1809 in a small town near Paris. His father was a saddle-maker. Louis wasn't blind from birth. He had an accident in his father's workshop when he was three. He was playing with an awl when he hit his eye with the tool.
Student C:	That's terrible! What an awful thing!
Student B:	Sorry. What's a nawl?
Student A:	It's not a nawl. It's an awl. A-W-L.
Student C:	I don't understand. Was he blinded in both eyes at once?
Student A:	No. He damaged his right eye and then his left eye got infected.
Student B:	That's dreadful.
Student A:	Yes, it is. Anyway, where was I?
Student B:	I can't remember.
Student C:	I've forgotten, too.
Student B:	Oh, yes. You were talking about the accident.
Student A:	That's right. He lost his sight in both eyes. He went to normal school for three years but he didn't learn much. From 1815 to 1819 he didn't go to school. Then in 1819, at the age of ten, he went to the National Institute for the Blind in Paris. While he was studying there, he learnt a system of reading for the blind. It involved large raised letters of the normal alphabet. Braille thought there must be a better way.

Presenter:	**2.13. Exercise D1. Listen and repeat some of the sentences from the presentation. Copy the pronunciation, including the pauses.**
Student A:	a. When he was three, he had an accident in his father's workshop.
	b. From 1815 to 1819, he didn't go to school.
	c. At the age of six, he left normal school.
	d. Then in 1819, at the age of ten, he went to the National Institute for the Blind in Paris.
	e. Sixteen years after his death, Braille became the worldwide standard.

Presenter:	**2.14. Exercise E2. Listen to a student presenting the information. What extra comments do the students make?**
Student A:	For eight years, from 1821, he worked on his own system. He raised dots instead of letters. In his system, he used …
Student B:	Sorry. What are dots?
Student A:	They're small circles. He used an awl to raise the letters. In fact, he used the same tool which blinded him.
Student B:	That's an incredible coincidence!
Student C:	I don't know. He was probably thinking about the accident all the time.
Student A:	That's true. Now, … I've forgotten what I was going to say.
Student B:	You were going to tell us about his system.
Student A:	Oh, yes. In his system, he used six dots. He finished it in 1829. A year before then, he became a teacher at the institute. However, he was not allowed to teach his own system. Isn't that stupid?! But while he was teaching the old method, he continued to work on his new one, and in 1837 he added symbols for maths and for music. So he didn't stop with symbols for the alphabet. Braille died in 1852 when he was only 43, but his system went on to be used all around the world. Just six months after his death, the National Institute switched to Braille's method and in 1868, his system was accepted as the world standard. So, a poor blind boy invented a system which is used all over the world today. Isn't it amazing, the way he dealt with his blindness and achieved so much?

Presenter:	**2.15. Everyday English: Talking on the phone**
	Exercise B2. Listen and complete the conversations.
	Conversation 1.
Voice A:	Hello. Could you give me David Marshall's e-mail address please?
Voice B:	Certainly. It's d dot marshall, with two l's, at hadford dot a-c dot u-k.
Voice A:	Thank you.
Voice B:	You're welcome. Bye.
Presenter:	**Conversation 2.**
Voice A:	*[recording]* The person you have called is not available. Please leave a message after the tone.
Voice B:	Hi Katia. It's Piera. Give me a call when you pick up this message. OK, talk to you later. Bye.
Presenter:	**Conversation 3.**
Voice A:	Hi Stef. It's Peter. How are you?
Voice B:	Hi. Fine. I can't hear you very well. Can you speak up?
Voice A:	Do you know Alan's mobile number?
Voice B:	You're breaking up. Can you hang up and redial?
Presenter:	**Conversation 4.**
Voice A:	Hi, is that Carlo?
Voice B:	Sorry, I think you've got the wrong number.
Voice A:	Oh, sorry.
Voice B:	No problem. Bye.
Presenter:	**Conversation 5.**
Voice A:	*[recording]* If you are calling about bus times, press 1. If you require information about family or student passes, or about Day Rover tickets, please press 2. For all other enquiries, please hold.
	… You are in a queue. One of our operators will be with you as soon as possible.
Presenter:	**Conversation 6.**
Voice A:	Send me a text this afternoon. My phone's always on.
Voice B:	OK. What's your number?
Voice A:	It's oh double-seven four, triple-five nine, one seven three.
Voice B:	Got it. I'll text you later.

Presenter: **2.16. Lesson 2.8. Learning new speaking skills: Repairing communication**

Exercise A2. Listen, check and practise.

Voice:
a. accept
b. accident
c. adopt
d. institute
e. inventor
f. standard
g. system
h. worldwide

Presenter: **2.17. Exercise B3. Listen, check and practise.**

Voice:
a. He was born in a small town near Paris.
b. He wasn't blind from birth.
c. He left normal school three years later.
d. He invented a system of reading.
e. He became a teacher at his old school.
f. He died in Paris in 1852.

Presenter: **2.18. Exercise C3. Listen to the extract. Check your answers.**

Voice A: He was playing with an awl when he hit his eye with the tool.
Voice B: Sorry. What's a nawl?
Voice A: It's not a nawl. It's an awl.
Voice C: I don't understand. Was he blinded in both eyes at once?
Voice A: No. He damaged his right eye and then his left eye got infected.
Voice B: That's dreadful!
Voice A: Yes, it is. Anyway, where was I?
Voice B: I can't remember.
Voice C: I've forgotten, too.
Voice B: Oh, yes. You were talking about the accident.
Voice A: That's right.

Presenter: **2.19. Pronunciation Check. Listen and copy the linking and suppressing.**

Voice A: He was blinded in an accident.
It's a pointed tool.

Presenter: **2.20. Lesson 2.9. Grammar for speaking: Using the past continuous**

Grammar box 7. Listen to the sentences in the tables.

Voice: Braille was playing with an awl when he hit his eye.
When he hit his eye, he damaged it.
While the children were studying at the institute, they learnt a system of reading.

Presenter: **3.1. Theme 3: Media and advertising**
Lesson 3.1. Vocabulary for listening: Violence in stories for children

Exercise B1. Listen to part of a talk about fairy tales. Answer the questions.

Lecturer: So, as we have heard, psychologists say that young children need to experience fear. Fairy tales, like Little Red Riding Hood, bring fear into the child's life. Fairy tales were very violent, originally. People were eaten, burnt in an oven, poisoned. The violence is often against children or young people – think of Hansel and Gretel, and Goldilocks. People are aggressive. Even animals are aggressive – the Father Bear in the Goldilocks story deals with Goldilocks with aggression. In the 18ᵗʰ century,

d. Of course, there are counter-arguments.
e. There was no increase in aggression.
f. These children are more likely to get into trouble with the authorities.

 3.7

Presenter: **3.7. Exercise B1. Listen to part of the lecture again. How does the lecturer introduce the counter-argument?**

Lecturer: *[fade in]* Watching TV violence is a bad thing and has bad consequences. If children see a lot of violence, you expect them to behave violently, don't you? But is that proposition actually correct?

Now, I accept that children have to experience fear, and learn how to deal with it. Clearly, this is why we have fairy tales, which are full of murders, kidnappings and violent acts. I agree that these stories are just as violent as kids' TV programmes. Just think of Hansel and Gretel, who push the witch into the bread oven and kill her. Or Little Red Riding Hood, in which Grandma is eaten by the wolf and then cut from his stomach, in some versions of the story at least. Fairy tales are very old and presumably perform a useful function in education, so this is a very powerful argument.

But we must take into account several factors. *[fade out]*

3.8

Presenter: **3.8. Exercise C. Listen to sections from three lectures. What's the lecturer's argument in each case? What counter-arguments does he or she concede?**

Lecture 1: Friendship in the 21st century

Lecturer 1: I'm here today to talk about friendship. Clearly, it's as old as human life on Earth. But there is evidence that it is changing for this new generation. Friendship used to mean meeting people, talking to them face to face, doing things together. Surely that is real friendship? Well, not according to some sociologists. They say that virtual friends are as real as physical friends. In fact, research in America suggests that some children do not distinguish between the two kinds of friend at all. I am not sure that this is a good thing. In my view, having friends involves meeting people face to face.

OK. I accept that online acquaintances serve a purpose. I agree that it is very nice to be able to exchange information with people in different towns, even different countries and continents. Obviously, a lot of people get a lot of benefit from virtual relationships. But people who you only meet online are not friends in the true sense of the word. Friendship means meeting people, talking to them face to face, doing things together.

Lecture 2: Time management

Lecturer 2: We've talked a lot about time management today. Let me end with a key point. It's called the Work–Life Balance. It means simply, you must balance your work and your social life. Now, of course, you have to keep up-to-date with your current work. Clearly, you must not get behind with projects and assignments because it is so much harder to manage your time if you have previous work to do as well as current. And I accept that work comes first a lot of the time.

But you must make sure you save enough of your time and your energy for your friends and your family. If you don't, you will find one day you have a wonderful job and a terrible life.

Lecture 3: Going green

Lecturer 3: I want to finish talking about environmental projects with a personal plea. Be careful about making so-called green decisions. The environment is a very complex place. It's absolutely true that we can make a big difference if every one of us makes a number of small changes to the way we live. It's right to turn down the thermostat on your central heating. Of course, you should save energy by switching off lights when you leave a room, and not leaving appliances on standby for hours and hours. But sometimes things are more complex than they seem. For example, growing tomatoes in Spain and shipping them to the UK uses less energy than growing them in greenhouses in the UK. So buying local produce may not be the greenest option.

3.9

Presenter: **3.9. Pronunciation Check. Listen to the pronunciation of each phrase. Can you hear the extra sound?**

Voice: a twelve-year-old
Grandma is eaten
used to aggression
you expect the average child
be able to cope

Presenter: **3.10. Skills Check. Listen. What other words and phrases can you use in place of each word in italics?**

Voice:
I *accept* that children have to experience fear.
It's true that children have to learn how to deal with fear.
Clearly, this is why we have fairy tales.
I *agree* that these stories are just as violent as kids' TV programmes.
It's a fact that Hansel and Gretel are violent.
Obviously there is violence in Little Red Riding Hood.
I *realize* that fairy tales perform a useful function in education.
Of course, this is a very powerful argument.

Presenter: **3.11. Lesson 3.4. Grammar for listening: verb + gerund; verb + *that*. Grammar box 10.**

Voice:
Children are used to seeing aggression.
Parents keep telling them not to fight.
TV executives deny being responsible for real-life violence.
Children spend a lot of time watching television on their own.
We should stop TV companies broadcasting violent children's programmes.
I recall my mother telling me fairy stories.

Presenter: **3.12. Exercise A. Listen to some sentences. Number the gerund you hear in each case.**

Voice 1: I remember using the television as a childminder.
Voice 2: I regret doing it now.
Voice 3: Have you finished reading the article about TV habits?
Voice 4: How can we prevent children watching too much television?
Voice 5: My lecturer suggested controlling TV for young children.
Voice 6: Dr Singer proposed stopping young children from watching TV on their own.
Voice 7: Do you mind your children seeing violence on TV?
Voice 8: I really resent people telling me how to bring up my children.
Voice 9: The TV executive defended producing violent cartoons for children.

Presenter: **3.13. Grammar box 11.**

Voice:
I accept that children need to experience fear.
Research suggests that children's programmes are more violent than adult TV.
Parke et. al. concluded that there was a significant increase in aggression.

Presenter: **3.14. Exercise B. Listen to some sentences. Number the function of the sentence in each case.**

Voice:
1. I predict that the problem will get worse.
2. I imagine that you have all seen violent children's programmes.
3. Researchers have calculated that children spend more time watching television than attending school.
4. Newton demonstrated that each force has an equal and opposite force.
5. Dr Singer said that TV should be treated as a stranger.
6. Doctors suspect that the disease started in chickens.
7. I recognize that many programmes are educational.
8. The results suggested that there was a serious problem.
9. People thought that the Earth was flat.

Presenter: **3.15. Exercise C. Listen to the start of some sentences. What do you expect to hear next – gerund or *that*?**

Voices:
1. I realize …
2. The lecturer dislikes …
3. Doctors suspect …
4. Dr Singer said …
5. Have you finished …?
6. People thought …
7. How can we prevent children …?
8. I imagine …
9. I predict …
10. Do you mind your children …?
11. Researchers have calculated …
12. I really resent people …
13. I recognize …
14. I remember …
15. Newton demonstrated …
16. The results suggested …

🕙 3.16

Presenter: **3.16. Lesson 3.5. Applying new listening skills: Let's ban television!**

Exercise A. Listen to the stressed syllables from each word or phrase. Number the correct word in each case.

Voice:
1. cour
2. gree
3. rea
4. stand
5. ob
6. clear
7. ev
8. rect

🕙 3.17 DVD 3.B

Guest speaker: I'm here today to ask for the impossible. I want you all to stop watching television. I'm not asking this because television programmes are bad, although that is a small part of the argument. I'm asking this because *television* is bad – bad for physical health, bad for mental health, bad for critical thinking and bad for good government. Where does this idea come from? In 1978, a man called Jerry Mander wrote a book called *Four Arguments for the Elimination of Television*. Let's have a look at each of those arguments.

OK. So … What's the first argument against television? It is that television reduces everything to very simple messages. Television is not a good medium for complex ideas. You need books for that. So instead, it gives us very simple ideas and repeats them again and again. There is only a small number of programmes which convey real information about the world, but those programmes are split into many small sections, with adverts in between, and, at the beginning of each section, the previous sections are quickly recapped. This is not the way to put across complex ideas. AC Nielsen, an organization that monitors television output, estimates that an average American child spends 900 hours a year at school, and 1,500 hours watching television. Incidentally, most of the statistics in this lecture are from Nielsen. Check them out on Nielsen.com. Anyway, I accept that television brings the world into your living room. I realize that television occasionally inspires children to learn something, do something, become something. And of course there are programmes about other countries, about the natural world and about history. But in most cases, the information is very limited.

Mander said that information is turned into repeated slogans. For example, foreign countries are 'exotic or scary'. Animals are 'furry or scary'. History is a few very famous events, particularly the Second World War, because they have lots of film of that historic event. On average, people in the United States see 20,000 adverts a year. People can recognize thousands of brands but only a few countries on the world map, a few plants, birds and trees. Television brings the world into our living rooms but it stops us having the time to go out and experience it for ourselves. Americans may think they know about the world because they have seen it on TV, but researchers have calculated that more than 75 per cent of Americans don't even own a passport. In the end, most people only know the world that is brought to them by television. Celebrity and sport, mindless quiz shows and reality shows – which aren't anything like reality – are more important than the environment and politics. Of course, people need to relax, and television is a wonderful way of unwinding. But the quality of programmes is getting worse and worse – we call it 'dumbing down' in Britain … and we'll come back to this later.

Guest speaker: The second argument concerns the control of television. The medium reaches millions of people in each country, but only a small number of people in each case – perhaps only one person – controls *all* of the broadcast output. That puts him – it is always a man – in the position of a dictator. According to freepress.net, six companies own nearly all of the television output in the United States. In many cases, they own the complete production and broadcasting process. The same six companies own large percentages of television output in many other countries in the Western world. Obviously, democratic countries have regulators who try to control the controllers. I agree that there are often laws which try to ensure some competition and some balance in news reporting. But television companies and their owners have become more powerful in many cases than the lawmakers in many countries. People watch Fox News – they don't look for news balance on a number of different channels.

The third argument involves the effect of television upon individual minds and bodies. Firstly, minds. The medium is addictive. According to psychologists, there are a number of measures of *dependency*, a mental health condition. If a person reports that two of the measures apply to them for a particular item – like drugs, or alcohol, or gambling – they are suffering from a clinical condition. They are dependent on the item. Just think about your use of television. Firstly, do you use it as a sedative – to wind down at the end of a stressful day? Secondly, do you use it indiscriminately – do you plan your viewing, or do you channel hop? Do you find there is nothing interesting on, but keep watching anyway? Thirdly, do you have control over your viewing – or do you just do it? The fourth measure is: Do you feel angry that you have wasted your time watching it? Number 5: Are you upset if you are not able to watch – because the hotel room doesn't have a television, for example? As I said, if you answered yes to two or more of those, you are dependent on television.

The problem is, watching television is largely a solitary occupation. I realize that, in a golden age, television brought the family together in one room. Everyone sat down together and watched the same programme, discussed it, laughed or cried at it. My parents recall watching television with their parents. But now many houses have three, four, five televisions. For example, 66 per cent of Americans have three or more televisions so, in most cases, each person is on their own, in a different room, watching a different, probably pointless programme. Research shows that, on average, parents spend 1,680 minutes a week watching television, and 3.5 minutes having meaningful conversations with their children. This must have an effect on the relationship between children and parents. And research indicates that it does. In a recent survey, 54 per cent of American children said they preferred the TV to their father.

So that's minds. What about bodies? Well, during their 28 hours per week watching television, children see a lot of adverts. Let's just think about one horrific statistic. In an average four-hour programme of Saturday morning cartoons, American children see 200 adverts for junk food. Is this why 11 per cent of 6- to 17-year-olds in the US are now obese – double the figure 20 years ago? Oh, and of course, all those beautiful people on television have a bad effect too. Seventy-five per cent of American women think that they are too fat. Of course, if they only eat the junk food from the adverts, it might be true.

Finally, the fourth argument claims that television has no *democratic* potential. In other words, it is impossible for ordinary people to become involved. Obviously, ordinary people are *on* television all the time now, as participants, in silly quiz shows and talent contests. Of course, they are asked their opinions in the street, and they are interviewed after a crime or an accident. But they cannot contribute to the *making* of programmes, or the decision-making on the content of programmes. I realize that there is community television in some areas but this is a tiny, tiny percentage of the total output, which nobody watches anyway.

OK. So, to sum up … Mander had four arguments against television. He believed that television reduces everything to simple messages in a complex world. He thought that a small number of people controlled television and therefore could control people. He said that television was bad for minds and bad for bodies. And finally, he maintained that television was bad for democracy – the people could not get involved. What do you think? Thank you very much.

🔊 3.19

Presenter: **3.19. Exercise E2. Listen and check.**

Voice: a. AC Neilsen estimates that an American child spend 900 hours a year at school and 1,500 hours watching television.
b. On average, people in the States see 20,000 adverts a year.
c. Researchers have calculated that 75 per cent of Americans don't own a passport.
d. Only six companies own the majority of television output in the United States, and in large parts of the Western world.
e. Sixty-six per cent of Americans have three or more televisions.
f. On average, an American parent spends 1,680 minutes a week watching television and 3.5 minutes having a meaningful conversation with their children.
g. In a survey, 54 per cent of American children said they preferred television to their father.
h. In the average four-hour programme of Saturday morning cartoons, children see 200 adverts for junk food.
i. In the US, 11 per cent of 7- to 17-year-olds are obese.
j. Seventy-five per cent of American women believe they are too fat.

3.20. Lesson 3.6. Vocabulary for speaking: Selling a product

Exercise A2. Listen to a group of students doing the first choice in the assignment. Complete the advertising brief.

Student A:	So, how are we going to sell this product?
Student B:	We could use a star from the movies … or is that too expensive?
Student C:	Yes, I think so. What about a TV personality, someone from sports television – Elliot Horn?
Student A:	OK. Do we ask him to present the advert?
Student B:	No, just to endorse it. You know, he says: 'I always drive Hitoshi,' or something like that.
Student C:	Is that the slogan?
Student B:	No, that's the endorsement. We need something catchy for the slogan.
Student C:	Yes, something that will appeal to the target market. What is the audience, by the way?
Student B:	It says here: 'Young men' … and sporty women, perhaps?
Student A:	OK. It's a convertible, right? And a sports car? So what about 'Get in the open air … fast!'
Student B:	Maybe … Shall we have a special offer of some sort?
Student A:	There's one already. The manufacturers will pay the VAT if you order before 31ˢᵗ July.
Student C:	That's fantastic!
Student A:	But we should have a competition, too. Maybe get them to register for a test drive to enter, then we get their names and e-mail addresses for future marketing.
Student C:	What's the prize? A brand new ZX, I suppose.
Student B:	The car will be released on 1ˢᵗ August, by the way.
Student C:	So what's the main selling point?
Student B:	Value for money. It's a sports car but they say it does 80 kilometres to the litre.
Student A:	They're exaggerating, of course.
Student B:	Yes, but the tests show that it's very economical.

🌐 3.21

Presenter: **3.21. Exercise B2. Listen and check.**

Voice: a. endorse, order, audience, August, money, sports
b. appeal, release, litre, competition, e-mail, need
c. slogan, show, product, offer, suppose, economical
d. exaggerate, catchy, value, star, personality, address

🌐 3.22

Presenter: **3.22. Exercise C2. Listen and check.**

Voice A:	So, how are we going to sell this product?
Voice B:	We could use a star from the movies.
Voice A:	Do we ask him to present the advert?
Voice B:	No, just to endorse it.
Voice A:	We need something catchy for the slogan.
Voice B:	Yes, something that will appeal to the target market.
Voice A:	Shall we have a special offer of some sort?
Voice B:	There's one already.
Voice A:	We should have a competition, too.
Voice B:	What's the prize?
Voice A:	What's the main selling point?
Voice B:	I think it's 'value for money'.

🌐 3.23

Presenter: **3.23. Lesson 3.7. Real-time speaking: Jingles, tag lines, punchlines and other tricks**

Exercise B3. Listen to some students and complete the information about the second method.

Tutor:	So, I hope you all know about TV ads now, and you've got lots of examples of TV advertising to share with us today. Joe, could you start us off with one of the methods?
Joe:	OK. Um. I worked with Sarah on this research. We chose BOGOF, which is Buy One, Get One Free.
Student 1:	Sorry. I don't understand.
Joe:	What I'm saying is, it's the first letter of each one. Buy One, Get One Free.
Student 1:	Oh, I see.
Joe:	So, customers who buy a packet of biscuits, for example, get another packet free.
Sarah:	The advertisers who use this method usually start with the normal price, then give the offer. They emphasize the value for money.
Student 2:	So what's the science behind this method?

Sarah:	I'm just coming to that. Apparently, people don't want cheap products. They want expensive products cheaply.
Student 3:	Did you find any good examples of BOGOF on TV at the moment? We couldn't find any.
Sarah:	Sorry. Can I deal with that in a second? So they pay full price for one product and get the second one free. And, um … ah. I've forgotten what I was going to say.
Student 3:	You were going to give us examples on TV at the moment.
Sarah:	Oh, yes. There's an advert which uses BOGOF for Superbuy supermarkets. Twenty products which are basics are in the promotion, like bread and milk.
Student 2:	But going back to Joe's example for a minute. BOGOF is the same as half price, isn't it? You get two of them for the price of one. So why don't they just say 'Get these biscuits half price'?
Joe:	Yes, I wondered about that too. So I did a bit more research. Psychologists say that the word *free* is very powerful, more powerful than *half price*.
Student 3:	So BOGOF sells more products than 'Get one half price'?
Joe:	Yes. Apparently, it does.
Student 3:	That's weird.
Joe:	Not really. As Sarah has said, people want something for nothing.
Student 3:	I still think they're the same thing.
Joe:	Perhaps you're right.
Student 4:	I don't know if this is relevant, but I read that supermarkets use BOGOF with products that are loss-leaders.
Tutor:	Yes, that's a good point.
Student 5:	Sorry I'm late!
Tutor:	That's OK. We're talking about adverts that use BOGOF. We've discussed customers who want free things. The example is the Superbuys campaign.
Student 5:	Right. Has anyone mentioned that BOGOF products are often loss-leaders?
Tutor:	Yes, we've just talked about that.
Joe:	That's it, really.
Sarah:	Yes. That's what we found.

🌐 3.24

Presenter: **3.24. Exercise C2. Listen to some expressions from the extracts. Repeat, copying the stress and intonation.**

| Voice: | I worked with Sarah on this research.
We chose BOGOF, which means Buy One, Get One Free.
Sorry. I don't understand. Is it a word?
I still don't get what you mean.
What I'm saying is, it's the first letter of each word. Buy One, Get One Free.
Apparently, people don't want cheap products.
I'm just coming to that.
Sorry. Can I deal with that in a second?
And, um, ah. I've forgotten what I was going to say.
You were going to give us examples on TV at the moment. |

🌐 3.25

Presenter: **3.25. Everyday English: Complaining**

Exercise B1. Listen to the conversations below. What is the complaint in each case?

Conversation 1.

Voice A:	Hello, reception.
Voice B:	Ah, yes. This is Mr Adams in Room 306.
Voice A:	Yes, Mr Adams. How may I help you?
Voice B:	I'm afraid the air conditioning isn't working.
Voice A:	Have you tried changing the thermostat?
Voice B:	Yes, it doesn't do anything.
Voice A:	OK. I'll send someone up.
Voice B:	Thank you.

Presenter: **Conversation 2.**

Voice A:	Excuse me.
Voice B:	Yes, madam?
Voice A:	Well, we have been waiting a long time.
Voice B:	I'm sorry. Have you ordered yet?
Voice A:	No. We haven't even seen the menu.
Voice B:	OK. Sorry. Here you are.
Voice A:	Thanks.
Voice B:	Now, what would you like?
Voice A:	Could you give us a moment?
Voice B:	Oh, yes. Sorry.

Presenter:	**Conversation 3.**
Voice A:	Can I help you?
Voice B:	I hope so. I bought this iPod here a few days ago but when I unpacked it, I found the screen was cracked. See?
Voice A:	Oh, dear. OK, so have you got the receipt?
Voice B:	No, I think I've lost it.
Voice A:	Well, we can replace the item but I'm afraid we can't give you a refund.
Voice B:	No, that's OK. I want a replacement.
Voice A:	Right. Just give me a moment. I'll get the form.
Voice B:	Thanks.

🌐 **3.26**

Presenter:	**3.26. Learning new speaking skills: Linking to a previous speaker**
	Exercise A3. Listen, check and practise.
Voice:	a. BOGOF products are often loss-leaders.
	b. I worked with Sarah on this research.
	c. It's on TV at the moment.
	d. So I did a bit more research.
	e. The word *free* is very powerful.
	f. You get two of them.

🌐 **3.27**

Presenter:	**3.27. Exercise C. Listen to some sentences about information in this course so far.**
Voice:	1. Visual learners don't like noise.
	2. Whales are the largest mammals on Earth.
	3. Carbon is released by trees at night.
	4. Braille was not allowed to teach his system.
	5. The Ogallala Aquifer will be dry in 200 years.
	6. Aural learners need to talk about information.
	7. Fleming was studying bacteria at the time.
	8. Rote learning is useful for lists of things.
	9. British sign language is different from American sign language.
	10. The Indian government may privatize water supply.

🌐 **3.28**

Presenter:	**3.28. Pronunciation Check. Listen and copy the intrusive sounds.**
Voice:	They are all in the promotion.
	They are all in the promotion.
	Have you all looked at the examples?
	Have you all looked at the examples?

🌐 **3.29**

Presenter:	**3.29. Skills Check. Listen to some sentences with linking expressions.**
Voice:	As Joe has said, advertisers sometimes use bribes.
	Taking up Sarah's point, tag lines are very important.
	Going back to Joe's point, jingles sell products.
	Returning to Sarah's point, people believe big lies.
	I don't know if this is relevant, but the word *free* is very powerful.
	I'm not sure if this is related, but advertisers use bribes a lot to sell children's products.
	Has anyone mentioned that viral advertising is very important nowadays?

🌐 **3.30**

Presenter:	**3.30. Lesson 3.9. Grammar for speaking: Noun phrases with relative clauses**
	Grammar box 12. Listen to the sentences. Where do the speakers pause?
Voice:	We are talking about adverts which use BOGOF.
	Adverts are targeted at people who might buy the product.

🌑 3.31

Presenter:	**3.31. Exercise A. Listen and check.**
Voice:	a. There are many ads which use BOGOF. b. A jingle is a tune which is memorable. c. A tag line is a slogan which contains the name of the product. d. A big name is a person who is famous for movies, sport or television. e. A big name ad contains a personality who endorses the product. f. A bribe is money which encourages someone to do something. g. A punchline is an ending which is funny and makes people laugh. h. Ads with punchlines have a set-up which prepares people for a particular ending. i. A narrative is a story which is usually in many episodes. j. People may like the characters who appear in narrative ads.

🌑 3.32

Presenter:	**3.32. Grammar box 13. Listen to the sentences. Where does the speaker pause?**
Voice:	Customers who buy a packet of biscuits get another packet free. Twenty products which are basics are in the promotion.

🌑 3.33

Presenter:	**3.33. Exercise B2. Listen and check your ideas.**
Voices:	a. Advertisers who use BOGOF start the advert with the normal price. b. People who are aural learners need to hear new information. c. Farmers in the States who use irrigation are worried about the future. d. A third of the water which is used for irrigation comes from the Ogallala Aquifer. e. People who apologize a lot often give a reason for their actions.

🌑 4.1

Presenter:	**4.1. Theme 4: Living life to the full** **Lesson 4.1. Vocabulary for listening: Cells, tissues and organs** **Exercise A1. Listen and write the number of each word in the correct place on the diagram.**
Voice:	1. ankle 2. arm 3. chest 4. elbow 5. foot 6. hand 7. hip 8. knee 9. neck 10. ribs 11. shoulder 12. thigh 13. wrist 14. head

🌑 4.2

Presenter:	**4.2. Exercise C1. Listen to part of a lecture about physiology. When the lecturer stops, number the next word.**
Lecturer:	1. OK. So first let's look at the levels of organization that make up the human … 2. At the lowest level, we have the cell. This is the smallest unit of life and every part of the body is composed of … 3. These cells can take in nutrients, convert nutrients to energy or carry out specialized … 4. Cells are grouped into tissues. Each kind of tissue is designed for a particular … 5. For example, muscular tissue is able to contract while nervous tissue conducts … 6. At the next level, some tissues combine to achieve a particular objective. These tissues are called organs. For example, the stomach, the lungs and the … 7. At an even higher level of organization, we have organ … 8. In each system, different organs work together – for example, the mouth, the stomach, the small intestine and the large intestine all play a role in … 9. The highest level is a group of organs working … 10. Groups of organs in the same body are called organisms. For example, humans, animals and …

4.3

<table>
<tr><td>Presenter:</td><td>**4.3. Exercise C2. Listen and check your answers.**</td></tr>
</table>

1. OK. So first, let's look at the levels of organization that make up the human body.
2. At the lowest level, we have the cell. This is the smallest unit of life and every part of the body is composed of cells.
3. These cells can take in nutrients, convert nutrients to energy or carry out specialized functions.
4. Cells are grouped into tissues. Each kind of tissue is designed for a particular purpose.
5. For example, muscular tissue is able to contract, while nervous tissue conducts electricity.
6. At the next level, some tissues combine to achieve a particular objective. These tissues are called organs. For example, the stomach, the lungs and the heart.
7. At an even higher level of organization, we have organ systems.
8. In each system, different organs work together – for example, the mouth, the stomach, the small intestine and the large intestine all play a role in digestion.
9. The highest level is a group of organs working together.
10. Groups of organs in the same body are called organisms. For example, humans, animals and plants.

4.4 DVD **4.A**

<table>
<tr><td>Presenter:</td><td>**Lesson 4.2. Real-time listening: organ systems**</td></tr>
<tr><td>Lecturer:</td><td>Welcome, everyone, to this core course in Physiology. I understand we have BioMed students, Sports Science students and some others, so I hope you all find this a useful introduction to Human Biology. OK. In today's lecture, we're going to look at some of the different body systems and their functions in humans. Then next time, we will look briefly at problems associated with each system. I'm not going to talk about all the systems, because I just want to give you an overview. But I will talk about the function of each system and some of the components. I will also try to show you how systems fit together, I mean, the way in which one system helps another system or enables it to operate. How they are interrelated, in other words. I've given you a handout with the systems on – have you all got one of those? Good. You might want to fill in some of the detail as we go along.

Right. What I'm going to do in this session is firstly, the skeleton – the bones and so on that keep us upright. Secondly, I'm going to mention the way the muscles enable the bones to move, and then, thirdly, the nervous system which sends messages to the muscles from the brain. So that's the skeletal system, the muscular system and the nervous system. Next, the digestive system – the stomach, and so on. Of course, it's this system that supplies the nutrients to enable the other systems to work, to grow and to repair. OK. Where was I? Let's see. Skeleton, muscles, nerves, digestion – ah, yes, right. What comes next is the respiratory system – the mouth and nose – breathing, if you like, although I'm going to point out that it's a bit more than that. Then finally, we have the circulatory system, based on the heart, which sends the blood around the body.</td></tr>
</table>

4.5 DVD **4.B**

<table>
<tr><td>Lecturer:</td><td>Right, so … let's consider the first system. The skeleton. What the skeleton does, basically, is keep us upright. It also gives the body its basic form, its basic shape. The human *skeletal system* is made up of 206 bones. The structure forms a strong internal framework for the body, which protects the organs involved in the other human body systems. It provides the basic strength for the rest of the body. Did you know bone can be four times as strong as concrete? Anyway, the main bones are, of course, the skull, which contains the brain, the ribs which protect most of the main organs – the heart, the lungs, the liver, the kidneys, and so on – and the pelvis, or hips, to give the bones their common name. Oh, and of course, the spine – the bones which run down the back. The spine, or vertebral column, comprises 33 bones or vertebrae. Just going back to the function of the skeleton for a moment … Bones don't only provide strength. They also store important minerals and vitamins. The bones meet at joints – for example, the hip joint and the shoulder joint, which are ball and socket joints. They give maximum movement, up, down, left, right. Then there are the knee joints and elbow joints, for example. They are hinge joints, like on a door. Oh, and I forgot to say – bones make red blood cells, too.

The next system is the *muscular system*. The muscles are attached to the skeletal bones and, basically, the primary function is to enable the body to move. Muscle tissue has the unique ability to contract. However, and this is quite interesting, it cannot then expand to its former position by itself. That's strange, isn't it? It contracts, but then it needs another muscle to work in opposition, to pull it back to its original position. These groups are called antagonistic pairs, and are the basis for human movement. *Antagonistic* … it comes from *antagonist*, clearly. Like the person in a story who opposes the hero, the protagonist. Sorry, perhaps you don't know anything about literature. Still, you get the basic idea. I understand we have a lot of people from Sports Science on this course. Well, for you, important muscles in the arms are the biceps and triceps. Across the stomach we have the abdominal muscles – from *abdomen*, of course. These are sometimes called *abs* for short. We also have the important muscles in the back of the thigh, which are often called the hamstrings. Oh, and of course, the Achilles tendon in the back of the ankle. Athletes often injure that part of their body. Now, what was I talking about? Right, the muscles are attached to the bones in pairs. Each one can only contract, but when one contracts, the other expands and vice versa. But how do we make the muscles contract? That's the next system. Oh, um, did I mention, there are over 600 muscles in the human body? And you have to learn them all. No, only joking!

It is the central nervous system that controls muscle contraction. The system is two-way. What I mean by that is, the system gathers information from nerves throughout the body and takes it to the brain through the spinal column. It uses electrical impulses. The brain is the primary processing centre for the body. If the decision is taken to react to a particular stimulus, the brain sends the necessary impulses to the muscles – electricity again. The main parts of the nervous system are the nerves, as I've just said, the brain, obviously, and the spinal cord, which runs down the spine. We can see now why the skull and the spine are so important. They protect key parts of the central nervous system. So we could say that it's the</td></tr>
</table>

nervous system that interfaces with the external environment. I mean, it gets messages *from* the environment and it tells the body to move *through* the environment. For example, it senses heat with the nerves in the fingers and tells the hand to move away.

Right, so we have seen that the skeletal system provides the basic structure for the body and the muscular system is attached to the skeletal system. The muscles need instructions to move and they come from the central nervous system. But what provides the body with the necessary energy to do things, and the nutrients to enable the body to grow and repair? Well, the *digestive system* is responsible for converting foods into usable substances along the digestive tract. These substances are then absorbed into the blood. We take food in through the mouth and down the oesophagus in the neck and chest. The food is broken down in the stomach and then absorbed into the blood stream through the walls of the intestines. But, and this is very important, at this stage, the nutrients are in the blood, they are *not* in the muscles and nerves and so on. We'll see how they get there in a few minutes.

Right, so we have supplied the blood with nutrients, but, in fact, the body cannot use those nutrients without oxygen. So we need another system. What we need is the respiratory system. Now, some people think that respiration is the same as breathing but that's not true. Respiration is not just about taking in air and giving out CO_2. It's the exchange of oxygen and carbon dioxide between cells, the blood and air in the lungs. It's the lungs which suck in air using strong muscles between the ribs … Oh, I should have talked about those muscles on the way through! They are called the *diaphragm* and they sit under the lungs. They move up and down to contract and expand the chest cavity, and that movement pulls air in and pushes carbon dioxide out. Sorry about that. Can you add the diaphragm to the muscular system?

Oh dear, I see we are nearly out of time. So, very quickly, the last system for today. We've seen that nutrients enter the blood from the digestive system, and oxygen enters the blood from the respiratory system, but of course all this is pointless if the blood just sits there and doesn't move. We need a system to move the blood around the body. We need … the circulatory system. It was an English physician, William Harvey, who discovered this system in the 17ᵗʰ century. The blood is pumped out of the heart through the arteries to the skeletal system, the muscular system, the nervous system, the digestive system and the respiratory system. The nutrients and oxygen leave the blood and enter the cells of the organs and then the blood returns to the heart through the veins.

That's enough for now. There are other systems and I'd like you to research those before the next lecture. The details are on the handout. OK. Thanks very much. In the next lecture, we'll be looking at what happens when something goes wrong with one of the systems. Oh, and I meant to point out that we have tutorials on Wednesday. I'm going to ask you questions about the systems we've talked about today, so have a look at your notes between now and then.

🌐 4.6

Presenter:	**4.6. Lesson 4.3. Learning new listening skills: Additional information in lectures** **Exercise A3. Listen to the correct pronunciation and check your ideas.**
Voice:	a. bronchi b. colon c. larynx d. nasal e. sciatic f. pharynx g. cerebellum h. trachea i. trapezius j. brachi

🌐 4.7

Presenter:	**4.7. Exercise C. Listen and make notes. Add extra information in the correct place.**
	Lecture 1: Studies of the effects of TV violence
Lecturer 1:	I'd like you to do some work on research studies into violent television. I'll give you some references to start you off and then I'd like you to find at least three more. OK, so in order, then, we have Berkovitz, 1969. He carried out a laboratory experiment with university students. The study involved participants watching violent films to see if they acted more violently than the control group. Parke et. al. worked with young offenders in an institution. The result was similar to Berkovitz. And on the other side? Well, nothing really, although there is one well-known study – this was Charlton et. al., 1999 – which looked at the introduction of television on the island of St Helena. Their results were not significant. There was no increase in aggression. Did I mention the date for Parke et. al.? It was 1977. Oh, and sorry. I forgot to say that Williams did a study with 6- to 11-year-olds in Canada. This is an interesting study, actually. The researcher looked at the impact of television on a community which did not have television before. It was in the early 70s – you'll have to find the exact date. The introduction of TV led to a significant increase in aggression in the community.
Presenter:	**Lecture 2: The history of the Internet**
Lecturer 2:	So where have we got to? Right … The late '70s. By then, we had most of the parts for the Internet in place. But an important piece was missing. The big breakthrough was made by Tim Berners-Lee, a British scientist working in Switzerland. He wanted all the scientists in his laboratory to be able to look at each other's documents. He realized that every document needed an address so you could find the document on another computer. So Berners-Lee invented a way

of addressing documents. He called the address *http – hypertext transfer protocol*. Berners-Lee also invented a simple program, called a browser. This program allowed the user of one computer to look at documents on another computer. And, hey presto – we had the Internet. Sorry, I see some of you are looking a little blank. I should have explained *hypertext*, shouldn't I? The ht in http. Berners-Lee knew about hypertext but you didn't! The idea of hypertext was invented by a man called Ted Nelson in the 1960s. It is a way of connecting documents so you can jump from one to another. And while we're going back over this, I meant to point out that this was in 1990. The Berners-Lee breakthrough, I mean.

Presenter:	**Lecture 3: A comparison of Chile and Pakistan**

Lecturer 3:

Let's look at population now. As before, I'm going to look at three sub-areas under this heading: the total population, the density and the urban:rural split. Pakistan has a large population, but Chile's is quite small. The population of Pakistan is 185 million, whereas Chile's population is about ten per cent of that size. Pakistan has a much higher density of population than Chile – 177 people per square kilometre against 20 per square kilometre. Um. Sorry. Did I mention the actual population of Chile? It's 17.3 million.

Next, land. As you know, we consider area, percentage of agricultural land and availability of natural water, that is, lakes and rivers. Both countries are large. In fact, they are almost about the same size. Pakistan has an area of 803,000 square kilometres whilst Chile is slightly smaller. Both countries have quite a high percentage of agricultural land. Pakistan has 30 per cent agricultural land and Chile has 21 per cent. Just going to back to area, Chile is 756,000 square kilometres. Where was I? Oh, yes, natural water. Both countries have permanent lakes and rivers. The most important river in Pakistan is the Indus, while the most important river in Chile is the Loa.

Ah … I forgot to give you the urban:rural split, didn't I? I think I did. Well, the population of Pakistan is more rural than the population of Chile. The split in Pakistan is 34 to 66, whereas in Chile it is 87 to 13.

🌐 4.8

Presenter: **4.8. Skills Check. Listen. What has the lecturer forgotten in each case?**

Lecturer 1:
1. I forgot to say that Harvey discovered the circulation of the blood in the 17th century.
2. Did I mention that Harvey was English?
3. I should have told you about white blood cells.
4. I meant to point out that arteries are normally bigger than veins.
5. Just going back to the skeletal system for a minute, the bones in the lower part of the spine are joined together.
6. Can you go back and add that there are special heart muscles?

🌐 4.9

Presenter: **4.9. Lesson 4.4. Grammar for listening: Cleft and pseudo-cleft sentences**

Grammar box 16. Listen to the sentences. Does the speaker pause in any of the sentences?

Voice:
What I'm going to do first is [PAUSE] talk about each system.
What the skeletal system does is [PAUSE] support the body.
What Harvey did was [PAUSE] experiment with fish and snakes.

It will be next week that we look at sports injuries.
It is the brain which controls the nervous system.
It was Harvey who discovered the circulation of the blood.

🌐 4.10

Presenter: **4.10. Exercise A1. Listen to the beginning of some questions or statements.**

Voice:
a. What is …
b. What we'll look at …
c. What Alcmaeon did …
d. What doctors …
e. What were …
f. What can …
g. What did …
h. What I'm going to …
i. What Kendrew …
j. What was …
k. What Schwann …
l. What the arteries …

Presenter:	**4.11. Exercise A2. Listen to the whole of each question or statement and check your answers.**
Voice:	a. What is the solution? b. What we'll look at first is the digestive system. c. What Alcmaeon did was distinguish between veins and arteries in 520 BCE. d. What doctors are hoping for is more research during the next ten years. e. What were we talking about? f. What can we do about the problem? g. What did Aristotle say about the heart? h. What I'm going to concentrate on next week is the functions of the cells. i. What Kendrew described in 1960 was the structure of the oxygen-carrying protein in muscles. j. What was the date of the first heart transplant? k. What Schwann discovered in 1836 was the first animal enzyme. l. What the arteries do is take oxygenated blood from the heart.

Presenter:	**4.12. Exercise C1. Listen to the beginning of some pseudo-cleft sentences. Letter the logical way to complete each sentence.**
Voice:	a. It will be next week … b. It was a man called Bell … c. It was the invention of the telephone … d. It was the telephone … e. It was in 1879 … f. It was after the invention of the telephone …

Presenter:	**4.13. Exercise C2. Listen to the whole sentence in each case and check your answers.**
Voice:	a. It will be next week that we look at the history of the telephone. b. It was a man called Bell who invented the telephone. c. It was the invention of the telephone which really began high-speed communication. d. It was the telephone which Bell invented. e. It was in 1879 that Bell invented the telephone. f. It was after the invention of the telephone that the telegraph declined in popularity.

Presenter:	**Lesson 4.5. Applying new listening skills: The PRICE of sports injuries**
Lecturer:	Welcome, everybody. This session is on dealing with sports injuries. So today we are going to look at fascinating issues like the difference between strains and sprains, and bruises and contusions. You'll know all about those by the end of today. We'll also talk here about compression and elevation, but they're not injuries. They're treatments.
	OK. Let's start by looking at this photograph. *[points in direction of screen]* What has happened here? She has hurt her leg, but what has she done, exactly? Fallen over? Twisted her ankle? Pulled a muscle? We say all these things, don't we? But what do we mean by 'twisted an ankle' or 'pulled a muscle'? These expressions don't tell us about the actual injury. To understand that, we need to look inside the body.
	Now, I hope you remember your Core Physiology course, but just in case you've forgotten everything already … let's quickly look at this illustration. What have we got here? Yes, the knee joint. Let's make sure that we can recognize the important parts of this joint – and any joint, in fact. So first, we have bones, of course. These give strength and support to the body. But we must connect the bones together. How do we do that? We use ligaments. Ligaments connect bone to bone. To put it simply, they stop the bones from pulling apart. But ligaments don't *move* the bones. What we need to move the bones are muscles. In this case, the muscles make the knee bend and straighten. So here, we have some muscles. But muscles don't connect directly to bone. We need another kind of tissue, which is called tendon. Tendons connect muscle to bone. Right, so here we have the muscle again, and this is the tendon, connecting the muscle to the bone.
	OK. Now, let's start the lecture proper. What we're going to talk about is, first, the common causes of injury and then, the basic treatment. As far as causes are concerned, there are two basic types of injury – trauma and overuse. So what we need to do is look at each of those in turn. Now, after all kinds of traumatic injury, there is always inflammation and swelling, so what I'm going to do is look at trauma – the minor types and then the major types, then what I'll do is discuss inflammation and swelling. What are they and why are they important? Then, with regards to treatment, there is a very useful acronym, PRICE – that's P-R-I-C-E – which helps us remember the basic actions. So causes of sports injury and the price of treatment, if you like. Oh, and physiotherapy. Very important kind of treatment nowadays.

Lecturer:

Right. So let's begin. Types of sports injuries. We can divide sports injuries into two types. The first is the result of trauma. The second is the result of overuse. Let's look in detail at the first kind and then I'll just say a few words about the second kind.

OK. Trauma. *Trauma* means 'a wound or shock produced by sudden physical injury'. Traumatic injuries are most common in contact sports. That is, sports where the athletes are supposed to come into contact with each other. So football is a contact sport and so is rugby, but tennis and basketball aren't. If the players come into contact with each other in basketball, for example, one or both of them will be disciplined by the referee.

Now, under trauma, we need to distinguish between minor items and major items. The first minor item is the bruise, which is the colouring of the skin after an injury. You know what happens. You bang your knee and, sometime later, it changes colour. It goes blue or purple. This change of colour is caused by blood leaking from damaged cells. So that's the first kind of minor injury.

The second minor item is called a strain – that's *strain* ... Oh, by the way, I should have said, we don't use the word *bruise* in physiology. We call this colouring of the skin a contusion. Contusion.

Now, where was I? Ah yes. The second minor item is a *strain* with a *t* and the third one is called a *sprain* with a *p*. So strain and sprain. Yes, I know. It's annoying that they are so similar in pronunciation but it is important to distinguish between these two. In a *strain*, it's the muscles that are affected. Strains happen when the muscle is torn. In a *sprain*, it's the ligaments that are damaged. They can get damaged in traumatic injuries by being displaced – I mean moved – out of alignment. And that's what we call a *sprain*. How can you remember the difference between a strain and a sprain? Well, just think of *muscle* strain and *ligament* sprain.

The fourth kind of minor injury is related to the tendons. Do you remember that tendons connect muscle to ... bone? That's it. There is one very well-known tendon in the back of the foot, in the heel. It's called the Achilles tendon. It's named after the Greek hero, Achilles, because the story goes that it was the only part of his body that could be injured. But that's not important really. Damage to the tendons is quite common in sport, although it mainly happens through overuse – so we'll come on to that in a minute.

What we need to look at now is inflammation and swelling. In all cases of traumatic injury, the body responds in the same way. The dead or damaged cells release chemicals. These chemicals carry messages to the body's immune system – that's the system that protects the body – and the immune system sends cells to repair the damage. The result of this is ... you've guessed it – inflammation and swelling. So, we can see that inflammation and swelling are natural parts of the healing process. However, and this is very important for sports scientists so listen carefully – too much inflammation or swelling can slow down healing.

Did I talk about *major* trauma? No, I don't think I did. OK, so *major* trauma involves fractures in bones. A *hairline* fracture is, as the name implies, very small, the width of a human hair. There is no displacement of the pieces of bone. A complete fracture means the bone is broken in two or more parts.

Now, one more thing to say about inflammation and swelling. Inflammation and swelling happen at the same time, but they are not the same. Inflammation means getting hot or inflamed. As you know, the site of an injury always gets hot. Swelling, on the other hand – or foot, of course – means getting bigger, which you are also familiar with after an injury. Fluid leaks into the tissue and it swells. Now, back to inflammation. It was Lan Zhou in 2010 who conducted a study of inflammation – it's cited on your handout – Lan Zhou, 2010. The professor found that inflamed cells produce *insulin-like growth factor 1* ... don't worry about the full name, it's always called IGF-1. Now IGF-1 is a chemical that increases the speed of muscle regeneration. In other words, it helps the muscle to grow again. It also helps to heal damaged tissue. So can you see the importance of this research? It's clear from the work of Lan Zhou that inflammation should be *managed* but not removed altogether. We need some inflammation ...

Ah, just going back to fractures for a minute. I think I forgot to ask a crucial question. What's the difference between a fracture and a break? The answer is – they are the same thing. It's a bit like contusion and bruise. One is the medical term, the other is the common word.

OK. So that's the first type of injury – *traumatic*, mainly from contact sports. The second type is *overuse* injury and it can happen in all sports, contact and non-contact. In fact, some people are saying now that overuse injuries are far too common, and are the result of sportspeople playing too much sport, or training too much or both. But that's not relevant to this lecture. The most common overuse injury for sportspeople is RSI, or repetitive strain injury, which, obviously, results from an athlete repeatedly using the same joint or set of muscles. For example, a tennis player will use the elbow joint on one arm all the time which is why injury to that joint is sometimes called 'tennis elbow'. One official name though is *tendinitis*, which of course refers to the tendon. The tendon becomes inflamed because very, very small tears in the muscle do not repair properly.

Which brings us on to the second main overuse injury – major muscle tears. This can happen, for example, in weightlifting. However, there is a strange point about muscle tears. They are actually the way the muscle grows. If you use a muscle a lot, it tears a little. It's sometimes called a micro-injury. Then, if you rest the muscle, it repairs itself, but in the process, it grows bigger, so next time it can deal with the load that you put on it. The problem comes if you do not give the muscle enough time to repair the micro-injury and then you develop a real injury. So remember that. It's tearing muscles slightly which makes them grow.

OK. So, we have seen a little about the types of sports injuries. Clearly, trainers and coaches should do everything they can to reduce the risk of injury during training and in matches themselves. But I'm not here to talk to you about this now. I'm more interested today in the treatment.

Lecturer:	Obviously, there are specialist treatments for each individual injury and companies make a lot of money selling special creams and bandages and pills and so on, but they all work on some general principles. These principles are sometimes given the acronym PRICE – we'll see why.
	Firstly, the P stands for *protection*. This means 'stop playing as soon as you notice the injury' to prevent making the damage worse. If possible, don't put any weight on the injured part. Sounds easy, but of course a lot of athletes are encouraged to play through the pain and carry on even if their leg is falling off. This is just stupid. It's pain that warns you to stop! If you ignore it, you will injure your body more, maybe much more.
	R is pretty simple. It stands for *rest*. What your body needs after an injury is to stop using the hand or arm or leg or whatever. In most cases, the body will recover from a sports injury by itself, if it is given enough time without stressing the injured area.
	I is for *ice*, which can be a bag of frozen peas or a specialist cold pack. Cold serves two purposes. Firstly it is a mild anaesthetic so it reduces the pain, but, more importantly, it reduces the amount of swelling, which is caused by blood rushing to the injured area. The ice reduces blood flow, which is a good thing for a short time, but you should never leave ice on for more than 20 minutes. You could damage the area more than the original injury. In fact, there is quite a lot of uncertainty about ice treatment. Read the article by Macauley from the *Clinical Journal of Sport Medicine*, 2001 – it's in your reading pack.
	Finally, what does E mean? It's *elevation*, or raising. Once again, it is a way of reducing blood flow to the injury, and basically you must just get the affected part higher than the heart. So for an injured ankle, the patient can rest in bed with the foot on a cushion or pillow. It's a little harder for an injured arm, but most sporting injuries happen to feet, ankles, legs and hips.
	Hang on. I've missed one out. Just going back for a minute, C is *compression*, or squeezing. This also reduces swelling and we can achieve it by wrapping the affected area in a bandage – particularly a compression bandage. But, just as with ice, we have to be a little careful. If the patient experiences throbbing around the area, the bandage is too tight. The blood cannot flow properly and bring the repair cells to the affected area. So unwrap the bandage and rewrap with less compression.
	Right. I think I've done them all now. But there is another huge area of treatment for sports injuries that will interest many of you here. Physiotherapy. PRICE is clearly an initial treatment, to ensure that the injury repairs as quickly as possible. But there is another element to getting the athlete back into training and competition – rehabilitation. The aim of physiotherapy is to prepare the body, particularly the injured part, for full use again, and to try to ensure that the injury does not recur.
	I mentioned specialist treatments earlier. Some of these are controversial because they are owned by companies which, of course, want to make money from them, but some are accepted now by the majority of sports scientists, at least. For example, the hyperbaric chamber. *Hyperbaric* means 'high weight' or 'high pressure'. The chamber is big enough to take one person or even two or three. The injured patient gets inside and the chamber is then sealed from the atmosphere. The pressure inside is raised. In addition, the patient puts on breathing apparatus so that they are inhaling pure oxygen. Blood supply is reduced by the pressure, which reduces swelling, but more oxygen reaches the damaged tissue which means that healing is speeded up. Some people claim that recovery can be cut by a third or even a half by these chambers. That's sports scientists, by the way, not just the manufacturers of hyperbaric chambers. On your handout you have a reference to one endorsement for this treatment in the *Sports Injury Bulletin*.
	Right, so, to sum up. What we have looked at today are the types of sports injury – trauma and overuse, and the basic treatment – PRICE and physiotherapy. Next time, we'll look at a few case studies to see how these general points apply in real life. Thank you.

🌐 4.17

Presenter:	**4.17. Lesson 4.6. Vocabulary for speaking: Mental and physical conditions**
	Exercise B2. Listen to an interview with a sports psychologist. Check your answers to Exercise A.

Interviewer:	Hi. Welcome to Sports Hour. To start with today, I'm talking to Emma Gibson, who's a sports psychologist. Welcome, Emma.
Sports psychologist:	Thank you. Nice to be here.
Interviewer:	OK, so your job is to help sportspeople to perform better, right?
Sports psychologist:	Yes, that's part of my job, certainly.
Interviewer:	What factors can affect the performance of a sportsperson?
Sports psychologist:	Well, we can divide the factors into mental and physical.
Interviewer:	What does *mental* mean?
Sports psychologist:	'To do with the brain'. And *physical* means 'to do with the body'.
Interviewer:	So can mental factors affect performance?
Sports psychologist:	Yes, indeed. Most people think that only physical factors are important, things like colds and flu.
Interviewer:	Why do we think that? Because when you have a cold or flu, you get tired easily?
Sports psychologist:	Yes, that's right, so that affects your performance, but there is also fatigue, which is extreme tiredness.
Interviewer:	Is fatigue a physical condition in itself?
Sports psychologist:	Well, yes and no. Fatigue is a symptom of a physical condition. It might be something very simple like lack of sleep or something more serious like heart problems.

Interviewer:	Right. So that's physical conditions.
Sports psychologist:	Yes – but I must just mention asthma. It's very common now, at least in the West. Many sportspeople have asthma, which is a respiratory problem.
Interviewer:	What are the symptoms of asthma?
Sports psychologist:	Well, during an attack, people experience shortness of breath. They can't breathe properly.
Interviewer:	OK. So we've got colds and flu, fatigue and asthma. What about mental conditions?
Sports psychologist:	Well, this is interesting. Mental conditions are probably more important than physical conditions for the top sportsperson.
Interviewer:	In what way are mental conditions more important?
Sports psychologist:	Well, top athletes often have an obsession with their sport. They think about it all the time.
Interviewer:	Isn't that a good thing?
Sports psychologist:	It can be. It depends. Sometimes it is good because it means they train harder and perform better. Sometimes obsession is bad because it leads to depression or anxiety – you know, worrying about your performance – your last performance and the next one. Sometimes, you become so obsessive that it causes neurosis.
Interviewer:	And what does that mean?
Sports psychologist:	Well, neurosis covers a huge range of mental conditions, including unpleasant or disturbing thoughts, aggression, fear and perfectionism – you know, everything has to be absolutely perfect.
Interviewer:	And that's bad?
Sports psychologist:	Yes. Because it is impossible for anything to be *absolutely perfect*, so you will always disappoint yourself. And you will suffer from depression.

🌐 4.18

Presenter: **4.18. Exercise B4. Listen and check your answers.**

Sports psychologist: a. When you go down with a cold or flu, you get tired easily.
b. Fatigue is a symptom of a physical problem.
c. Many sportspeople have asthma, which is a respiratory condition.
d. During an attack, people with asthma experience breathing difficulties.
e. Top athletes often have an obsession with their sport. They think about it all the time and train hard because they are obsessed.
f. Sometimes obsession is bad because it leads to anxiety – worrying about your performance.
g. Sometimes, you become so obsessive that you experience neurosis.

🌐 4.19

Presenter: **4.19. Exercise C2. Listen and check your answers.**

Voice: 1. aggression
2. aggressive
3. anxiety
4. anxious
5. asthma
6. asthmatic
7. depressed
8. depression
9. fatigue
10. fatigued
11. neurosis
12. neurotic
13. obsession
14. obsessive
15. breath
16. breathe

🌐 4.20

Presenter: **4.20. Exercise C3. Listen again and repeat.**

[REPEAT OF SCRIPT FROM 🌐 4.19]

🌐 4.21 [DVD] 4.F

Presenter: **4.21. Lesson 4.7. Real-time speaking: Physical factors in sport**

Student 1:	Right. Umm. OK. Er … fatigue. Um. Fatigue means … well… tired. Really, really tired. So when you are doing exercise, sometimes you give up. You stop doing it – the exercise, I mean. Um … because you're tired. And maybe you don't really feel like it. That's it really.
Tutor:	OK. So, those are the symptoms. What about the research?
Student 1:	Oh, yes, right. Research. Um. If people do a cognitive task – *cognitive* means 'thinking', right?
Tutor:	Yes. 'Connected with thinking'.
Student 1:	OK. Where was I? Um, yes, if they do that before a physical task, er, then they think the physical task is … um … harder.
Tutor:	And why do they think that?

Student 1:	Um. I don't really know. Oh yeah. I think maybe it changes their view.
Tutor:	OK. So it changes their perception. Now, what's your source?
Student 1:	Oh, yeah. Um … some people called – um – Marcora, Stai – um – ano and er someone.
Tutor:	Manning. And when was that?
Student 1:	In 2009.
Tutor:	What were they writing in?
Student 1:	English?
Tutor:	No, I mean the name of the book or the journal …
Student 1:	Um, let me check. Yeah. *The Journal of Applied Psychology.*
Tutor:	Psychology?
Student 1:	Oh, no. Physiology.

Student 2:	I researched asthma, which is an illness of the respiratory system. The symptoms of asthma are an inability to breathe properly. In severe cases, the illness can be fatal. Physical exertion can bring on an attack.
Student 3:	So what you're saying is, it could be dangerous for people with asthma to do sport.
Student 1:	Well, to some extent. But it's possible that certain sports affect asthmatics more than others. For example, Fitch and Godfrey, writing in the *Journal of the American Medical Association*, 1976, found that swimming very rarely brings on an asthma attack.
Student 4:	In other words, asthmatics should only take part in swimming?
Student 1:	No, I'm not saying that. The point is that asthma is controllable in most cases.
Student 3:	Are you saying that the majority of asthmatics can control the illness with medication?
Student 1:	Yes, exactly. In fact, I think there are several top athletes who are asthmatic.
Student 2:	What's your source? *[laughter]*

🔊 4.22

Presenter:	**4.22. Everyday English: Talking about health problems**
	Exercise B1. Listen and match each conversation to a photograph above.
	Conversation 1.

Voice A:	What seems to be the trouble?
Voice B:	Well my throat is really sore. And I think I've got a temperature.
Voice A:	Mm. I'm just going to feel your glands. Mm. OK. It's nothing too serious. Just strep throat.
Voice B:	Oh right. My friend had that recently.
Voice A:	Yes. It's very infectious. I'll write a prescription for some antibiotics.

| Presenter: | **Conversation 2.** |

Voice A:	Are you feeling alright?
Voice B:	Not really. I've got a really bad headache. Feel sick too.
Voice A:	You look terrible. And you're very hot.
Voice B:	Yeah? But I can't stop shivering. I really don't feel too good.
Voice A:	OK, I'm going to call the health centre.

| Presenter: | **Conversation 3.** |

Voice A:	What is the matter?
Voice B:	Nothing really. Just feeling a bit stressed.
Voice A:	Oh. Do you want to talk about it?
Voice B:	Well, my student loan hasn't come yet. I've got two essays to finish and I can't sleep.
Voice A:	OK … well … let's go and get some fresh air. Then you can tell me all about it.

| Presenter: | **Conversation 4.** |

Voice A:	Have you ever had TB?
Voice B:	I don't think so. What is it?
Voice A:	Tuberculosis. It's a respiratory disease.
Voice B:	Oh, right. No, I have never had it.
Voice A:	Are you currently taking any medication?

🔊 4.23

Presenter:	**4.23. Lesson 4.8. Learning new speaking skills: Summarizing and reacting to summaries**
	Exercise B1. Listen to three extracts from the discussion in 4.7.
	Extract 1.

Student 1:	Physical exertion can bring on an attack.
Student 2:	So what you're saying is, it could be dangerous for people with asthma to do sport?
Student 1:	Well, to some extent.

Presenter:	Extract 2.

Student 2: In other words, asthmatics should only take part in swimming?
Student 1: No, I'm not saying that. The point is that asthma is controllable in most cases.

Presenter:	Extract 3.

Student 2: Are you saying that the majority of asthmatics can control the illness with medication?
Student 1: Yeah, exactly.

🎧 4.24

Presenter:	**4.24. Pronunciation Check. Listen and repeat.**

Voice: It's possible that certain sports affect asthmatics more than others. For example, Fitch and Godfrey 1976, writing in the *Journal of the American Medical Association*, found that swimming very rarely brings on an asthma attack.

🎧 4.25

Presenter:	**4.25. Skills Check. Listen and repeat the expressions above. Copy the stress and intonation.**

Voice: So what you're saying is, exercise is a good thing?
Are you saying that exercise is a bad thing?
In other words, everyone should do exercise?
Yes, that's right.
Well, to some extent.
No, that's not really the point. The point is, we should do the right kind of exercise.

🎧 4.26

Presenter:	**4.26. Lesson 4.9. Grammar for speaking: Review of modals**
	Grammar box 17. Listen to the sentences in the table. Which part of the verb is stressed in each case?

Voice: 1. We must support statements in essays.
2. People's ideas mustn't be quoted without a reference.
3. Asthma can be fatal.
4. People with flu should avoid exercise.
5. Asthmatics don't have to stop all sport.
6. Fatigue might be caused by lack of sleep.

🎧 4.27

Presenter:	**4.27. Exercise A2. Listen and check your answers. How does the speaker say the modal in each case?**

Voice: a. Academic essays must include a list of references.
b. References must follow conventions, for example, brackets for dates.
c. You mustn't include other people's words without a reference.
d. Page numbers must be given for direct quotes.
e. In most cases, personal opinions mustn't be included.
f. Wikipedia mustn't be used as a source.

🎧 4.28

Presenter:	**4.28. Exercise A3. Listen again and practise.**

[REPEAT OF SCRIPT FROM 🎧 4.27]

🎧 4.29

Presenter:	**4.29. Exercise B1. Listen and repeat the examples.**

Student 1: Nuclear power is the future for energy supply.
Student 2: Well, it might be the future. But more solar power could be used instead.

Student 1: Lack of clean water is the greatest world problem.
Student 2: Well, it could be the greatest, but food might be a bigger problem.

Presenter:	**5.1. Theme 5: The past, present and future of food** **Lesson 5.1. Vocabulary for listening: Producing and protecting** **Exercise B2. Listen to the first part of Malcolm's talk.**
Radio presenter:	Good morning. Welcome to this week's *Talking Point*. As always, we have someone in the studio this week who feels very strongly about a current issue. With his wife, Heather, Malcolm farms 10,000 hectares in Norfolk, which is in the east of England. Welcome, Malcolm.
Malcolm:	Thank you. Good morning.
Radio presenter:	Now, Malcolm, I understand that you are worried about where we are going with farming?
Malcolm:	Yes, indeed. I am very worried.
Radio presenter:	But we're not talking about the EU or supermarkets …
Malcolm:	No, something much more important.
Radio presenter:	OK. Over to you then, Malcolm.
Malcolm:	Thank you. I need to start with a little bit of history. At one time, all farmers were organic. By that I mean that they only used natural products to help their plants grow and to protect them. Let's look at growth first. Now, we know, of course, that plants need sunlight and water, but plants need nutrients, too. The nutrients are chemicals like nitrogen, potassium and phosphorus. Nutrients exist naturally in soil, but the problem is, crops take nutrients out of the soil during the growing process. Eventually, the soil becomes exhausted. At this point, farmers must put nutrients back. At one time, farmers put nutrients back organically, with animal waste, particularly manure from the cows and horses on the farm. So that's growth. Now, what about protection? Farmers must protect their crops from pests, like birds, insects and bacteria. Birds and insects eat the crops, bacteria can give them diseases. From the earliest times, farmers have used natural pesticides like sulphur to destroy pests. It is a vital part of farming because certain pests can completely destroy a crop. On many occasions in history, pests have been responsible for famine in a large area, with farms producing few or no food crops. For example, the Great Famine of the 1850s in Ireland, which was caused by bacteria, destroyed the complete potato crop of the country. This was the main food crop and, as a result, approximately one million people died through starvation. OK, so that's the past. What about the present? Nowadays, most farmers use artificial fertilizers to help crops to grow. The fertilizers are made in a laboratory. They also use artificial pesticides to protect their crops. However, a small number of farmers, like Heather and me, have gone back to older ways. We are very afraid that artificial fertilizers and pesticides are running out of the soil and polluting the water system – I mean, the streams and rivers and finally the water supply to private houses. In the rivers and streams, they are damaging the environment, killing fish and aquatic plants. In our water supply, they are an enormous danger to public health.
Radio presenter:	Thank you, Malcolm. So what's your solution?

Presenter:	**5.2. Exercise B4. Listen to the final part of Malcolm's talk. When he stops, number the next word or phrase.**
Malcolm:	My solution is [PAUSE] simple. The future is going back to the [PAUSE] past. Farmers should return to organic [PAUSE] farming. They should stop using chemicals which are made in a [PAUSE] laboratory. They should use only natural fertilizers and natural [PAUSE] pesticides. If these chemicals escape from the farm, they do not damage the [PAUSE] environment. They do not pollute rivers and kill [PAUSE] fish. They do not endanger public [PAUSE] health. Organic farming is not only the [PAUSE] past. It is also the [PAUSE] future.

Presenter:	**5.3. Lesson 5.2. Real-time listening: Agriculture – the beginning of civilization**
Lecturer:	Agriculture is the name we give to the industry of farming. It has two main branches – producing crops and rearing animals for food. It has been happening for over 14,000 years, according to most sources. Today we are going to look briefly at the history of the industry, and then consider some of the theories of how agriculture started. In later lectures, we will review the *current* situation of agriculture, or 'agribusiness' as we should probably call it now, and, of course, the *future* of agriculture, which concerns all of us on this planet.

| Lecturer: | Right, so, what I'm going to do first is take you on a quick trip through the history of agriculture. It all started about 14,000 years ago, as I said, in about 12000 BCE, in the area we now call Lebanon. This is part of an area now called the Fertile Crescent – basically, the Middle East. It was the cradle of agriculture – the place where it all started. Actually, perhaps I should have said, *one* place! Recent research suggests that agriculture started independently in many places at about the same time. But, anyway, at the moment, the only important thing is, it started! The local tribes started to harvest wild grasses. If that sounds strange, remember, wheat is just a kind of grass. I remember harvesting wild grass myself. When I was young, I used to pick wild grass and chew the kernel, the bit at the top. There was hardly anything in it, of course, because the grass was wild, but it's interesting to think that 14,000 years ago, people must have done the same thing and thought – hey, we can eat this! OK. So, getting back to the history … |

Early people made flour from the seeds, but the yield – I mean, the amount of flour that they got from each seed – was very, very low. *Yield* is a very important concept in agriculture, so make a note. Oh, of course, I should have said what was happening *before* agriculture started. Well, early man was a hunter-gatherer. In other words he, or in some tribes, she, hunted and killed wild animals for food, or gathered wild berries and fruits from the trees and bushes. Incidentally, when you are a hunter-gatherer, you spend all day hunting and gathering to get enough food to feed yourself and your family. Also, if the animals migrate each season to another area, you have to follow them. I want you to think about that when we consider the theories of the origins of agriculture.

OK. Jump forward to about 8500 BCE. It was then that people first began to grow crops such as barley, wheat, peas and lentils. We know this, of course, from the remains of food that has been found with the bones of early man. Oh, did I mention? … there is some evidence that rice was domesticated in China in about 11500 BCE. OK, let's get back to Lebanon. About 7000 BCE, people began to tame animals such as goats and sheep in Greece and other parts of the eastern Mediterranean. About 1,000 years after that – so where are we now, about 6000 BCE – cows and chickens were added to the list of domesticated animals … that was in Pakistan. It's strange, isn't it, to think of farmyard animals like sheep and cows as wild, but they certainly used to be.

OK. Where did I get to? Oh, yes, 6000 BCE. That's about 8,000 years ago. A thousand years later, in about 5000 BCE, the horse was domesticated, first in the area that we now call the Ukraine. Obviously, some people ate the meat of the domesticated horse – some people still do today – but horses were really much more important as work animals, to pull ploughs, for example, or to transport harvested crops. Actually, I've jumped the gun on the plough – that didn't appear until about 4000 BCE in the area we now call Iraq. That reminds me. I was in a village on the southern edge of the Sahara and I saw *camels* pulling ploughs. They are still using animals because tractors break down too often in the sand, and you can't get the spare parts. Anyway, where was I? Ah, yes – 5000 BCE.

Over the next 5,000 years, there were a lot of small improvements to agriculture, including irrigation and power supply – I mean windmills and watermills to grind corn. I'm not going to spend ages on that today because you have a project on Chinese agriculture and another on Arab agriculture later in the course. So what we'll do now is jump right forward to the Agricultural, or Agrarian, Revolution in 18th-century Britain.

Why is it called a revolution? Because it revolutionized the way people worked the land. Until about 1700, land all over the world was worked mainly by people, with the help, as I mentioned, of horses and other animals. Then, in 1701, a man called Jethro Tull decided to mechanize a basic part of farming. What he invented was the seed drill. This was a mechanical method of sowing seeds. Although it was more than 150 years before the method was widely adopted, it was the start of the mechanization of agriculture. In 1786, for example, Andrew Meikle invented a mechanical threshing machine, which could thresh, or separate, the edible parts of cereal crops from the rest. There was also the steam plough, in the 1850s. It finally replaced horses in many places after about 7,000 years. Other inventions in the Agrarian Revolution were crop rotation and selective breeding, which we'll talk about in another lecture.

Just before we go back to look at theories, I must just mention one more revolution – the Green Revolution, which started in the early 1960s. Because the population of countries like India and China was rising so fast at the time, agriculturalists were terribly worried about famine. Many researchers around the world thought that millions of people were going to die of starvation in the near future because improvements in agriculture could not keep up with the increase in population. But a man called Norman Borlaug suggested an answer. He introduced a new variety of rice to India that had a much higher yield – remember that important word? – a much higher yield than the indigenous variety. It could produce ten times the crop in the best conditions. It was called 'Miracle Rice' by the people of Asia and started a revolution in yield that is still continuing to this day.

🌐 **5.5** [DVD] **5.C**

Lecturer:

So, we've had a brief overview of the history. But how did it all start, 14,000 years ago? Well, there are six main theories about why people moved from hunting and gathering to organized farming. Yes, sorry about that, six! But some, in my view, are much better than others. Here they are, in no particular order. We've got the Oasis theory, the Hilly Flanks theory – that's flanks, or sides – you'll see why in a minute. Next, the Feasting model. Feasting means having a lot of food at one meal. Then we have the Demographic theory – I'm sure you know about demographics. The fifth theory is the Evolutionary theory. And, finally, the Domestication theory. I expect you can guess what some of these theories involve, but let's look at each one in turn.

First, then, the Oasis theory. This was propounded by Raphael Pumpelly in 1908. It's described in Rosen, 2007, on your reference list. The theory argues that climate change caused the start of agriculture. He says that the climate in some areas became drier. When this happened, people moved to oases – or actually, more accurately, to watering holes. Because wild animals came to the watering hole to drink, people came into closer contact with them. Gradually, the animals accepted the humans, which in turn led to their domestication. At least, that's the theory. Also, because the people did not move from the oases or watering holes, they started to plant seeds. It makes sense to me, but it seems that this theory has not received much support, due to the lack of evidence of climatic change at the relevant time.

The second theory is the Hilly Flanks theory, put forward by Robert Braidwood. This is in Sutton and Anderson, 2009. Braidwood did not believe that there was a climatic change, as Pumpelly proposed. Instead, he thought that people living in grassy habitats began to cultivate the edible species such as wheat and barley. This occurred in the subtropical wooded hills of Turkey, Iran and Iraq on the flanks, or sides, of rivers – hence the Hilly Flanks theory. Although this theory sounds reasonable, Sutton and Anderson state that no evidence for it has been found.

A man called Brian Hayden – that's Hayden, 2002 on your list – proposed another theory, the Feasting model. He argues that leaders came to regard feasting as a display of power – in other words, they organized big meals for hundreds of people, to show how powerful they were. This led to agriculture because leaders had to have a reliable source of large amounts of food. It is difficult to evaluate this theory. There is no evidence for or against. I remember, though, when I lived in Arabia, it was clear that feasting was still very important. There was always too much food for the people invited to a meal – and in the case of rich people, that was often hundreds of people. In fact, I believe, in that culture, if the guests eat all the food, the host is ashamed. In Europe, of course, when people come to dinner, we like them to finish everything on their plate. Anyway, back to the point …

Theory number 4 – Demographic theory … or perhaps we should say *theories*, because there are several based on the same idea. You will see some sources in your Reading Pack. Basically, they all take the view that people became more sedentary and began to stay in the same place, so the population grew and they needed more food than the area supplied. So they had to plant seeds and grow more food themselves. In my view, these theories start from the wrong end. They suggest that people stopped moving and then started planting crops. But why did they stop moving? If we are to believe this theory, we must understand why people stopped moving. If you are a hunter-gatherer and the animals move away and the berries go out of season, surely you must follow them?

The fifth theory that has been suggested by several scholars is the Evolutionary theory. There are sources for this in your Reading Pack, too. The Evolutionary theory is the idea that agriculture began with the gradual protection of wild plants in order to preserve the resource. You know, they said to each other, 'We must look after these wild plants because we need them to produce fruit or berries next year.' Except of course, there was no spoken language at the time, but maybe they said it with sign language. This in turn led to an understanding of different locations for different plants. This theory gets my vote. If you use something every day, you begin to realize that it is important to protect it. I realize that we still haven't really learnt this lesson, but perhaps early man was closer to nature than us and therefore more protective … which reminds me of one local council in Britain. They realized that a lot of visitors were coming to their town. They were coming, in fact, to see the old trees in the area. The problem was, there was nowhere for them to park. So the council cut down the trees to make a car park. Sorry. That's a silly story and probably not even true. So let's get back to the theories …

The final theory is the Domestication theory propounded by Daniel Quinn, amongst others. Sorry, I haven't got the reference for him. You'll have to look it up. This theory suggests that people became more domesticated, staying in one area and beginning to domesticate that area. This involved looking after plants and taming the wild animals. Like the Demographic theory, this just doesn't work for me. Why did people become more domesticated? What was the impetus? Again, it seems to be the wrong way round. We need to explain why people became more domesticated in the first place.

So there we have the theories concerning the start of agriculture. Which do you think is most likely?

🌐 5.6

| Presenter: | 5.6. Lesson 5.3. Learning new listening skills: Dealing with digressions |

Exercise A2. Listen and check your ideas.

| Voice: | agriculture, agricultural, climate, cultivate, domesticated, edible, famine, fertile, harvest, indigenous, irrigate, irrigation, machine, mechanize, preserve, resource, starvation, tractor |

🌐 5.7

| Presenter: | **5.7. Exercise C. Listen and make notes. When the lecturer digresses, write one or two words to help you remember.** |

Lecture 1: The development of Qatar and Lebanon

| Lecturer 1: | OK. Now we are going to compare two countries, using these areas and sub-areas. Both countries are located in the Middle East but Qatar is in the Gulf whereas Lebanon is in the eastern end of the Mediterranean Sea. Qatar is a peninsula, only bordered to the south by Saudi Arabia, while Lebanon is almost completely surrounded by Syria. I remember I once had to visit Qatar – that was over 35 years ago – and when I told people where I was going, none of my friends even knew where it was. I went back recently and it's incredible to see the progress that has been made in such a relatively short time. Lots of modern buildings and wide roads. I think perhaps the outlook has changed too. Anyway. Where was I? OK, Qatar in the Gulf, Lebanon on the Mediterranean. Does the location of these countries affect their human development? |

| Presenter: | **Lecture 2: Long-distance communication: semaphore** |

| Lecturer 2: | In 1793, a man called Claude Chappe invented the long-distance semaphore in France. The French government built a network of 556 relay stations all over the country. These were houses with arms on the roof. The arms could move to make different symbols. Urgent messages could travel at about 20 miles an hour now – faster and much more secure. That reminds me of a part from a French novel by Alexandre Dumas, *The Count of Monte Cristo*. He is falsely imprisoned for years and when he gets out, he takes revenge on all the people who falsely accused him. He destroys one man by bribing a semaphore station clerk to send a false message – something about Napoleon winning a battle or losing one – I can't remember which. So of course, this shows that semaphore wasn't completely secure. But getting back to the point, it was very difficult to intercept and stop a message from reaching its destination. It was in code, too, so even if you did intercept it, you couldn't understand it. But the system was very expensive, to build and to maintain. It was very expensive for the customers who wanted to use it, too. But Napoleon used it all the time to send urgent messages about troop movements – you know, how his armies were moving around the country. |

Presenter:	**Lecture 3: Children and violence on television**
Lecturer 3:	Now, I accept that children have to experience fear, and learn how to deal with it. Clearly, this is why we have fairy tales, which are full of murders, kidnappings and violent acts. Fairy tales are very old and presumably perform a useful function in education, so this is a very powerful argument. But we must take into account several factors. Firstly, children are visual learners, and television is a visual medium. It actually *shows* the violence, whereas fairy tales *talk* about it. There is a big difference. I remember when I was a child of about eight, I had to watch a particular TV science fiction programme, with robots and aliens and green monsters with ten heads and so on from behind the sofa, or peeking through my hands because it was so scary. But I could read about the same sort of thing and it had no effect on me at all. Anyway. Why was I saying that? Oh yes, because fairy tales are not visual. Also, most fairy tales are initially told to children by a parent. So the parent has a chance to mediate the experience for the child – in other words, to tone it down, if they think the child will not be able to cope with the events as written. The parent is the medium by which the child receives the story, and they can change the story if necessary. But television is a very different medium. It is unvarying. It does not change to suit the viewer, even if the viewer is eight years old, alone with the television in the sitting room and terrified.
Presenter:	**Lecture 4: The central nervous system**
Lecturer 4:	It is the central nervous system which controls muscle contraction. The system is two-way. What I mean by that is, the system gathers information from nerves throughout the body and takes it to the brain through the spinal column. It uses electrical impulses. The brain is the primary processing centre for the body. If the decision is taken to react to a particular stimulus, the brain sends the necessary impulses to the muscles – electricity again. Which reminds me that when I was at school, I suppose in about Year 8 or 9, we had to do this experiment with frog's legs – don't worry, the animals were dead, and in fact, the legs were not even on the animal, they had been cut off. We touched them with the two ends of an electrical circuit and the legs twitched, which shows the effect of electricity on the muscle tissue even when the animal is dead. The girls all screamed, I remember, when the legs jumped – I think most of the boys did, too. Anyway, that's enough of that. Let's get back to the nervous system. The main parts are the nerves, as I've just said, the brain, obviously, and the spinal cord, which runs down the spine. We can see now why the skull and the spine are so important. They protect key parts of the central nervous system.

🔊 **5.8**

Presenter:	**5.8. Lesson 5.4. Grammar for listening: Complex sentences (1)**
	Grammar box 21. Listen to the examples. Where does the speaker pause in each case?
Voice:	When I was young, I used to pick wild grass. If the animals migrate, you must follow them. Because the population was rising fast, agriculturalists were afraid of famine. Although this theory could be correct, scientists have found no evidence.

🔊 **5.9**

Presenter:	**5.9. Exercise B1. Listen to the first clause of some complex sentences. Find a suitable ending.**
Voice:	a. When you are a hunter-gatherer, … b. If you use something every day, … c. If guests eat all the food, … d. Because people stayed in one place, … e. Because there is a global shortage of fresh water, … f. Because Lebanon doesn't have any oil resources, … g. If the Sumerians wanted to communicate over a long distance, …

🔊 **5.10**

Presenter:	**5.10. Exercise B2. Listen and check your answers.**
Voice:	a. When you are a hunter-gatherer, you spend all day hunting and gathering. b. If you use something every day, you begin to protect it. c. If guests eat all the food, the host is ashamed. d. Because people stayed in one place, they started to plant seeds. e. Because there is a global shortage of fresh water, we must retain rainfall in reservoirs. f. Because Lebanon doesn't have any oil resources, it imports from countries in the region. g. If the Sumerians wanted to communicate over a long distance, they could send a letter.

🔊 **5.11**

Presenter:	**5.11. Exercise C1. Listen to the main clause of some complex sentences. How could the speaker finish each one?**
Voice:	a. I'm not going to talk about Chinese agriculture very much because … b. The nerves in your fingers send a message to the brain if … c. There is much more agriculture in Lebanon than in Qatar because … d. In children's television programmes, people don't die when … e. It is possible that children become aggressive because … f. You shouldn't let young children watch television when …

Presenter:	**5.12. Exercise C2. Listen and check your ideas.**
Voice:	a. I'm not going to talk about Chinese agriculture very much because you are going to do a project on this. b. The nerves in your fingers send a message to the brain if they touch something hot or sharp. c. There is much more agriculture in Lebanon than in Qatar because it has more fertile land. d. In children's television programmes, people don't die when they are blown up and shot. e. It is possible that children become aggressive because they watch violent TV programmes. f. You shouldn't let young children watch television when they are alone.

🎵 5.13

Presenter:	**5.13. Exercise D1. Listen to the first clause of some sentences. When the speaker pauses, discuss possible endings to the sentence.**
Voice:	a. Parents often tone down fairy tales if … b. Muscles work in pairs because … c. When Napoleon had an urgent message for his army … d. Civilization started when … e. Sports injuries usually get better faster if … f. Although customers buy *products* … g. If you provide higher benefits …

🎵 5.14

Presenter:	**5.14. Exercise D2. Listen and check your ideas.**
Voice:	a. Parents often tone down fairy tales if they are very violent. b. Muscles work in pairs because they can only contract. c. When Napoleon had an urgent message for his army he sent it by semaphore. d. Civilization started when people stayed in the same place. e. Sports injuries usually get better faster if you rest. f. Although customers buy *products* they actually want benefits. g. If you provide higher benefits, some customers will pay more.

🎵 5.15

Presenter:	**5.15. Lesson 5.5. Applying new listening skills: Same land, more yield** **Exercise A2. Listen and check.**
Voice:	a. It all started about 14,000 years ago in an area which we now call Lebanon. b. I've jumped the gun on the plough – that didn't appear until about 4000 BCE. c. Improvements in agriculture could not keep up with the increase in population. d. Here are the theories, in no particular order. e. But before we look at the theories, I must just mention the Green Revolution. f. Gradually, the animals accepted the humans, which, in turn, led to their domestication. g. The Evolutionary theory says that agriculture began with the gradual protection of wild plants to preserve the resource. This theory gets my vote. h. The Domestication theory suggests that people became domesticated and then stayed in one area. But this seems to be the wrong way round to me.

🎵 5.16 [DVD] 5.D

Lecturer:	This week we're going to look at developments in agriculture. For the whole of its long history, agriculture has been an industry that has constantly improved. Or, to put it another way, it has recognized problems and found solutions. The driving force for improvement for thousands of years has been a rising population. If you have more mouths to feed, you need more food. It's obvious. The industry has risen to that challenge time and time again – as we saw to some extent in the last lecture. Which reminds me … I was reading a blog the other day and the guy was suggesting that the driving force behind agriculture has changed now. He reckoned the driving force now was profit, and now the stronger need is to make bigger and bigger profits from farming. We're not talking about agriculture anymore but 'agribusiness'. Although agriculture does not employ the majority of the population of a particular area anymore, it does make huge profits as a business. Sorry. That's enough of that! As I was saying, agriculture is about constant improvements. There have been literally thousands of improvements since the first person picked some wild grass and ate the seeds. But nearly all the improvements have been aimed at the same objective – more yield. There are three main ways to increase yield. Firstly, farmers have always tried to get more yield from a particular piece of land. Same land, more yield. Secondly, farmers have tried to get more yield from a particular crop. Same crop, more fruit, more berries, or bigger roots or stems. And thirdly – you've guessed it – farmers have tried to get more yield from a particular animal. Same animal, more meat or milk. Today, we're only going to look at the first way – same land, more yield. Because I'm going to ask *you* to research the other two ways.

Right, let's look at how we can get more yield from the same piece of land. Remember, we're talking about problems and solutions all the time. For the first solution, we need to go back to 3500 BCE. Plants need sunlight, which is probably why early agriculture developed in some of the sunniest parts of the world, the modern-day areas of Iraq, Syria and Egypt, for example. So what's the problem? Well, plants also need *water* to grow, obviously. And those same areas – Iraq, Syria, Egypt – are some of the driest areas on earth, with very little rainfall and hardly any natural rivers or lakes.

So the plants in these areas often did not get enough natural water to grow well. The solution? Irrigation. Throughout the centuries, different peoples have used different methods to irrigate their crops, to provide them with the water they need to grow well. For example, the Ancient Egyptians built reservoirs to retain water and to stop it running to the sea. They also built canals that were filled when the Nile flooded. Because they had to get the water from these canals on to the actual plants, they invented the *shaduf*. This was a pole with a bucket on one end and a heavy weight on the other. The Phoenicians, from what we now call Lebanon, used wells, tunnels and pumps powered by animals or people to bring water to their land. I remember when I lived in Oman in the Gulf, people in the villages on the edge of the desert were using water from a falaj system which brought water hundreds of miles underground from mountain streams. Nothing very strange about that, really, but the irrigation system was built by the Phoenicians hundreds of years before. Incredible. Anyway, irrigation is still needed all over the world, and farmers use systems such as sprinklers or trickle irrigators. This can be done automatically and electronically and so requires no labour and, in some cases, no attention at all once it is set up. Some irrigation systems even move automatically up and down the field to cover every part. So, problem? Not enough water. Solution? Irrigation.

So that's irrigation. Plants need sunlight and water, but – here's the next problem – they also need *nutrients*, like nitrogen, phosphorus and potassium. Although early farmers didn't know exactly what nutrients plants needed, they realized that growing plants on a particular piece of land destroyed the soil. If they farmed the same piece of land for several years, the yields went down. Eventually the soil was exhausted. For thousands of years, some tribes solved this problem by moving on to another piece of land. They were nomadic, in other words, moving from one area to another, and perhaps eventually returning to a previous area. But this is not an efficient use of time. The solution creates a new problem. If you have to keep moving to new areas, you cannot establish towns and cities. In other words, you cannot start a civilization. Which reminds me of my Latin at school because *civis* in Latin is 'town', so *civilization* means something like 'making a town'. Incidentally, *agricola* is Latin for 'farmer' so that's two connections between the ancient world and modern English. I was hopeless at Latin at school so I don't know why I remember that!

Anyway, where was I? Oh, yes. Eventually, someone discovered that if they left the field 'fallow', or unused, for a year, it returned to being good for growing food crops. So the solution, in some areas, was a system in which each person had three strips of land. They grew crops on two of them – so they didn't starve – but left the third one fallow in *rotation*. That's an important word – *rotation*. Remember it. The solution created a new problem. If you leave one-third of your land fallow, you can only produce two-thirds of the potential crop on it. But some cultures solved the problem when they realized that certain crops actually put goodness back into the soil, for example, plants of the pea family. We know now why. Because some plants gather or fix nitrogen from the soil, they replace the nitrogen that other plants use up. Peas, of course, are edible, so with this kind of crop rotation all of the land produced food crops all of the time. Same land, more yield, year after year.

The system of crop rotation is still widely used all over the world today on small farms. But it leads to other problems. Because many farms are worked by huge machines nowadays, you cannot divide a field up into strips. Also, an agribusiness has a particular market for specific products, so it is not possible to change the crop every year. If your business is called Tomatoes Direct, you cannot become Peas Direct every third year. Farmers had to find a way to put nutrients back into the soil without planting different crops. In other words, they had to feed the crops with nitrogen and phosphorus and potassium and other important minerals. What do we call these chemicals, which improve the yield or the fertility of the land? Of course – *fertilizers*.

Actually, I've rather jumped the gun on fertilizer, because animal waste has been used for hundreds of years as a natural fertilizer. Animal waste is rich in nitrogen, so farmers spread this waste, or manure, on the land to improve the yield. Bird waste – called *guano* – was particularly successful in some areas of the world. But of course, if you do not have a local source of animal waste, there is a problem. In the early 19th century, chemists began to solve the problem. They started to experiment with the chemicals in manure. Justus von Liebig was one of these chemists. It was von Liebig who first created an artificial fertilizer but it was not successful. Although it contained useful nutrients, crops could not absorb them. Gradually, the science improved until, in the 1900s, two German chemists, Carl Bosch and Fritz Haber, developed a cheap process for synthesising ammonia, which contains nitrogen. Which reminds me of an interesting piece of information that I came across the other day. Apparently, after the Second World War, the US government had a lot of ammonium nitrate, because it is the main substance in explosives. It also happens to be one of the best sources of nitrogen for crops. Agronomists persuaded the government to spread the chemical on farmland, and yields rose. Look up the story in Pollan, 2006 – it's on the net. I don't know if you realize, but the United Nations motto is 'We shall beat the swords into ploughs', meaning move from war to peaceful occupation. Perhaps we should add, 'And turn the bombs into crops.'

Anyway. What was I talking about? Oh, right. Artificial fertilizers. I should mention that many people feel these artificial fertilizers are damaging the environment. They wash out of the soil and pollute streams and rivers. So, as so often in the past, a solution leads to a new problem. Some farmers have kept traditional methods in order to produce better quality crops and not damage the environment. These traditional methods include crop rotation and the use of natural fertilizers like cow manure. This process is called *organic farming* and we'll talk a lot more about that later in the course. Unfortunately, crops from organic farming often cost more – solution leading to a problem again – so it is a question of whether the consumer is willing to pay more to protect the environment more.

So, where have we got to? We're talking about raising the yield of a particular piece of land, and we can do that with irrigation, crop rotation and with fertilizers, natural or artificial. But there is one final problem to deal with. Once the land is producing a good crop, how are we going to protect it from pests? Farmers call them pests, but of course we are just talking about other inhabitants of the environment – birds and insects, in the main. Pests are a big danger to agriculture.

Birds or insects can completely strip a crop, so protection is needed. Early farmers used simple methods, such as scarecrows – models of people standing in fields – to scare off the birds, or they covered the crops in some way. But chemicals that deter or kill harmful creatures have a very long history. There is evidence that the Sumerians used insecticides in about 2500 BCE. The substance was sulphur, which was burnt to kill the creatures. Salt was used in Ancient Rome, and in Europe in 1600 CE, ants were attracted away from crops by honey and then killed with arsenic. But it was in the 1940s that the first mass use of pesticide occurred. The substance was called DDT, and it became extremely popular in the 1950s because it killed plant pests and insects that carried malaria, yellow fever, etc.

However, in 1962, a woman called Rachel Carson published a book called *Silent Spring* in which she described the dangers of DDT. She said the chemical was washing into rivers. When animals and birds drank from the polluted water, they became ill and sometimes died. DDT was banned in the USA shortly after. Pesticides are still widely used but they are much more targeted at specific pests, and now there are even organic insecticides that use natural ingredients so they do not harm animals or humans. Interestingly, some environmentalists are now calling for a return to DDT spraying on a large scale. Richard Liroff of the World Wildlife Fund said in 2005, 'If the alternatives to DDT aren't working, you've got to use it.' But others still feel that the dangers are too high, with insects that are basic to agriculture, like bees, being killed as well as harmful creatures.

 5.17

Presenter: **5.17. Lesson 5.6. Vocabulary for speaking: Using genetics in farming**

Exercise B1. Listen to a student talking to a tutor. Check your answers to Exercise A.

Tutor: Can farmers modify plant species – I mean, change them in certain ways?
Student: Yes. It's called selective breeding.
Tutor: And you do it in a laboratory?
Student: No. Farmers do it on their farms. They have been doing it for thousands of years.
Tutor: What can you breed for, selectively?
Student: Any desirable characteristics, anything you want. For example, size or shape or taste. Put two plants together with the same characteristic and the offspring will probably inherit that characteristic.
Tutor: What about pest resistance? I understand some plants do not suffer so badly from attacks by insects, for example.
Student: Yes, you can breed for that, too. The code for that characteristic is in every cell.
Tutor: OK. Here's a stupid idea. Can you breed from one plant which has large fruit and another one which is resistant to pests?
Student: Yes, and you will probably get large fruit which has pest resistance, because the characteristics are independent. Like blue eyes or green eyes and black hair or brown hair. It's heredity.
Tutor: So is it based on genetics?
Student: Yes, that's right. Each characteristic comes from a gene or a number of genes in the DNA. So you can breed a plant which has a gene for size and a gene for pest resistance, for example.
Tutor: Does it work with animal species, too?
Student: Yes. It works with all organisms.
Tutor: Because they all have a similar genetic code?
Student: Exactly.
Tutor: What if both plants or both animals have a genetic defect? All the offspring might have the same defect.
Student: Well, that could be a problem.

 5.18

Presenter: **5.18. Exercise C2. Listen and practise some of the words in sentences.**

Voice: 1. Farmers modify plant species.
2. It's called selective breeding.
3. Any desirable characteristic can be chosen.
4. Offspring inherit characteristics through the genes.
5. Some plants have more pest resistance than others.
6. All living organisms have a similar genetic code.
7. Sometimes parent plants have a genetic defect.
8. They may produce offspring with the same defect.

 5.19 [DVD] 5.E

Presenter: **5.19. Lesson 5.7. Real-time speaking: The power of the supermarkets**

Student 1: I'm going to talk about one effect of supermarkets on farmers and farming. As we all know, supermarkets are very powerful nowadays. They buy a very large proportion of the output of farming – between 50 and 80 per cent, depending on the country – so they can control the way that farmers operate. For example, they can demand a uniform product. In other words, all the edible parts are a similar size and shape.
According to the website Waste 2, 2011, supermarkets maintain that uniform products appeal more to their customers. But uniformity leads to a lot of waste. It also means food is more expensive for farmers to produce. Let me explain. Uniformity is achieved by selective breeding ...
Student 2: Did you say the website was called Waste 2?
Student 1: Yes, that's right. Waste 2 dot co dot uk.
Student 2: Thanks.

Student 1:	OK. Where was I?
Student 3:	You were talking about selective ... something.
Student 1:	Ah, yes. Selective breeding. Uniformity is achieved by selective breeding. When a farmer notices a desirable characteristic, he or she saves the seeds and breeds from the plants. The result of selective breeding is that the plant species gradually changes. Now, although selective breeding is very effective ...
Student 2:	I don't understand. Does selective breeding change the genetic code of the plants?
Student 1:	Yes, it does.
Student 2:	So what you're saying is, selective breeding is the same as GM ... genetic ... um ... modification?
Student 1:	No, not at all. When you breed plants selectively, the genetic changes occur naturally in the plants, whereas if you modify plants genetically, the changes are done artificially in a laboratory.
Student 3:	I don't know if this is relevant, but GM crops are banned in my country.
Student 1:	Yes, they are in mine, too. But as I said, plant breeding is not the same as GM. It's natural heredity. OK. Um. Sorry. I've forgotten what I was going to say.
Student 2:	I think you were going to give us some disadvantages. You said 'Breeding is .. .good ...', or something.
Student 1:	Right, yes. Although selective breeding is very effective, it has some drawbacks. Firstly, the British Society of Plant Breeders or BSPB states that it is very time-consuming. Joliffe, writing in *Plant Breeding*, 2006, says it can take up to 12 years to develop a new breed. Because it takes a long time, it is very expensive for farmers.
Student 2:	Are you saying that it raises the cost of the products?
Student 1:	Yes, exactly. Secondly, there is a lot of waste with uniformity. If a fruit or vegetable does not conform to the uniform size or shape, it is thrown away. For example, Mather et. al., 2010, describe the problem in California. Hundreds of tons of edible fruit and vegetables are ploughed back into the soil because they are the wrong shape or the wrong colour.
Student 3:	Sorry. Do you mean *millions* of tons?
Student 1:	Yes, sorry. I meant to say *millions*. Finally, Duffy, 2005, argues that breeding for uniformity actually gives us inferior produce. For example, the Italians actually pay more for potatoes with silver scurf, which is a disease affecting the skin colour of potatoes. When you bake them, they are crispier. Duffy also quotes a farmer as saying 'blemishes – that's marks – on melons, for example, are a sign of high sugar content. It means they taste better.'
Student 2:	So are you saying that supermarkets want uniform products but nobody else does?
Student 1:	I'm not sure. Certainly supermarkets want them and farmers don't want them. But what about customers?

🎧 5.20

| **Presenter:** | **5.20. Exercise C1. Listen to extracts from the presentation and discussion. Complete each phrase or sentence with one word in the space.** |

Student 1:	According to the website Waste 2, 2011, supermarkets claim that uniform products appeal more to their customers. But uniformity leads to a lot of waste and more expensive produce. Let me explain. Uniformity is achieved by selective breeding ...
Student 2:	Did you say the website was called Waste 2?
Student 1:	Yes, that's right. Waste 2 dot co dot uk. OK. Where was I?
Student 2:	You were talking about selective ... something.

Student 1:	The result of selective breeding is that the plant species gradually changes. Now, ...
Student 2:	I don't understand. Does selective breeding change the genetic code of the plants?
Student 1:	Yes, it does.
Student 2:	So what you're saying is ... plant breeding is the same as GM ... genetic ... um. .. modification?
Student 1:	No, not at all.

Student 2:	I don't know if this relevant, but GM crops are banned in my country.
Student 1:	Yes, they are in mine, too. But, as I said just now, plant breeding is not the same as GM. It's natural heredity. OK. Um. Sorry. I've forgotten what I was going to say.
Student 2:	You were going to give us some disadvantages. You said 'Although breeding is ... good ...', or something.

Student 1:	Because it takes a long time, plant breeding is very expensive for agribusinesses.
Student 2:	Are you saying that it raises the cost of the products?
Student 1:	Yes, that's exactly right. Secondly, there is a lot of waste with uniformity ... Hundreds of tons of edible fruit and vegetables are ploughed back into the soil because they are the wrong shape or colour.
Student 2:	Sorry. Do you mean *millions* of tons?
Student 1:	Yes, sorry. I meant to say *millions*.

🎧 5.21

| **Presenter:** | **5.21. Exercise C2. Listen again and check your answers.** |

[REPEAT OF SCRIPT FROM 🎧 5.20]

Presenter:	**5.22. Exercise C4. Listen to the phrases and sentences in C1 and copy the stress and intonation.**
Voice:	a. Did you say the website was called Waste 2?
	b. Where was I?
	c. You were talking about selective … something.
	d. Does selective breeding change the genetic code of the plants?
	e. So what you're saying is, plant breeding is the same as GM.
	f. No, not at all.
	g. I don't know if this is relevant, but GM crops are banned in my country.
	h. But, as I said just now, plant breeding is not the same as GM.
	i. I've forgotten what I was going to say.
	j. I think you were going to give us some disadvantages.
	k. Are you saying that it raises the cost of the products?
	l. Yes, that's exactly right.
	m. Do you mean *millions* of tons?
	n. Yes, sorry. I meant to say *millions*.

Presenter:	**5.23. Everyday English. At the supermarket**
	Exercise B3. Listen and check your ideas.
	Conversation 1.
Voice A:	Hiya. Can you put the basket on here?
Voice B:	Sure.
Voice A:	Do you need a bag? They're 5p.
Voice B:	Er, no thanks. I can manage.
Presenter:	**Conversation 2.**
Voice A:	That's £14.50. Have you got a loyalty card?
Voice B:	No, I haven't.
Voice A:	Are you paying by cash or card?
Voice B:	Um, card. Shall I put it in the machine?
Voice A:	Yes, please and check the amount.
Voice B:	Um. Is it working?
Voice A:	Other way round.
Voice B:	Oh, yeah. Oh, and can I have cashback?
Voice A:	How much would you like?
Voice B:	£10, please.
Voice A:	OK. Enter your PIN number, please.
Presenter:	**Conversation 3.**
Voice A:	I'm sorry. Could you go to the next checkout?
Voice B:	Why? What's the problem?
Voice A:	This checkout is 'baskets only'.
Voice B:	Oh, OK. I didn't see the sign.
Presenter:	**Conversation 4.**
Voice A:	Hi. You alright there?
Voice B:	Well, can I return this shirt? It's in this bag.
Voice A:	Is there anything wrong with it?
Voice B:	No, it's just too small.
Voice A:	Do you want to change it for a bigger size?
Voice B:	No, thanks. I'd like a refund.
Voice A:	OK. Have you got your receipt?
Voice B:	Um, oh dear. Did I leave it in the bag?
Voice A:	Yes, here you go. Did you pay by card?
Voice B:	Yes, here you are.
Voice A:	Cheers.

Presenter:	**5.24. Lesson 5.8. Learning new speaking skills: Referring to research** **Exercise A2. Listen to the phrases above and practise.**
Voice:	a. selective breeding b. uniform product c. desirable characteristic d. genetic code e. edible fruit f. sugar content g. plant species h. supermarket buyers

Presenter:	**5.25. Skills Check. Listen and practise the pauses and the intonation pattern.**
Voice:	Duffy, 2005, argues that breeding for uniformity actually gives us inferior produce. Mather et. al., 2010, describe the problem in California. The British Society of Plant Breeders, 2006, states that selective breeding is very time-consuming. Joliffe, writing in *Plant Breeding*, 2006, says that it can take up to 12 years to develop a new breed. Duffy quotes a farmer as saying 'blemishes on melons, for example, are a sign of high sugar content.' According to the website, Waste 2, 2011, supermarkets claim that uniform products appeal more to their customers.

Presenter:	**5.26. Lesson 5.9. Grammar for speaking: Complex sentences (2)** **Grammar box 22. Listen and repeat the examples. Copy the pauses and the intonation.**
Voice:	Supermarkets can control food prices [PAUSE] because they buy so much produce. Genetic changes occur naturally [PAUSE] when you breed plants selectively. Selective breeding has drawbacks [PAUSE] although it is very effective.

Presenter:	**5.27. Exercise B2. Listen and check your answers.**
Voice:	1. Farmers can breed from the seeds of the plants when they notice a desirable characteristic. 2. If you breed plants selectively, genetic changes occur naturally in the plants. 3. The changes are done artificially in a laboratory if you modify plants genetically. 4. Selective breeding is very expensive for farmers because it takes a long time. 5. Fruit can actually taste better if a plant has a disease. 6. Because they are the wrong shape, millions of tons of fruit and vegetables are wasted.

Presenter:	**5.28. Exercise C2. Listen and check. Try saying the full sentences.**
Voice:	a. If you buy a BOGOF product, you get a second one free. b. Film and television personalities sometimes endorse products although they probably don't use them. c. Bad reviews can kill a new movie, although some people go to see if the reviewer was right or wrong. d. When a film company puts a trailer of a new movie onto a website like YouTube, it hopes that the film will go viral. e. Athletes should listen to music during training because it decreases the perception of effort. f. The majority of asthmatics can prevent attacks if they take medication before doing exercise. g. Although Braille invented a better system of reading for the blind, he was not allowed to teach it at his own institute. h. Because Braille's system only used six dots, it is easier to read than previous methods. i. Because the Yangtze River floods most years, the Chinese government is diverting some water to other parts of the country. j. The government of Egypt has threatened to use force if any country takes water from the Nile without permission.

Presenter: **5.29. Lesson 5.10. Applying new speaking skills: Cloning and intensive farming**

Exercise A. Listen to some sentences. Which photograph is each sentence related to?

Voice:
1. Chemicals are used to improve growth.
2. Each animal is an exact copy in genetic terms.
3. Farmers can create animals which are consistent in terms of productivity.
4. There have been several successful trials, although genetic defects mean that many animals die young.
5. The animals live in cramped conditions because it is easier to look after them.
6. Scientists grow cells from selected animals in a laboratory.
7. The living conditions mean that many animals experience stress.
8. The practice has been banned in the European Union.

A					
a good case	4.11		authority (n) [= expert in a field]	3.16	
abandon (v)	4.11		availability (n)	1.1	
abolish (v)	4.11		available (adj)	1.11	
absence (n)	1.1		average (v)	1.1	

A		
a good case	4.11
abandon (v)	4.11
abolish (v)	4.11
absence (n)	1.1
abstract (adj) [= opp. of concrete]	4.11
accelerate (v)	4.16
accept (v)	3.1
access (n)	1.16
accident (n)	2.6
account for (v)	1.16
additional (adj)	5.16
adopt (v) [= take up]	2.6
adventure (n)	3.11
advocate (v)	5.11
affect (v)	1.1
against (prep)	1.1
ageing (adj)	4.16
aggression (n)	3.1, 4.6
aggressive (adj)	3.1, 4.6
agribusiness (n)	5.6
agriculturalist (n)	5.1
ahead of its time	2.11
alien (n)	3.11
allocate (v)	2.1
alphabet (n)	2.6
analogue (adj)	2.1, 2.16
analysis (n)	2.16
analyze (v)	2.16
animation (n)	3.11
announce (v)	1.6
antagonist (n)	3.11
anxiety (n)	4.6
anxious (adj)	4.6
appeal (v)	5.6
aquifer (n)	1.6
archaeological (adj)	1.11
archaeology (n)	1.11
argument (n) [= thesis]	3.1
artery (n)	4.1
artificial (adj)	5.1
artificially (adv)	5.6
asthma (n)	4.6
asthmatic (adj)	4.6
attack (n) [= physical illness]	4.6
audience (n)	3.16
audience (n) [= target market]	3.6
authoritative (adj)	4.6
authorities	3.1

authority (n) [= expert in a field]	3.16
availability (n)	1.1
available (adj)	1.11
average (v)	1.1

B		
ban (v)	3.1
ban (n and v)	5.6
bar-code (n)	2.11
battery farming	5.6
be the basis of	2.11
because of	1.16
because of (adv)	5.16
beehive diagram	4.16
beneficial (adj)	2.1
benefit (n and v)	2.1, 4.16
berry (n)	5.1, 5.11
billboard (n)	3.6
binary (adj)	2.6
biotech (n)	5.16
biotechnology (n)	5.16
blind (adj and v)	2.6
blindness (n)	2.6
blood stream	4.1
BOGOF (n)	3.6
bone (n)	4.1
Braille	2.6
brand (n) [= named product]	3.1
brand (v)	2.16
breathe (v)	4.6
breed (v)	5.6
breeding (n)	5.1
breeding (n)	5.6
bribe (n and v)	3.6
bright (adj) [= clever]	2.11
bring on [= cause to start]	4.6
browser (n)	2.1
buddy (n)	3.6
bulb (n)	2.11

C		
cable (n)	2.1
calculate (v)	3.1
campaign	4.11
cancel (v)	2.16
cancellation (n)	2.16
carbon emissions	1.11
carnivore (n)	5.11
carnivorous (adj)	5.11
cartridge (n)	2.16
catchy (adj)	3.6

CD (n)	2.16	
cell (n)	4.1	
cellar (n)	2.11	
cereal (n)	5.1	
CGI	3.6	
channel (n)	1.6	
character (n)	3.11	
chemical (n)	5.6	
child-bearing age	4.16	
childminder (n)	3.1	
circulation (n)	4.1	
circulatory (adj)	4.1	
cite (v) [= quote]	3.16	
citizen (n)	4.11	
citizenship (n)	4.11	
civil war	1.16	
class (n) [= social division]	4.11	
clearly (adv)	3.1	
cloning (n)	5.6	
code (n)	2.1, 2.6, 3.11	
cognitive (adj)	4.6	
collapse (v)	1.11	
come into its own	2.11	
come to pass	5.16	
come up with	2.11	
commercial use	2.11	
commit (v)	3.1	
compelling (adj) [= very strong]	5.16	
compete (v)	2.16	
competition (n)	2.16	
competition (n)	3.6	
complete (adj)	5.11	
complex (adj)	2.1	
compress (v)	2.16	
compression (n)	2.16, 4.1	
comprise (v)	1.11, 1.16	
concrete (adj) [= opp. of abstract]	4.11	
condition (n)	4.6	
conflict (n)	3.11	
conform (v)	3.1, 3.11, 5.6	
congregation (n)	5.11	
consensus (n)	1.6	
consequence (n)	2.6	
consider (v) [= regard as]	1.16	
constant (adj)	2.11	
constraining	3.11	
contemporary (n)	5.11	
contestant (n)	3.16	

contract (n)	2.16	
contribute (v)	1.16, 4.16	
contributory (adj)	1.16	
control (v) [~ a disease]	4.6	
controllable (adj)	4.6	
convention (n)	3.11	
convention (n) [= rule]	3.16	
conventional (adj)	5.16	
conversion (n)	2.16	
convert (v)	2.16	
copper (n)	1.1	
copyright (n)	3.11	
correct (v)	2.16	
correction (n)	2.16	
counter-argument (n)	3.1	
courier (n)	2.1	
creative (adj)	3.11	
criterion (n) [pl. = criteria]	1.16	
critic (n)	3.11, 3.16	
crop (n)	1.6, 5.1	
cruel (adj)	5.11	
cruise (n and v)	1.11	
cultivation (n)	1.1	
curriculum (n) [pl. = curricula]	4.11	
customer base	2.1	
D dam (n and v)	1.6	
damage (n and v)	2.6	
damage (v)	1.11	
deal with [= cope]	2.6	
decide against	4.16	
decline (n and v)	4.16	
decode (v)	3.11	
deliver (v)	1.6, 2.1	
delivery (n)	2.1	
demand (n)	1.11	
demonstrate (v)	2.16	
demonstration (n)	2.16	
density (n)	1.1	
dental (adj)	5.11	
deny (v)	3.1	
dependency (n)	3.1	
dependency ratio	4.16	
dependent (adj)	3.1, 4.16	
depressed (adj)	4.6	
depression (n)	4.6	
deprive (v)	4.6	
desalination (n)	1.1, 1.6	
design (n and v)	2.16	

desirable (adj)	5.6	
despite (adv)	5.16	
destroy (v)	1.6	
developed (adj) [~ countries]	4.16	
device (n)	2.1	
diaphragm (n)	4.1	
diet (n) [= normal food]	5.11	
digestion (n)	4.1	
digestive (adj)	4.1	
digital (adj)	2.1, 2.16	
digress (v)	5.1	
digression (n)	5.1	
direct (adj)	1.11	
disability (n)	2.11	
discriminate (v)	5.16	
disease	1.16	
disgusting (adj)	3.6	
distinguish (v) [= mark the difference]	3.11	
divert (v)	1.6	
diving (n)	1.11	
documentary (n)	3.16	
domesticate (v)	5.11	
domesticated (adj)	5.1	
donor (n)	3.11	
dot (n)	2.6	
downstream (n)	1.6	
drama (n)	3.11	
dramatic (adj)	3.16	
draw (v) [= take out]	1.6	
drawback (n)	2.1	
drought (n)	1.6	
dry (v)	2.16	
dry up (v)	1.6	
dumb (adj)	2.6	
dumb down	3.1	

E

economic indicator	1.16	
edible (adj)	5.1, 5.6	
educationalist (n)	4.11	
educator (n)	4.11	
elderly	4.16	
eliminate (v)	3.1	
encounter (v)	3.11	
endangered species	5.11	
endorse (v)	3.6	
endorsement (n)	3.6	
entrepreneur (n)	4.11	
environmental (adj)	5.11	
episode (n) [= part of a series]	3.6	

episodic (adj)	3.16	
equilibrium (n)	3.11	
equivalent (n)	5.16	
escapism (n)	3.16	
establish (v) [= make clear]	3.11	
etailer (n)	2.1	
ethical (adj)	5.11	
evil	3.11	
exaggerate (v)	3.6	
exceed (v)	1.11	
exception (n)	1.16	
exchange (n)	4.1	
exertion (n)	4.6	
exist (v)	1.16	
existing (adj)	2.16	
experience (v)	3.1	
experiment (v)	2.11	
experiment with	2.16	
expire (v)	2.11	
extension (n) [= next step]	5.16	
extract (v)	1.6	
extraction (n)	1.6	
extremely	1.16	
eye-catching (adj)	3.6	
eyesight (n)	2.6	

F

fairy tale	3.1	
famine (n)	5.1	
fantasy	3.11	
fatal (adj)	4.6	
fatigue (n)	4.6	
feature (v)	3.11	
feed (v) [= supply]	1.6	
feedback (n)	4.6	
feel strongly about	2.11	
fertile (adj)	5.1	
fertility (n)	4.16	
fertilizer (n)	5.1	
fiction (n)	3.11	
fictional	3.11	
fictional (adj)	3.1	
film (v)	3.16	
finger (n)	2.6	
flat (adj)	2.6	
flexible (adj)	4.11	
flood (n and v)	1.6	
flow (v)	1.6, 2.16	
follow a way of life	5.11	
follower (n) [of religion]	1.11	

food chain	5.11	
food miles / kilometres	5.6	
format (n)	3.16	
fossil fuel	1.1	
foster (v) [= encourage]	4.11	
fracture (n)	4.1	
franchise (n and v) [= type of programme]	3.16	
franchise (n) [= successful series]	3.6	
furthermore	4.11	

G

gather (v)	5.11
GDP	1.16
gene (n)	5.6, 5.16
generally speaking	1.16
genetic (adj)	5.6
genetic code	5.6
genetic defect	5.6
genetic modification	5.6
genetic modification (GM)	5.16
genetically (adv)	5.6
genetics (n)	5.16
genius (n)	2.11
genre (n)	3.6, 3.11
get by (v) [= manage to survive]	1.11
get in the way of	2.11
get through [= contact]	2.11
give an indication of	2.11
give one's name to	2.6
global (adj)	1.1
GM	5.6
go deaf / blind	2.6
go on to be [= result]	2.6
go on to do	2.11
goal (n) [= target]	4.6
golden age	3.1
grain (n)	1.6
grind (v)	5.1
gross domestic product	1.16

H

hand	2.6
handmade (adj)	2.16
harm (n)	5.16
harmful (adj)	5.16
harvest (v)	5.1
have an influence on	2.11
hazardous chemical	5.11
head towards	2.11
health care	4.16
hearing (n)	2.6
hemisphere (n)	1.16

herbivore (n)	5.11
herbivorous (adj)	5.11
hereditary (adj)	2.11
heredity (n)	5.6
heretic (n)	5.11
hero (n)	3.11
high street (n)	2.1
Human Development Index (n) [= list]	1.1
humanities (n pl)	4.11
hunt (v)	5.11
hunter-gatherer (n)	5.1, 5.11

I

ibid.	3.11
ignorance (n)	3.11
immune (adj)	4.1
impaired (adj)	2.6
impairment (n)	2.6
impetus (n)	4.11
impulse (n) [= electrical]	4.1
in general	1.16
in terms of	1.16
incidence (n)	4.16
incidentally (adv)	3.1
inconvenient (adj)	2.1
inculcate (v)	4.11
independence (n)	2.11
independent shop	5.6
index (n) [= list]	1.1
indigenous (adj)	5.1
industrialist (n)	2.11
infected (adj)	2.6
infectious (adj)	1.16, 5.16
infer (v)	1.11
inference (n)	1.11
inflammation (n)	4.1
infrastructure (n)	2.1
inherit (v)	5.6
initially (adv)	3.1
injury (n)	4.1, 4.6
ink (n)	2.16
insecure (adj)	2.1
inspiration (n)	2.11
intensity (n)	4.6
intensive farming	5.6, 5.11
intercept (v)	2.1
interface (v)	4.1
intestines (n pl)	4.1
intriguing (adj)	3.6
invade (v)	1.16

invasion (n)	1.16	
iron ore	1.1	
irrigate (v)	1.6	
irrigation (n)	1.6	

J jingle (n)   3.6

joint (n)	4.1
joke (n)	3.6
journal (n)	3.11

K kill (v)   5.11

L labour force   4.11, 4.16

lack (n)	1.1
lack of sleep	4.6
largely (adv)	1.16
laser (n)	2.16
leak (v)	1.6
leather (n)	2.6
leisure (n)	4.11
life expectancy	4.16
lifelong (adj)	4.11
limit (v)	1.6
link (n and v)	4.16
lip (n)	2.6
literacy (n)	1.1, 4.11
live action	3.6
livestock rearing	5.11
living organism	5.6
longevity (n)	4.11, 4.16
look like	2.11
lose your sight / hearing / voice	2.6
loss-leader	3.6
lung (n)	2.6
luxury (n)	2.16

M mainly (adv)   1.16

maintain (v) [= keep in good condition]	1.11
maintain (v) [= say is true]	5.16
make a fresh start	2.11
manufacture (v)	2.16
manufacturer (n)	2.16
manure (n)	5.1
manuscript (n)	2.16
marina (v)	1.11
market (n) [= general place to sell goods]	1.16
market (v)	2.1
marketing strategy	2.16
mechanization (n)	5.1
mechanize (v)	5.1
media (n pl)	3.1

mediate (v)	3.1
medical innovation	4.16
medication (n)	4.6
medium (n)	3.1
medium (n) [= way of sending message]	2.1
meet (v) [= equals]	1.16
member	1.16
membership (n)	1.16
mental (adj)	4.6
message (n) [= meaning]	3.1
messenger (n)	2.1
migrate (v)	5.16
migration (n)	5.16
mineral (n)	1.1
model (v) [= copy]	3.1
modification (n)	5.16
modify (v)	5.6, 5.16
monster (n)	3.11
motion picture	2.11
mouth (n)	2.6
MP3 (n)	2.16
muscle (n)	4.1
muscular (adj)	4.1
mutate (v)	5.16
mutation (n)	5.16
mute (adj)	2.6

N narrative (n)   3.6, 3.11

natural gas	1.1
natural resource	1.1
navigable (adj)	1.16
navigate (v)	2.1
Neolithic	5.11
nerve (n)	4.1
nervous (adj)	4.1
network (n)	2.1
neurosis (n)	4.6
neurotic (adj)	4.6
nightlife (n)	1.11
nitrogen (N) (n)	5.1
nose (n)	2.6
numeracy (n)	4.11
nutrient (n)	4.1, 5.1, 5.16
nutrition (n)	5.16

O observe (v)   2.11

obsessively (adv)	4.6
obstacle (n)	3.11
obviously (adv)	3.1
offend (v)	1.11

omnivore (n)	5.11	
omnivorous (adj)	5.11	
on location	3.16	
one-off	3.6	
organ (n)	4.1	
organic (adj)	5.1	
original (adj) [= new]	2.11	
outbreak (n)	5.11	
output (n)	5.6	
outsell (v)	5.16	
outweigh (v)	5.16	

P

packaging (n)	5.6
partial (adj)	5.11
partly (adv)	1.16
passionate (adj)	4.6
patent (n)	2.11, 2.16
per capita	1.16
perceive (v)	4.6
perception (n)	4.6
performance [= outcome]	1.16
personal education	4.11
personality (n) [= star]	3.6
personnel (n)	2.1
perspiration (n)	2.11
pest (n)	5.1, 5.6, 5.16
pesticide (n)	5.1, 5.11
phosphorus (P) (n)	5.1
physical (adj)	4.6
physiology (n)	4.1
physiotherapy (n)	4.1
pipe (n and v)	1.6
place (v)	1.16
planting (v)	5.1
plot (n)	3.11
plough (n and v)	5.1
plough (v)	5.6
population (n)	1.1
population ageing	4.16
populous (adj)	1.6
positive thinking	4.11
post (v) [= put in mail box]	2.1
postal system	2.1
postpone (v)	4.16
potassium (K) (n)	5.1
potentially (adv)	5.16
practical (adj) [= able to work]	2.16
precise (adj)	5.16
pregnancy (n)	4.16

prequel (n)	3.6
presence (n)	1.1
preserve (v)	5.1
principle (n)	2.1
privatize (v)	1.6
produce (n and v)	5.6
producer (n)	3.16
proofreader (n)	2.16
proportion (n)	4.16
proposal (n)	4.11
proposed (adj)	1.6
proposition (n)	3.1
prosperity (n)	4.16
protagonist (n)	3.11
protection (n)	5.1
provider (n)	4.16
provision (n)	4.11
proximity (n)	1.11
psychological (adj)	4.6
psychological need	3.16
public (n)	3.16
punchline (n)	3.6
put pressure on (v)	4.16
put X ahead of Y	2.11

Q

quotation (n)	3.16
quote (n and v)	5.6

R

radical (n)	4.11
raise the question	4.11
raised (adj) [= above the surface]	2.6
range (n) [= extent]	1.1
range (v)	1.16
ration (n)	5.11
reach a conclusion	1.16
react (v)	2.16
readiness (n)	4.6
reality TV	3.16
rear (v)	5.1
reasonable (adj) [= quite good]	1.11
reasoning (n)	2.11
rebrand (v)	2.16
rebuild (v)	2.11
receiver (n) [= object]	2.11
recognize [= see the value of]	2.11
recommended daily intake	5.11
reconciliation (n)	3.11
recover (v) [e.g., sales]	2.16
recycle (v)	5.6
reef (n)	1.11

reference (n)	3.11	sedentary (n)	4.11
refill (v)	1.6, 2.16	seed (n)	5.16
reflect (v) [= be related to]	4.11	seemingly (adv)	4.16
reflect (v) [= show]	1.1	selective breeding	5.6, 5.16
register (v)	2.11	self-starter (n)	4.11
related (adj) [= connected]	3.16	sense of self-worth	4.6
relative (adj) [= compared to something else]	5.16	sensitive (adj)	4.6
relay station	2.1	sequel (n)	3.6
release (v and n) [= a film]	3.6	serial (n) [= story in parts]	3.16
relinquish (v)	5.16	serve (v) [= help]	1.11
remains (n)	1.11	setting (n)	3.16
renovate (v)	1.11	shared (adj)	1.11
renowned (adj)	5.11	shelf-life (n)	5.16
republic (n)	1.11	shortage (adj)	1.1
reservoir (n)	1.6	shortage (n)	1.6
resistance (n)	5.6	shrink (v)	1.6
resistant (adj)	5.16	shrinkage (n)	1.6
respiration (n)	4.1	sight (n)	2.6
respiratory (adj)	4.1, 4.6	sign language	2.6
restore (v)	1.11	signal (n)	2.1
result (n)	2.6	significantly (adv)	4.16
retailer (n)	2.1	similarity (n)	1.1, 3.16
retire (v)	4.11	skeleton (n)	4.1
retirement (n)	4.11	skull (n)	4.1
review (v and n) [= of a film, book]	3.6	slogan (n)	3.6
revolutionize (v)	5.1	smudge (v)	2.16
rise / rose / risen (v)	4.16	social education	4.11
risk (n)	5.16	social security benefit	4.16
romance (n)	3.11	socialize (v)	3.1
ruins (n)	1.11	source (n)	1.6
run out of (v)	1.6	speaker (n) [= object]	2.11
rural (adj)	1.1	species (n)	5.6
		spinal (adj)	4.1
safari (n)	1.11	spine (n)	4.1
saturated fat	5.11	split (n)	1.1
save (v) [= stop death]	2.11	spouse (n)	4.16
scan (v)	2.16	sprain (n)	4.1
scanner (n)	2.11	spread (v)	3.6
scarce (adj)	2.1	stability (n)	4.16
Schadenfreude	3.16	stable (adj) [= fixed]	1.16, 3.11
schema (n)	3.11	stage (n)	3.11
script (n)	3.16	stand-alone (adj)	2.1
scripted (adj)	3.16	standard (n) [= norm]	2.6
seaport (n)	1.16	standard of living	1.1
seasonal (adj)	1.11	starvation (n)	5.1
sect (n)	5.11	state	4.11
secure (adj)	2.1	state (n) [= government]	4.11
security (n)	2.1	stock (adj) [= unchanging]	3.11
sedative (n)	3.1		

S

store (n) [= shop]	5.6	
store (v)	1.6	
strain (n)	4.1	
stranger (n)	3.1	
stream (n)	1.6	
strict (adj) [= very clear]	3.11	
struggle (n)	3.11	
sub-area (n)	1.1	
suffer (v) [= feel pain / stress]	5.6	
suffer (v) [~ from]	1.6, 1.11, 1.16, 2.16	
sulphur (S) (n)	5.1	
supervise (v)	3.1	
supervised (adj)	3.1	
supplement (v)	1.11	
supply (v)	1.6	
support (n and v)	4.16	
supposition (n)	4.11	
survival (n)	3.16	
sustainability (n)	5.16	
sustainable (adj)	5.11	
swelling (n)	4.1	
symbol (n)	2.1, 2.6	
symptom (n)	4.6	
synopsis (n)	3.11	
synthesis (n)	2.6	
synthesizer (n)	2.6	

T tag line (n) 3.6
take into account 4.11
tame (adj) 5.1
technology (n) 2.1
teeth (n pl) 2.6
telegraph (n) 2.1
temperate (adj) 1.1
tension (n) 4.6
the EU 1.16
the extent of 3.16
the interior (n) [= of a country] 1.16
the issue of 3.16
the relationship between 3.16
the similarities between 3.16
the WHO 1.16
the World Bank 1.16
thriller (n) 3.11
throw away 5.6
thumb (n) 2.6
tissue (n) 4.1
tone down 3.1

tongue (n) 2.6
topsoil (n) 5.11
tractor (n) 5.1
trailer (n) 3.6
treatment (n) [i.e., water] 1.11
trend (n) 4.16
tropical (adj) 1.16
tube (n) 2.16
turn your back on 5.16
TV schedule 3.16

U uncertainty (adj) 3.6
underground (adj) 1.1, 1.6
uniform (adj) 5.6
uniformity (n) 5.6
unit of production 5.6
unknown (adj) 3.6
unsupervised (adj) 3.1
unvarying (adj) 3.1
upmarket (adj) 1.11
upstream (n) 1.6
urban (adj) 1.1
urbanization (n) 4.16
useless (adj) 2.1

V vaccine (n) 5.16
value for money 3.6
variation (n) 4.16
vast (adj) 1.11
vegetarian (n and adj) 5.11
vegetarianism (n) 5.11
vein (n) 4.1
victim (n) 3.11
viewer (n) 3.16
viewing (n) 3.16
villain (n) 3.11, 3.16
violence (n) 3.1
violent (adj) 3.1
viral (adj) 3.6
vocal chords 2.6
volume (n) [= journal] 3.11
volume (n) [= quantity] 3.16
vote (v) 3.16
voyeurism (n) 3.16
vulnerable (adj) 3.1

W waste (n and v) 5.6
waste (n) 5.1
well (n) 1.6
wheat (n) 5.1

widely *(adv)*	1.11
wild *(adj)*	5.1
with regard to	1.1
working class(es)	4.11
worldwide *(adj)*	2.6
worth *(n)*	2.11
wrap *(v)*	2.11

 yield *(n)*　　　　　5.1, 5.16